NMAЯDHTIW

HAWKEYE COMMUNITY COLLEGE

3 7944 1007 8161 2

333.9115 S359
Schneiders, Robert Kelley,
1965-
Unruly river : two centuries
of change along the Missouri
48092

D1264846

Unruly River

DEVELOPMENT OF WESTERN RESOURCES

The Development of Western Resources is an interdisciplinary series focusing on the use and misuse of resources in the American West. Written for a broad readership of humanists, social scientists, and resource specialists, the books in this series emphasize both historical and contemporary perspectives as they explore the interplay between resource exploitation and economic, social, and political experiences.

John G. Clark, University of Kansas, Founding Editor
Hal K. Rothman, University of Nevada, Las Vegas, Series Editor

333.9115
S359

Unruly River

Two Centuries of Change Along the Missouri

Robert Kelley Schneiders

University Press of Kansas

048092

© 1999 by the University Press of Kansas
All rights reserved

Published by the University Press of Kansas (Lawrence, Kansas 66049),
which was organized by the Kansas Board of Regents and is operated and
funded by Emporia State University, Fort Hays State University, Kansas
State University, Pittsburg State University, the University of Kansas, and
Wichita State University

Library of Congress Cataloging-in-Publication Data

Schneiders, Robert Kelley, 1965–
    Unruly river : two centuries of change along the Missouri / by
Robert Kelley Schneiders.
        p.   cm. — (Development of western resources)
    Includes bibliographical references and index.
    ISBN 0-7006-0937-7 (alk. paper)
    1. Missouri River Watershed—Environmental conditions.   2. Water
resources development—Missouri River Watershed.   3. Missouri River
Watershed—Description and travel.   I. Title.   II. Series.
GE155.M85S36   1999
333.91'15'0978—dc21   98-33976

British Library Cataloguing in Publication Data is available.

Printed in the United States of America

10 9 8 7 6 5 4 3 2 1

The paper used in this publication meets the minimum requirements of
the American National Standard for Permanence of Paper for Printed
Materials Z39.48-1984.

I dedicate this history to a number of people, all of whom have contributed to my understanding of water and rivers

To David Wieling, for introducing me to fly-fishing and a more intimate relationship to streams

To my brother, Tom Schneiders, for the moments at Wolf Creek and that huge rainbow that got away

To my mom and dad, Mary Jean (Lang) and Robert Joseph Schneiders, for allowing me to go to the river as a boy nearly every day in the summertime and for teaching me to respect the river's power

To James Weyer and William Meier, for the shared imagination that inspired the "WeyMeiSchnei" expeditions along the Big Sioux

To Gail Evans, for teaching me to see the river as ever-changing and forever wild

And to my wife, Elizabeth Ann Wieling, for the 105-degree day at Big Bend, the ten-foot-high elephant grass at Hudson, and the wonderful times at Niobrara.

Contents

Figures and Maps

Acknowledgments

I want to thank James Whitaker for his support and critical evaluation of the manuscript and for his ceaseless insistence that I write, rewrite, and then write some more. I also want to thank Gail Evans for her encouragement and her untiring efforts to improve the quality of my writing. I extend a thank-you to Trevor Nelson, director of the Study Abroad Center at Iowa State University, for his patience and understanding while I worked on this project. I am indebted to Sister Ramona Colling, O.S.F.; she believed in me and in my abilities as a young scholar. I also thank Father Vernon Stapenhorst for making his passion for nature my own. Others who lent support to this project over the years include, in alphabetical order, Michael Brodhead, Thomas Bruegger, John Ferrell, Robert Hipple, Gerald Jauron, and Mrs. Philip Weaver. John Ferrell deserves special recognition. He repeatedly pointed me in the direction of new sources and willingly shared his vast knowledge of the Missouri River. An anonymous librarian, or librarians, at the Sioux City Public Library collected newspaper articles related to the Missouri River from 1930 to 1980. Those clippings provided an invaluable resource during the research and writing of this history; a thank-you goes out to the librarian(s) in Sioux City. I also want to acknowledge assistance from the Kansas City Public Library; National Records Center (Kansas City, Missouri); Sioux City Public Library; River Bluffs Regional Library (St. Joseph, Missouri); Sioux City Public Museum; Sergeant Floyd Museum; Omaha District of the Corps of Engineers, Missouri River Division; Joslyn Art Museum; Onawa Public Library; University of South Dakota, I. D., Weeks Library; South Dakota State Historical Society; Iowa State University Parks Library; Dakota Wesleyan College Library; Dakota State College Library; Woodbury County Conservation Board; Iowa Department of Natural Resources; and the Siouxland Interstate Metropolitan Planning Commission.

1 | Introduction

The Missouri River, and its valley, has been transformed in the past 190 years through human action. Once a wide, shallow, silt-laden stream with islands, sandbars, side channels, and oxbow lakes, the modern Missouri, over much of the reach above Yankton, South Dakota, is a series of clear, cold, deep lakes behind massive earthen dams. The river below Yankton also possesses few of its original characteristics, having been narrowed and straightened by the Corps of Engineers. This is the story of how the Missouri changed from a broad, meandering river to a partially regulated stream consisting of dams, reservoirs, and thousands of channelization structures.

The modern Missouri resulted from the cooperative efforts of local, grassroots organizations and federal entities. Numerous individuals and organizations worked together to develop the river, but they did not operate within a political vacuum. The Missouri itself had a tremendous influence on the formulation and implementation of their development plans. The Corps of Engineers altered the Missouri River for a number of reasons, but the establishment of a navigation channel in the river to aid agriculture and the rural population of the Midwest and northern Great Plains served as the primary justification for the construction projects. Yet completion of a series of dams, reservoirs, and channelization structures from Montana to the river's mouth produced mixed results for the agricultural sector. The Corps initiated the development plans without sufficient information about the river's complex environment. Inadequate information and hasty construction of dams and channelization structures caused disastrous and costly environmental repercussions.

In this history I focus on events in the lower river valley (the area downstream and south of Sioux City, Iowa) because it served as the center of efforts to alter the Missouri. Furthermore, environmental changes along the lower river valley led its residents to seek the construction of dams across the upper Missouri.

Much has been written about the Missouri River. The literature can be categorized into four periods. During the first period, from approximately 1804 to 1880, explorers, adventurers, and European travelers kept notes of their impressions of the river and valley and then published the accounts. The most noteworthy are the journals of the Lewis and Clark expedition (1804–1806), which contain extensive records of the flora and fauna the explorers saw on their trek. They also wrote detailed descriptions of Indian tribes, especially those living above the mouth of the Big Sioux River, including the Mandan, Hidatsa, Arikara, and Blackfeet. Unfortunately, Lewis, who was to supervise publication of the journals, committed suicide soon after the expedition, and the complete report was not published until late in the nineteenth century. Elliot Coues's three-volume edition, *History of the Expedition Under the Command of Lewis and Clark* (1893), and Gary Moulton's *Journals of the Lewis and Clark Expedition* (1983–) are two of the most historically accurate editions.[1]

Other writers followed Meriwether Lewis and William Clark up the Missouri and quickly published their descriptions of the region. In 1811 Henry M. Brackenridge accepted Manuel Lisa's invitation to accompany a fur-trading party to the Mandan villages (near present-day Bismarck, North Dakota) and in 1814 published his journal, which described Indians, the river's unpredictable nature, and the animals living in the valley.[2] British botanist John Bradbury traveled on a keelboat to the upper Missouri in 1811 and published a report of his trip in 1817, *Travels in the Interior of America in the Years 1809, 1810, and 1811.*[3] The journals of the Stephen Long expedition to the present-day Omaha, Nebraska, area in 1819–1820 appeared in 1823, *Account of an Expedition from Pittsburgh to the Rocky Mountains.*[4]

Tourism to the American West and upper Missouri became fashionable in the 1830s and 1840s among European and eastern U.S. intellectuals, aristocrats, and artists. George Catlin (1832), Prince Maximilian of Wied and Karl Bodmer (1833), and ornithologist John J. Audubon (1843) provided Americans and Europeans with a glimpse of the Missouri Valley's natural wonders and indigenous peoples. Their published paintings, drawings, and writings spurred further interest in the upper Missouri. Thaddeus Culbertson followed the lead of the earlier adventurers and artists and floated on a steamboat to the upper river in 1850.[5] The reports of Lewis and Clark, Brackenridge, Bradbury, Long, Prince Maximilian, Audubon, and Culbertson, and the illustrations of Catlin and Bodmer, provide a wealth of information on the environment of the Missouri River Valley prior to the settlement of large numbers of European-Americans.

Historians and anthropologists wrote during the second period, which lasted from roughly 1890 to 1920. Historians focused on the history of European-American settlement in the Missouri River region, especially on the exploits of early pioneers as they confronted the free-flowing river and the rugged, unsettled land. Anthropologists examined what many considered a vanishing Indian presence in the river valley.

Hiram Chittenden's two-volume account, *History of Early Steamboat Navigation on the Missouri River* (1903), is an extensive history of the role the steamboat played in the settlement of the Missouri Valley. The two volumes also explain the Missouri River's seasonal character and flow rates, along with the difficulties of navigating the stream by keelboat and steamboat.[6] In 1909 John G. Neihardt, a Nebraska native, poet, and college professor, wrote *The River and I*, which chronicles his journey down the Missouri from Great Falls, Montana, to Sioux City, Iowa, in a small motorized boat. Neihardt describes the river along this route, explains the history of several significant points in the valley, and concludes by predicting the eventual development of the river for hydroelectric generation.[7]

Anthropologists traveled to the upper Missouri region in increasing numbers in the early twentieth century to record the histories, culture, and agricultural techniques of the area's indigenous inhabitants. Believing Indian peoples and their cultures faced extinction soon, these anthropologists sought to record, for posterity's sake, the traditional cultural characteristics of various tribes. George F. Will's *Corn Among the Indians* (1917) examines Mandan and Hidatsa agricultural practices; Gilbert Wilson's *Agriculture of the Hidatsa Indians* (1917) is an account of his relationship with a traditional Hidatsa agriculturist and details the agricultural information he learned from his teacher. Melvin R. Gilmore's *Uses of Plants by Indians of the Missouri River Region* (1919) presents an ethnobotanical report of past Indian uses of plants for medicinal, religious, and dietary purposes.[8]

The third period of historical writing about the Missouri occurred between 1944 and 1960. During these years, authors promoted the building of dams and channelization structures along the river. Books in this category include Stanley Vestal's *The Missouri* (1945), Bruce Nelson's *Land of the Dacotahs* (1946), LeRoy W. Schaffner's *Economic Aspects of the*

Missouri River Project with Special Reference to Iowa (1946), Rufus Terral's *Missouri Valley: Land of Drouth, Flood, and Promise* (1947), Otto G. Hoiberg's *Missouri River Basin Development Program: A Study Guide* (1950), and Richard Baumhoff's *Dammed Missouri Valley: One Sixth of Our Nation* (1951). These writers portray the Missouri in its natural state as an enemy of civilization and material progress. Furthermore, the authors viewed development and control of the river's water as crucial to the stability and future prosperity of the agricultural economy of the Midwest and the northern Great Plains. Stabilization of this economy could be achieved only through the construction of large dams across the Missouri main stem, which would curtail the occasional high flows that had previously disrupted the production of crops in the valley and which would provide irrigation water for growing produce during drought periods. In 1955 Marian E. Ridgeway wrote a legislative history, *The Missouri Basin's Pick-Sloan Plan: A Case Study in Congressional Policy Determination*. Encyclopedic in scope and detail, the book reveals the political machinations that preceded congressional passage of the Pick-Sloan Plan.

The final period of historical writing on the Missouri River began in 1970 and continues to this day. It is characterized by a plethora of scientific studies on the river and valley environments. Government agencies, including the Corps of Engineers, the Interior Department's U.S. Fish and Wildlife Service, and the Iowa Geological Survey, have sponsored several of these studies. They examine such diverse environmental topics as water quality, streambed degradation, aquatic habitat, and the migration patterns of fish in the altered river system. A few titles illustrate the general theme of this period: William Persons's *Use of Open and Closed Backwater Ponds of the Missouri River: Iowa as Spawning and Nursery Areas for Fish* (1979), George R. Hallberg's *Changes in the Channel Area of the Missouri River in Iowa, 1879–1976* (1979), the Corps of Engineers' *Final Report and Final Environmental Impact Statement for Fish and Wildlife Mitigation for the Missouri River Bank Stabilization and Navigation Project* (1981), and Forrest Holly's *Computer-Based Prognosis of Missouri River Bed Degradation: Refinement of Computational Procedures* (1984).

Four political histories have been written during this last period. Michael Lawson, *The Dammed Indians: The Pick-Sloan Plan and the Missouri River Sioux, 1944–1980* (1982), examines the plan's effects on the Indians of North and South Dakota. The Pick-Sloan Plan authorized the construction of five dams across the main stem of the Missouri River.

The Corps of Engineers built these five earthen behemoths between 1946 and 1966. Lawson focuses on the social, economic, and political consequences of dam construction for those Indians who lived in the valley and places special emphasis on the issue of monetary compensation to the tribes for the inundation of their lands.[9] John E. Thorson, *River of Promise, River of Peril: The Politics of Managing the Missouri River* (1994), briefly examines how the Missouri River has been managed since the 1940s. Thorson addresses current water-management issues confronting the Corps of Engineers and recommends institutional changes in order to allocate the river's water more effectively. In particular, Thorson believes a new, nonpartisan institution should be established to manage the Missouri River.[10] His book is timely because of the current political controversy between the upper and lower basin states over the methods used by the Corps of Engineers to apportion Missouri River water. Upstream states are pushing the Corps to adopt a new management plan to replace the one that has favored downstream interests for the past fifty years. The third recent book on the Missouri River is John Ferrell's *Big Dam Era: A Legislative and Institutional History of the Pick-Sloan Missouri Basin Program* (1993). Ferrell probes the legislative origins of the Pick-Sloan Plan and discusses current management problems confronting the Corps of Engineers, including the difficulty of meeting the water demands of many interest groups during drought periods.[11] Ferrell also published *Soundings: 100 Years of the Missouri River Navigation Project* (1996), in which he briefly explores several of the local political initiatives that led to channelization of the Missouri. He also shows through the use of photographs the techniques and technologies employed by the Corps of Engineers in its channelization work. Histories that describe both the political origins of Missouri River development and the long-term environmental changes induced by that development are absent from the literature.

These recent histories fit into the larger historiography of water development in the United States, which itself has four identifiable characteristics. First, the majority of the histories examine topics related to river development in the American West during the twentieth century, particularly after 1930. Second, the literature focuses on the role of local, state, and federal organizations in implementing development schemes and managing completed projects. Third, authors either indict the developers or absolve them of any wrongdoing for changing the West's rivers. Fourth, these histories do not emphasize the actual environmental change that resulted from the construction of dams, diversion canals, and channelization works; instead, they emphasize the politics of river development, especially the role of interest groups in pushing for the construction of projects.

The recent historiography of water-resources development in the United States has been greatly influenced by environmental historian Donald Worster. In his book, *Rivers of Empire* (1985), Worster argues that the modern American West (the region extending from the Mississippi River west to the Pacific Ocean) is organized into a hydraulic society characterized by the concentration of wealth and power in the hands of a few individuals and organizations, whom he refers to as the water, or power, elites.

Worster defines the water elites as large agribusiness firms and the federal government, represented by the Bureau of Reclamation and the Corps of Engineers. These water elites sit at the top of the West's social, political, and economic hierarchy, a status they achieved by possessing the capital, expertise, and technology to dominate nature, especially rivers. Their ability to control, and manipulate, rivers has enabled them to establish an undemocratic regime across the region.[12] Worster argues that because water is the source of wealth and power in the West, those individuals and organizations that monopolize it also control the masses who live in the region.

Worster contends that the water elites in the federal government and in agribusiness implemented water-development schemes in an undemocratic fashion by forcing great engineering projects on the people of the West. He argues that decisions concerning development of western rivers were made by the elites alone, without the participation of the masses (those persons without large reserves of capital, technology, or expertise). Worster condemns the capitalist economic system, asserting that capitalism, besides creating the water elites, is also responsible for the destruction of a multitude of riverine ecosystems. Yet Worster fails to discuss the details of environmental degradation. He does not explain how river ecosystems have been altered through development.

Since the publication of the first edition of *Rivers of Empire*, historians of water-resources development have repeatedly addressed the issues raised by Worster—in particular the issue of whether elites have controlled water development in the West. Historians have lined up to support or oppose his thesis. Worster's supporters argue that river/water development has been undemocratic, exploitative, and dominated by repressive state and federal governments and large corpora-tions. Historians in opposition to Worster, including John Opie, Norris Hundley, and James Sherow, have argued that water development in the West has been based on democratic principles. The initiative for development projects came not from the federal government but from grassroots farmers, town residents, and local businessmen.

John Opie, *Ogallala: Water for a Dry Land* (1993), states that demo-cratic-pluralism has determined the history of water development in the Great Plains region. According to Opie, the people of the Great Plains are not controlled by a water elite. No state, federal, or local organiza-tions dominate the region's political, economic, and social systems. The region is characterized by the dispersal of power among many indi-viduals and groups. Access to the region's primary source of water, the Ogallala Aquifer (a vast body of fresh water underlying the Great Plains from North Dakota to Texas), has been open to everyone; no one orga-nization ever controlled the aquifer's water supply. Open access to the aquifer's water led to the establishment of democratic institutions to manage that water supply. The clearest example of this democratic system of water management is the existence of irrigation districts man-aged by the farmers and ranchers themselves; these districts are self-regulating, establishing water withdrawal rates for their members.

Unlike Worster, Opie does not blame the capitalist economic system for environmental destruction in the Great Plains region. He believes the functioning of the capitalist system and democratic water-management practices resulted in the transformation of a desert into the breadbasket of the world. Although capitalist economics and democratic institutions have worked miracles on the plains in the past thirty years, both need to be modified in order to avert the complete depletion of the Ogallala Aquifer. Opie is confident that farmers and ranchers can modify their organizations to ensure that the aquifer's water is not entirely gone within the next thirty years.[13] Opie does examine environmental change on the Great Plains. In particular, he focuses on how this arid territory has been transformed into a wheat-, corn-, and cattle-producing region.

Norris Hundley does not agree with Donald Worster's conclusions either. In his book, *The Great Thirst: Californians and Water, 1770s–1990s*, Hundley argues that democratic principles have guided water-manage-ment decisions in California since the mid-nineteenth century. Accord-ing to Hundley, a water elite does not exist in California or in the West. To illustrate this point, he describes how state and city officials based in northern California are frequently in conflict in the state legislature with representatives from southern California over the use and development of the state's water resources. Furthermore, farmers, ranchers, city dwellers, and industrial users fight for the state's limited water supply, with no one political or economic entity dominating water policy and dictating use to the others. Hundley does not criticize, as does Worster, the capitalist system for "destroying" the environment. Instead, he argues that capitalism has created an incredibly sophisticated system of dams and diversion canals that have helped make California one of the world's economic powerhouses, with a state GNP ranking it eighth among the world's industrialized nations. Hundley concludes that California should develop a new water-management system that can deal with the ever-shrinking water supply in relation to rising demands.[14] He does not address the environmental transformations resulting from the creation of California's water-delivery system.

James Sherow, *Watering the Valley: Development Along the High Plains Arkansas River, 1870–1950,* argues that Worster is wrong about the western water elite but correct for blaming the capitalist economic and political system for ecological degradation. Sherow asserts that no one interest group in eastern Colorado and western Kansas came to dominate the Arkansas River's water supply or dictate its development and use. Instead, these groups competed for the river's water within the capitalist economy, and this competition led to the overexploitation of the Arkansas. Various individuals and interests eventually drew so much water from the Arkansas River that it dried up in certain reaches. For all intents and purposes, the Arkansas then ceased to be a river. Sherow does address environmental changes that resulted from the construction of the John Martin Dam and the unrelenting consumption of the river's water; however, he provides only cursory coverage of these environmental consequences.

Sherow concludes that the competitive capitalistic approach to river development and water allocation along the Arkansas River Valley must be replaced with a water-allocation system based on socialist principles. The long-term economic viability of the entire western Kansas and eastern Colorado region depends on regulating the further development of the river so that the people of the region as a whole benefit from the river's water, not just one economic interest group. Only long-term planning and a supragovernment agency can sustain balanced and ecologically sensitive development in the valley.[15]

Unruly River differs from previous writings on the Missouri River and water-resources development in the American West. Past accounts of the Missouri describe the river and valley environments in time, during a particular year or decade. In this history I chronicle the river and valley through time, explaining how these environments have changed since the early nineteenth century. In *Unruly River,* as in previous political histories related to the Missouri River, the political origins of Missouri River development plans are examined. But instead of describing only the actions of the human players in the political arena, I argue that the Missouri River was an active entity that had a tremendous and often unpredictable effect on the formulation and implementation of development plans. For example, the great flood of 1952 influenced the political decision-making process to alter the Missouri River. The flood led to the construction of two additional dams on the river, two dams for which federal funds had been eliminated or substantially reduced because they were deemed unnecessary for the control of the stream. In *Unruly River* I detail the environmental changes that resulted from the construction of the navigation channel below Sioux City, and to a lesser degree the effects of the dams and reservoirs north of Yankton. The only previous data on the environmental consequences of construction projects have been presented in scientific journals and reports. Unlike these scientific studies, this history presents the environmental changes in the Missouri River in narrative form, with attention to how the changes related to other events and actions.

Moreover, neither a water elite nor grassroots organizations dictated the direction of Missouri River development. Instead, the elites (as defined by Worster) and the democratic organizations (as defined by Opie, Hundley, and Sherow) cooperated to accomplish their respective goals. Missouri River development was designed to benefit the agricultural sector of the American economy, especially through the establishment of a navigation channel in the river. Proponents of channelization believed that deep-draft barge traffic on the Missouri would result in a lowering of commodity-shipment costs for farmers. Development progressed without sufficient information about the river environment. Even though the federal engineers continually learned about the Missouri and adapted their engineering techniques and technologies, they could not prevent negative and costly environmental repercussions. Development, in turn, produced mixed results. People paid a tremendous price for the benefits derived from damming and channelizing the river. For example, upstream dams decreased the flood threat south of Sioux City but required the inundation of several hundred thousands of acres of the most fertile agricultural land in Montana, North Dakota, and South Dakota.

Prior to the development projects of the nineteenth and twentieth centuries, the Missouri River radiated with life. Life pulsated in the river's darkest depths, percolated onto its sandbars, and burst through the brush and trees lining the banks. This life, this energy, was manifested in a symphony of sounds and a smorgasbord of smells. The wind blowing through the silver-lined leaves of a tall cottonwood, the splash of a rolling catfish, the subtle rush of a bird's wings, and the steady, ominous humming of millions of mosquitoes proclaimed life just as surely as did the rancid, decaying flesh of a beached buffalo fish or the dank, mustiness of vegetation rotting in stagnant pools. The Missouri River lived. There existed no distinction, no separation, between the river's water (its essential element) and all the life that drew nourishment from it.

Channelization, dam construction, and land-clearing adjacent to the stream quieted the river's noises, sanitized its robust odors, and redirected its waters for the sustenance of one species, Homo sapiens. Human self-interest fueled the development of the Missouri. Many river developers unashamedly sought to promote their own economic standing while others held a grander, more noble vision for the Missouri basin, one that entailed using the river to improve the lot of the human race. Historians have always found it difficult to distinguish the latter group from the former. But within the Missouri Valley, both forms of human self-interest harmed innumerable species, radically altered the riverine ecosystem, led to bitter conflicts between various political and economic organizations, and spawned a host of problems that plagued the Missouri basin into the 1990s.

This history is organized chronologically, except for Chapter 2, which describes the Missouri River as it exists today. Chapter 3 sketches the views of early nineteenth-century travelers who experienced the river before the beginning of large-scale American agricultural settlement in the river valley. Chapter 4 explains how the Missouri River and Valley environments facilitated this settlement. Chapter 5 examines the first efforts of lower valley residents, the Missouri River Commission, and the Corps of Engineers to improve the river for navigation purposes. Chapter 6 chronicles the rejuvenation of development plans following the flood of 1903 and records the political origins of the 1912 legislation authorizing the six-foot channel to Kansas City. The chapter also addresses the 1927 congressional authorization to extend the six-foot channel to Sioux City.

Missouri River development during the drought and depression years of the late 1920s and 1930s is depicted in Chapter 7, with an emphasis on the expansion of the federal presence along the river by the construction of the Fort Peck Dam and reservoir. Individuals and interests based in the upper Missouri Valley, particularly in South Dakota, sought to build dams across the river during the early decades of the twentieth century. Chapter 8 describes South Dakota's attempts to control the Missouri River and explains why those attempts failed to receive federal government support. Chapter 9 examines the river's history during the 1940s, focusing on the individuals, organizations, and events that led to congressional authorization of the Pick-Sloan Plan in 1944. The great flood of 1952, including its influence on public support for the construction of dams in the Dakotas, is described in Chapter 10, which also details the highly advanced construction techniques used to confine the Missouri to its navigation channel. Chapter 11 compares the benefits of river development to the costs. Chapter 12 concludes this history by summarizing the previous eleven chapters and suggesting what lessons might be learned from the development of the Missouri River.

2 | The Modern Missouri

The modern Missouri River serves millions of people. It provides irrigation water to farmers in Montana, hydroelectricity to city folk in Great Falls, Sioux City, and Omaha, walleye for sport fishers in the Dakotas, drinking water for the thirsty cattle of ranchers in Nebraska, and an occasional navigable water route for barge companies based in St. Louis. Only within the past 100 years has the river been engineered and managed to provide these benefits; the intensive use of the Missouri River is a twentieth-century phenomenon. The waterscape of the modern Missouri reflects the diverse individuals and interest groups it serves each day.[1]

The Missouri is a long river, longer than even the Mississippi. It flows approximately 2,466 miles from its headwaters in the foothills of the Rocky Mountains to its confluence with the Mississippi, roughly twenty miles north of St. Louis, Missouri. The river, its source streams, and its tributaries drain 529,000 square miles, or one-sixth the land area of the continental United States.[2] The source streams of the Missouri form in, or around, Yellowstone National Park and the Bitterroot Mountain Range of northwestern Wyoming and southwestern Montana. There, in the land of geysers, hot springs, pinnacles of sandstone, and deep canyons, rivulets and streams begin their descent to rivers that feed the Missouri. In the Bitterroot Range, to the west of Yellowstone National Park, the Ruby, Beaverhead, and Big Hole Rivers converge to form the Jefferson, named by American explorers Meriwether Lewis and William Clark for the third president of the United States and the primary supporter of their expedition to the western sea (Fig. 2.1).

The Madison River is created from the waters spewing forth from hot springs, from snowmelt, and from quick, violent summer thunderstorms that frequent the mountains; it exits the west end of Yellowstone National Park and veers to the north, its current moving rapidly over stone and gravel. Northwest of Quake Lake exists a stretch of water known in local parlance as the Fifty Mile Riffle, because the Madison is continuously choppy from shallow water moving over stones.

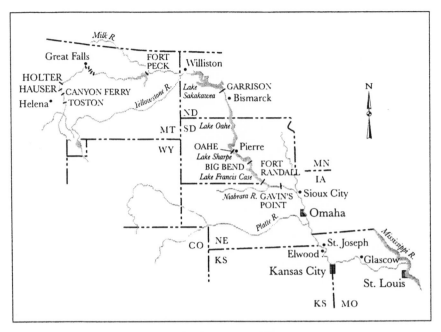

Fig. 2.1. The Missouri River.

The Gallatin River also rises in the park, only a few miles from the source streams of the Madison. From its starting point, the Gallatin travels nearly due north through a narrow valley, abutted by high cliffs on each side. The Missouri's largest tributary, the Yellowstone, begins at Yellowstone Lake in the center of the park. This stream, the only undammed major river remaining in the continental United States, has a spectacular beginning, exiting the lake and cascading over a 109-foot fall and then over another, more incredible 308-foot fall, before traveling north through a yellow- and red-walled canyon.[3]

As the Jefferson, Madison, and Gallatin course through the irregular land surrounding the park, their channel areas are straight and stable and possess rapid currents. However, each river is transformed as it descends to the foothills of the Rockies. There, in the gently rolling landscape near Bozeman, Montana, the rivers' currents slow down, the streams meander, and their silt content increases. By the time the Jefferson, Madison, and Gallatin meet at Three Forks, Montana, they meander so much that it is a challenge to discern which rivers are actually converging to form the Missouri. Three Forks is a low, alluvial plain interspersed with a confusing array of oxbow lakes and river channels. The Jefferson, Madison, and Gallatin do not join in an awe-inspiring torrent of water to create the Missouri. Rather, the Madison first, rather timidly, joins the Jefferson; then the Jefferson and Gallatin, each seemingly vying for dominance, meet under a steep, south-facing white bluff, giving birth to the Missouri River.

North from Three Forks, the clear, blue river glides past a land of wheat fields extending westward and the Big Belt and Little Belt Mountain Ranges rising to its east. Only twenty miles north of Three Forks, the river current is blocked by a low dam at Toston, Montana, built in the early twentieth century to provide irrigation water to local farmers and ranchers. Another twenty miles north-northwest of Toston Dam, the Missouri enters the headwaters of the Canyon Ferry Reservoir, the largest reservoir on the river above Fort Peck Reservoir, storing 2 million acre-feet (MAF) of water.[4] Thousands of white gulls regularly dance along air currents above Canyon Ferry Reservoir, menacing cruising fish as well as boaters wearing the latest sport fashions. Canyon Ferry Dam was built in the 1950s by the Interior Department's Bureau of Reclamation as part of the Pick-Sloan Plan for Missouri River Development, and its primary purpose is the generation of hydroelectricity.[5] Just below this dam the river enters the reservoir impounded by Hauser Dam.

Canyon Ferry Lake and Hauser Lake are located only fifteen miles to the east of the Montana state capital of Helena, which is situated above the two reservoirs on a sloping plain. Helena residents rely on the reservoirs for recreation. Summer weekends witness large numbers of people along the reservoirs' shores either fishing, camping, or boating.

Only four miles below Hauser Dam sits Upper Holter Lake. It rests on the upstream end of a deep gorge of the Missouri known since 1805 as the Gates of the Rocky Mountains. The river is squeezed through the Gates by high black and white cliffs that rise hundreds of feet directly above the river. The channel itself is confined to a width of a mere 100 to 150 yards. Lewis and Clark described this spectacular section of the river in late July 1805: "Nothing can be imagined more tremendous than the frowning darkness of these rocks, which project over the river and menace us with destruction. The river, of 150 yards in width, seems to have forced its channel down this solid mass; but so reluctantly has the rock given way that, during the whole distance, the water is very deep even at the edges, and for the first three miles there is not a spot, except one of a few yards, in which a man could stand between the water and the towering perpendicular of the mountain."[6]

After passing through the Gates of the Rocky Mountains, the Missouri's waters again spread out across the reservoir formed behind Holter Dam. The water exiting from Holter Dam's powerhouse is cold enough to support one of the best trout fisheries in the United States along the river from the dam to the town of Cascade, Montana. This section abounds with large rainbow and brown trout that feed on the river's rich aquatic insect life. During the summer months and in early fall the river here is crowded with fly-fishers who gain access to it from the Missouri River Recreational Road.

At and just below the town of Great Falls, Montana (named after the Great Falls of the Missouri located here), the Missouri has five dams across its path, which capture the river's hydroelectric capacity as it descends. In one section alone, the river drops an estimated 350 feet in a mere two-and-three-quarter-mile stretch.[7] A hydroelectric dam stands directly on top of the Great Falls of the Missouri, destroying what had once been considered the most beautiful falls west of Niagara (Fig. 2.2).

As the Missouri travels through the valley from Fort Benton, Montana, to the Charles M. Russell Wildlife Refuge—a section designated by Congress as a National Wild and Scenic River—it enters the longest stretch of the entire river system that has not been either dammed or channelized. Fantastic rock formations, known locally as the Stone Walls, stand above the river. In 1833 Swiss artist Karl Bodmer remarked that the sandstone formations here resembled ancient European fortresses and castles.[8] One formation is known as Citadel Rock, a sliver of stone that juts straight up from the waterline.[9]

Downstream from the Stone Walls, the river's current again slows as its waters enter the reservoir behind Fort Peck Dam. This reservoir extends 134 miles to the face of the dam. Fort Peck was the first and largest earthen dam built on the main stem of the Missouri. The dirt plug across the valley is four miles long and 220 feet high. The reservoir has a storage capacity of 18.7 MAF, enough to store nearly three times the average annual flow of the Missouri River past this point.[10]

Just below Fort Peck, the Milk River enters the Missouri from the north. The Milk River received its name because of the color of its water, which appears milky white due to sediments that leach into the stream from the surrounding countryside. The Milk River's sediment load spills

Fig. 2.2. The dams at Rainbow Falls and Great Falls, Montana. On 14 June 1805 Capt. Meriwether Lewis observed the Rainbow Falls *(top photograph)* for the first time. The explorer considered the falls "one of the most beautiful objects in nature." The grandeur of the Great Falls *(bottom photograph)* also deeply impressed Lewis and Capt. William Clark. (Photographs by author, 1996)

into the Missouri and slows its current, increases its channel sinuosity, and contributes to the formation of sandbars and islands. The changes in the character of the Missouri River accelerate as the waters of the Yellowstone, the Missouri's largest tributary (and some claim the Missouri's true parent) pour into the river just a few miles southwest of Williston, North Dakota. The sediment of the Yellowstone and Missouri Rivers is not allowed to flow as it did years ago; instead, the valley to the northeast of the mouth of the Yellowstone has become an immense, sandy delta. As the silt-laden waters of the Yellowstone run into the calmer water of the Missouri, the former's silt is dropped on top of the Missouri's streambed. Since the mid-1950s, the Missouri's carrying capacity (the amount of water the river's channel area can normally hold without flooding) at the mouth of the Yellowstone has decreased 50 percent because of these silt deposits. Furthermore, the buildup of silt has led to a higher water table, increased lowland flooding, and required the protection of Williston from ever-rising waters. The cause of these problems is Lake Sakakawea.[11]

Lake Sakakawea is a windswept monster of a lake, created in the 1950s with the downstream closure of Garrison Dam. Lake Sakakawea's storage capacity is 23.8 MAF, making it the largest reservoir on the river.[12] To create a lake of this size, all the Missouri Valley bottomlands on the Fort Berthold Reservation, home to the Three Affiliated Tribes of the Mandan, Hidatsa, and Arikara, were flooded. Beneath the reservoir's waters lie the remains of nine Indian towns, with such names as Old Sanish, Shell Creek, Charging Eagle, Elbowoods, and Nishu.[13] Garrison Dam stands 180 feet high and is 11,300 feet long.[14]

Below Garrison Dam, the Missouri again runs as a river. In an eighty-seven-mile stretch from the dam to the headwaters of the next reservoir, the river somewhat resembles its former self, before the massive, twentieth-century civil engineering projects completely remade it and its valley.[15] Here the river flows around sandbars, cuts away its banks, and glides past islands and timbered bottomlands. But this free-flowing river of today is not the river of yesterday. The Missouri's waters are clear and cold, not warm and silt-laden. The water flowing in this reach originates from the dark, sunlight-deprived depths of Lake Sakakawea. As this sediment-free water exits the dam, it erodes the riverbed. Over the years, the riverbed south of Garrison has dropped from four to five feet.[16]

Lake Oahe, formed by Oahe Dam, begins only a few miles south of Bismarck, the capital of North Dakota. This reservoir sustains one of the best sport fisheries in the United States. Chinook salmon, channel catfish, northern pike, white bass, sauger, trout, crappie, and walleye flourish in Oahe. The superb walleye fishing has earned the lake the title Walleye Capital of the World. The fishing is good because the South Dakota Game, Fish, and Parks Department annually stocks fingerlings in the lake and because Oahe's size provides a wide array of suitable habitat. Oahe's reservoir storage capacity is 23.1 MAF, which creates a shoreline of 2,250 miles. But the sheer size of the lake increases the dangers for fishers and recreational boaters. At the Little Bend of the Missouri, located thirty miles north of Pierre, South Dakota, the distance from bank to bank is twenty miles. Here, three- to five-foot-high waves are common, and during strong winds the waves breaking on the shore-line can reach heights above ten feet.[17]

Oahe Dam towers 200 feet above Pierre and Fort Pierre. Below the dam, the river runs again, but only for about six miles before it enters Lake Sharpe, named for Merrill Q. Sharpe, the South Dakota governor who gave unflagging support for large dam projects in South Dakota. Lake Sharpe lies in central South Dakota, country as wide open, impos-ing, and beautiful as any on the Great Plains.

Forty-five miles south-southeast of Pierre, the river makes a dramatic turn to the north-northwest and then loops around again toward the south-southeast. The Big Bend of the Missouri is twenty-six miles around, which distinguishes it as one of the longest natural river bends in the world. The neck of the bend is a mere one and one-half miles across. On the southeast corner of the bend, at the edge of the neck, sits the small town of Lower Brule, the government seat for the Lower Brule Sioux Reservation. A relatively new town, it was built in the early 1960s to replace the original community, which was inundated in the spring of 1964 by the rising waters behind Big Bend Dam.[18]

Approximately seven miles east-southeast of Lower Brule is another dam, named for the bend in the river and not for the bend in the dam itself. In the 1960s engineers considered Big Bend Dam to be an engi-neering marvel because of the construction techniques the Corps of Engineers employed to create the structure. The Corps built the dam in a unique S shape to make use of the favorable foundation conditions located on both sides of the Missouri Valley. In 1967 the American So-ciety of Civil Engineers nominated the dam for the Outstanding Civil Engineering Achievement Award.[19]

The Missouri does not become a free-flowing river again below Big Bend Dam. Instead, the headwaters of its next reservoir begin at the bottom of the dam wall. Lake Francis Case, named after the senator from South Dakota who was instrumental in promoting and procuring fund-ing for the construction of dams and reservoirs on the Missouri in the 1940s, 1950s, and 1960s, extends 140 miles downstream to Fort Randall Dam. Lake Francis Case may be the most unsightly Missouri River reser-voir; from Big Bend Dam to Chamberlain, South Dakota, the protrud-ing white stumps and branches of trees drowned in the 1950s outline the former serpentine river channel. The dead trees resemble the bleached bones of some giant, slithering beast now lying silent in the river and serve as a reminder of a once vibrant valley ecosystem that has been stilled.

Along the edges of Lake Francis Case is evidence of a phenomenon known as shoreline slumping. Officials of the Missouri River Division of the Corps of Engineers, who oversee the operation and maintenance of the main-stem dams and reservoirs, wrote, "Because these shorelines consist of highly erodible soils, wave and ice action leads to accelerated erosion in the form of slumping cut-banks. . . . The cut-banks are continually slumping into the reservoirs at rates as high as 20 feet per year. At such rates, there is not sufficient opportunity for protective vegetation to take root and protect the cut-banks from further erosion."[20] Besides decreasing the reservoir's storage capacity, slumping contributes to vast stretches of mud shoreline. These drab mudflats become painfully obvious during low-water periods.

Fort Randall Dam is not as big as Garrison or Oahe; it measures 185 feet from crown to riverbed, and its length approaches two miles.[21] Fort Randall was the first of the Pick-Sloan Plan dams to stem the Missouri's flow. At the foot of the dam sit the remains of Fort Randall, a U.S. Army post established in 1856 to observe the nomadic Sioux and to aid in the European-American settlement of the valley. The dilapidated Christ Church is the only structural evidence of the post's presence. About one-half mile due west of the post, on the slope of a grassy bluff overlooking the dam and the church, is a nineteenth-century cemetery that bears testament to the American frontier experience. Simple, white headstones have such inscriptions as Eugene Trask, killed by Indians, Sept. 3, 1863; John Thompson, found frozen, Jan. 16, 1870; H. B. E. Heiner, chronic diarrhea, Sept. 5, 1876; and John H. Bezent, struck by lightning, Aug. 20, 1874.[22]

South of Fort Randall Dam the river flows again, past hills that recede into the western horizon. The river and valley, extending for thirty-nine miles southeast of the dam, have been designated a National Recreational River under the National Wild and Scenic Rivers System. The National Park Service, which manages this area, hopes to preserve its wildlife habitat and develop its tourism potential. Forty-four miles below Fort Randall, the Missouri meets the Niobrara, emptying its waters from the west. The Niobrara River moves with such force into the Missouri that the Missouri, for a moment, is pushed aside to let this tributary enter. At the mouth of the Niobrara, a mass of silt has built up over the years to create a marshy delta. The silt has caused problems for the residents of the town of Niobrara, Nebraska, located on the south bank of the Niobrara River. In the 1950s the town had been spared initial inundation from the waters behind Gavin's Point Dam, but by the 1960s the silt pouring into the headwaters of Lewis and Clark Lake (behind the dam) raised the water table enough to cause frequent flooding of basements. To avoid future flooding, residents agreed to relocate to higher ground. In July 1977 they dedicated a new town site on the bluffs above the river valley.[23]

Gavin's Point Dam is the smallest of the five earthen structures built on the Missouri between 1946 and 1966. The dam stands 72 feet high and is 8,700 feet across.[24] Lewis and Clark Lake is roughly forty miles long. A major tourist attraction, the lake draws visitors from three metropolitan areas, including Omaha, Sioux City, and Sioux Falls. The number of visitors has steadily increased since the 1950s, with a major boom in the mid- and late 1980s. In one ten-day period in summer 1991, over 100,000 people visited the Lewis and Clark Recreation Area, a series of parks adjacent to the lake.[25] The scenery, fishing, boating, and sailing opportunities attract the high number of visitors. The calumet bluffs on the Nebraska side change color with the position of the sun, turning a brilliant gold at sunset on cloudless evenings. Furthermore, the lake's water level fluctuates less than the other reservoirs on the Missouri, which contributes to good fishing. Stable water levels have also allowed attractive shoreline vegetation to take root and grow.

From Gavin's Point Dam to Nebraska's Ponca State Park, a distance of fifty-seven river miles, the Missouri appears largely as it did in the nineteenth century, possessing sandbars, islands, side channels, and shifting, deadly currents.[26] A mile below the steep bluffs that front the river at Ponca State Park, the Missouri passes around the first stone wing dam built by the Corps of Engineers to prevent bank erosion and to provide a navigation channel for barges. The wing dams just below Ponca are designed to keep the river from shifting its channel away from Sioux City, Iowa, the supposed head of barge navigation on the stream. From Sioux City to the river's confluence with the Mississippi, over 8,000 wing dams and hundreds of miles of quarried limestone line the riverbank, forcing the water into a uniform, monotonous channel. There are no sandbars, only a handful of islands and a couple of side channels along this 740-mile stretch. The river maintains a near-constant 300-foot-wide, 9-foot-deep channel. Above its stone banks, an observer can easily see where the former river once meandered through its valley in western Iowa. The old shorelines are visible in the otherwise laser-leveled valley; they appear as gentle dips in the terrain, and after a good rain, former channel areas fill up with water, marking the river that once flowed through the area.

The Missouri glides past the skyscrapers of Omaha, Nebraska, the city where the Headquarters Office, Missouri River Division, U.S. Army Corps of Engineers, is located; here work the people entrusted with the day-to-day oversight of the dams, reservoirs, and navigation channel. The headquarters building houses the office that is referred to as the Missouri River Reservoir Control Center, the nerve center for regulating the flow of the river. In this room, with its maps of the basin, computers, and large-screen monitors displaying data on flow rates, Corps officials determine the water-release sequence for the main-stem dams.[27] If the land surrounding Pierre, South Dakota, received a drenching, six-inch rainfall the previous night, officials calculate how much of that water will enter the reservoirs behind Oahe and Big Bend Dams, when it will arrive, and how much and when to draw down the reservoirs in order to create storage space for the eventual runoff. Officials at the Reservoir Control Center can sharply curtail the flow of the river or dramatically increase it.[28]

Farther down, past the mouth of the Platte and into the states of Missouri and Kansas, the river moves on, rather quickly within its rock-lined, 300-foot-wide, Corps-designed channel. Just across from St. Joseph, Missouri, the historic starting point for Pony Express riders crossing the Great Plains, stand the remains of Elwood, Kansas, a town devastated during the great flood of 1993. Before sunrise on 25 July 1993, water from the Missouri rushed through the streets of Elwood, pulling down entire houses, digging deep channels, and moving mobile homes in helter-skelter fashion. Fewer than 12 of the town's 500 houses remained unscathed by the high water; an estimated 100 houses were totally destroyed.[29] On the outskirts of the ravaged town lie gigantic cottonwood trees, uprooted by the floodwaters and deposited in the valley, signposts showing where the torrents had passed.

The signs of the great flood of 1993 persist south of Elwood, down to Kansas City, and especially through central Missouri, which witnessed some of the worst flooding of that memorable summer. The river moved with such force through central Missouri that one town after another fell under the high water, and roads running down into the valley literally disappeared as their concrete or gravel bases melted away, forcing closures, detours, and delays. Bridges spanning the Missouri were also damaged by the relentless current. One entire span of a railroad bridge at Glasgow, Missouri, dropped into the river.[30] Even after the flood, the Corps of Engineers kept a close eye on the Missouri, especially along its final reach. During the flood, the river began flowing through one of its ancient channels that emptied into the Mississippi eight miles north of its present mouth. But the high waters of the Mississippi overpowered the floodwaters of the Missouri and prevented the Missouri from permanently occupying this prehistoric route. If the Missouri had been able to shift its entire flow to this older riverbed, it would have wreaked havoc on the new $850 million Melvin Price Lock and Dam on the Mississippi, which sits a couple of miles above the present mouth of the Missouri. If the Missouri's water is ever able to enter the Mississippi above the lock and dam, rather than below it, the effective life of the structure will be dramatically lowered by the silt and debris that will accumulate behind it. To safeguard the lock and dam, the Corps of Engineers built a massive stone barrier to keep the Missouri out of its ancient channel during the next flood. The Corps is determined to keep the river flowing along its current path. Claude Strauser, Corps of Engineers, St. Louis District, Mississippi Valley Division, emphatically stated, "As long as we have a viable government and people realize the consequences [of the river's meandering] we won't let it happen. The Corps will find some way to keep enough rock in front of the Missouri to keep it from establishing a major new channel across the low-lying peninsula. In the next 50 or 100 years we'll probably be able to keep things the way they are, but in the long run the Missouri will have its way. Over geologic time, nature will do what it wants to."[31]

The waterscape of the modern Missouri River is the result of changes that have occurred largely within the past century. In that relatively short span of time, the Missouri changed from a river lightly touched by the human presence to a river completely transformed to serve people. This transformation began with American agricultural settlement. Thus, an examination of the river and its valley before that settlement is necessary to understand subsequent events.

3 | The Missouri River Yesterday

During the nineteenth and early twentieth centuries, Americans gave the Missouri River a number of nicknames designed to describe, succinctly, the environmental character of the stream. People referred to it as the Big Muddy, the Mighty Mo, the Wide Missouri, and Old Misery. Big Muddy denoted the river's water; the Mighty Mo acknowledged its incredible power, especially during floods; the Wide Missouri described the great width of the river as it flowed through the Dakotas, and past eastern Nebraska, western Iowa, eastern Kansas, and Missouri; Old Misery expressed the sufferings of the thousands of individuals who had lost loved ones or property to the stream. A number of popular sayings also characterized the river. Valley residents said it behaved like a transient because it spent every night in a different bed; others asserted that farmers with crops in the bottomlands never knew whether they would harvest corn in the fall or a stringer full of catfish. Missouri Valley inhabitants declared the river's water too thick to drink and too thin to plow. These nicknames and remarks aptly applied to the Missouri River and Valley environments in the early and mid-nineteenth century, before large-scale American agricultural settlement occurred in the valley.[1]

In the early 1800s the Missouri River, below its confluence with the Yellowstone River, was much longer, from 150 to 200 miles longer than it is today.[2] Then, it meandered great distances within its valley. Two factors contributed to the river's sinuosity: valley width and the climatic cycle. Through the Dakotas, the width of the Missouri Valley is from one to three miles.[3] Thus the river meandered, but the valley walls limited its sinuosity by blocking its curving path. From present-day Yankton, South Dakota, south to the Platte River confluence, the Missouri Valley widens. Here the distance between valley walls is from five to eighteen miles, with the widest section found in northern Monona County, Iowa.[4] Because of the broad alluvial valley below Yankton, the Missouri wandered far and wide. Along this reach, the river created dramatic loops, or bends (Fig. 3.1). On 29 July 1804 Meriwether Lewis and William Clark wrote, "The Missouri is much more crooked since we passed the Platte, though generally speaking not so rapid."[5] The explorers also measured

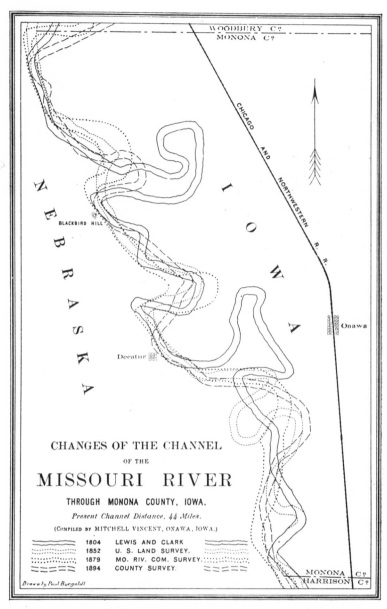

Fig. 3.1. Changes in the channel of the Missouri River. The Missouri
River constantly eroded its banks and changed the direction of its
channel. In the nineteenth century the Missouri naturally straightened
its channel area by cutting off long bends. Those changes are visible in
this illustration of the river channel adjacent to Monona County, Iowa.
(Map from Hiram Chittenden's *History of Early Steamboat Navigation on
the Missouri River*)

a bend in the river in present-day Monona County that extended eighteen and three-quarters miles around and only 974 yards across at its neck.[6] When John James Audubon traveled up the Missouri in 1843, he observed the change in the river above present-day Council Bluffs, Iowa: "We have now come to a portion of the river more crooked than any we have passed; the shores on both sides are evidently lower, the hills that curtain the distance are further from the shores, and the intervening space is mostly prairie, more or less overflowed."[7]

Climate also influenced the river's sinuosity. In the early 1800s a dry climatic cycle descended on the Missouri basin. Low annual precipitation amounts contributed to the river's meandering. The Missouri did not have the water volume or current velocity to move more directly south, so it moved from side to side. Beginning in the early 1840s and continuing into the twentieth century, precipitation patterns shifted; annual rainfall amounts increased and the valley became wetter. The river compensated for the increase in its water volume and current velocity by straightening itself, widening its channel area, and cutting off bends. From the 1840s to the 1920s, the river naturally changed from a meandering stream to a semibraided stream (a river with a straighter channel area that contains more side channels, sandbars, and dunes than a meandering river).[8]

This change in the river began soon after Audubon visited the Missouri Valley. In 1844 the lower reaches of the Missouri (south of the Platte River confluence) inundated its valley in the greatest European-American-recorded flood to that time and cut off a number of bends.[9] The straightening process accelerated in the early and mid-1850s.[10] During winter 1856–1857, the upper Midwest experienced heavy snows and bitter cold. According to Landon Taylor, an early settler in western Iowa, a snowstorm that struck in the first week of December 1856 lasted for three straight days and dumped over four feet of snow in the valley near Sioux City. The deep winter snows remained on the ground into May 1857.[11] When the snows finally melted and the rains fell that spring, the Missouri in western Iowa cut off more of its meander channels. The process continued with the huge floods of 1881, 1903, 1908, and 1915. Thus, the river was first shortened by changes in the climatic cycle and only later through human action.

In present-day western Iowa and in Missouri, the river channel area (the area of the floodplain that contains the main channel, secondary channels, chutes, sandbars, islands, and recent cut-off channels), had a width of 1,000 to 10,000 feet during normal flow periods.[12] During flood periods, however, the river's width expanded to 25,000 feet, 35,000 feet, or even 40,000 feet.[13] A river five to eight miles wide, running hurriedly through trees and brush and abutting the bluffs, appeared less like a river and more like some foaming, misdirected monster.

Every year, the Missouri experienced an annual spring and summer rise, which usually occurred in April and June. The spring rise resulted from the breakup of the river's ice, the melting of the snow cover on the plains, and the advent of thunderstorms. The spring rise struck quickly and violently, remained localized, and lasted perhaps a week or two. The summer rise resulted from the melting of the mountain snowpack, combined with prolonged precipitation in the lower valley, and it lasted longer and covered a larger area.[14] These rises occurred every year, like clockwork, and their height and duration depended on the amount of runoff entering the river.

Audubon witnessed the start of the summer rise when he visited Fort Union at the mouth of the Yellowstone on his 1843 voyage. He recorded how the swollen Yellowstone (which drains the short-grass plains and mountainous regions to the southwest) entered the Missouri, causing it actually to stop flowing, back up, and flood low-lying areas.[15] Henry Brackenridge, who went up the Missouri by keelboat in 1811 out of "idle curiosity," wrote about the summer rise near the Whitestone River (the Vermillion River in present-day southeast South Dakota). "A delightful day, the water has risen to its utmost height, and presents a vast expanse, the current uniformly rapid, in some places rolling with the most furious and terrific violence. . . . [The water in] the middle of the river appeared several feet higher than the sides. . . . The high waters enable us to cut off points, which is no small saving of the distance. . . . Great quantities of drift wood descend [the stream] and thirty or forty drowned buffaloes pass by every day."[16] Another observer noted that during floods the river's tremendous water volume pushed with such force against the outer banks of bends that the water level there stood several feet higher than the level along the inner banks. The Missouri resembled a sloping racetrack as its water careened downstream around its bends.

The river's elevation in relation to the adjacent valley floor exacerbated the flooding that occurred. Over the ages, the deposition of the Missouri's silt load raised its immediate bank line above the surrounding bottomlands. Iowa geologist B. Shimek noted that the valley floor in western Iowa sloped downward from five to six feet from the banks of the river to the Loess Hills on the eastern edge of the valley. This phenomenon also existed along the Missouri's course through Kansas and Missouri. Thus, once the Missouri overtopped its banks, its waters went cascading through the lowlands.[17]

The river experienced extreme fluctuations in water volume, and corresponding depth, during any given year or even during a particular week. The river rose several inches or even feet in a few hours following a severe thunderstorm, and it dropped just as quickly once the skies cleared. The higher reaches of the river had more stable water levels than the lower reaches because above the mouth of the Yellowstone most of the runoff entering the Missouri came from snowmelt, which slowly trickled into the stream. Moreover, the upper river has a smaller drainage area, along with a stone and gravel bed, two factors that kept the river level from fluctuating wildly. Along the Missouri's upper reaches, the variation in water level during the average year equaled 7.3 feet, and during a year with a major flood, the difference in level went as high as 19 feet. Further downstream, in the reach through western Iowa, the ordinary fluctuation measured 10.4 feet, and the highest fluctuation approached 25 feet. The reach extending through central Missouri experienced oscillations as high as 38 feet in a year. Thus, the river stage at Hermann, Missouri, might jump from as low as 3 feet to as high as 41 feet between January and July.[18] Even more fascinating, as water levels rose, the Missouri's bed rose. Higher volumes of water meant more silt in the river. This heavier silt load settled onto the established bed, raising it from a few inches to several feet, depending on the height of the flood. The elevated bed then propelled the river outward and down, commanding the Missouri to tear a new course through the lowlands and spread far afield.

Besides floods, extreme fluctuations in volume, and the periodic elevation of its bed, the river experienced a phenomenon known as ice-out. This usually occurred in March, when the frozen river awoke from its winter slumber. Ice-out began with the popping and cracking and occasional booming of the ice as it thawed. Then the ice broke into pieces, and the whole mass started to move. As the jumbled, cold mixture hurried downstream, the blocks of ice rammed into each other, as if jockeying for position, and the larger ice cakes pulverized the smaller ones into slush or forced them skyward, accompanied by a low groan.

Ice-out always coincided with localized flooding, as ice jams formed and the river backed up into the surrounding bottomlands.[19] The worst flooding from ice jams occurred on the river in spring 1881. That year, the Missouri's tributaries poured a large volume of meltwater into the still frozen river. Instead of the usual, gradual breaking up of the river's ice, the inflow quickly dislodged the ice, resulting in the formation of massive ice cakes.[20] One cake, witnessed near Yankton, South Dakota, reportedly measured ten acres across and four feet thick.[21] These cakes flowed downstream and jammed around logs, sharp bends in the channel, or on top of sandbars and islands. Once an obstacle blocked the flow of ice, it piled up behind the obstruction until the river became dammed. It was common for the water to rise three, four, five feet or more in a matter of hours behind ice jams.[22] After sufficient water pressure built up behind the structure, the ice jam gave way.

A succession of ice jams above and below Old Vermillion, Dakota Territory, demolished that town in 1881 (Fig. 3.2). The river's ice and water shattered a total of 132 buildings. In one day alone the Missouri carried downstream fifty-six buildings, eventually smashing them up against an ice jam south of town.[23] When the waters receded, Old Vermillion resembled a junkyard. Ice cakes covered with greasy black mud lay strewn all over the streets, and a large section of the town had been wiped clean, its buildings gone with the river (Fig. 3.3).

The depth of the river's main channel, or thalweg, varied with the season of the year. In spring and early summer, the thalweg attained its greatest depth, peaking in late June. Beginning in early July, the river dropped, retreating to its lowest level in December and January.[24] Although highly variable, the depth of the thalweg below the mouth of the Yellowstone confluence averaged between three and four feet. But on the outside edge of abrupt bends (where the water tore against the bank) or off the end of gravel bars, the thalweg achieved depths approaching ten or even twenty feet, and there were holes in the Missouri that exceeded forty feet in depth.[25]

The Missouri also contained rapids, cascades, and riffles. The river above the Yellowstone had the majority of rapids and falls. Two famous rapids, named during the steamboat era, were Bird's and Daulphin's Rapids.[26] Even the lower river, with its predominantly sand, gravel, and clay bed, possessed rapids and riffles.[27] In 1811 Brackenridge reported that on 24 April, his party attempted to pass over a sand and gravel riffle where the water flowed with considerable force.[28] Lewis and Clark documented large boulders in the middle of the river near the Big Bend region. Massive, water-worn round stones blanketed the Missouri River

Fig. 3.2. Old Vermillion, Dakota Territory, 1880. The founders of the original Vermillion platted the town on the valley floor to access steamboats hauling cargo on the Missouri River. (Courtesy of the W. H. Over Museum, Vermillion, South Dakota)

channel near the mouth of the Cannonball River; the presence of these stones gave the Cannonball its name. William (Steamboat Bill) Heckman of Hermann, Missouri (one of the few steamboat pilots to work the lower Missouri in the twentieth century), detected sizable stone slabs in the river through central Missouri, which had slipped into the river from adjoining bluffs. At points where the river dashed against the base of a limestone bluff, Heckman noticed rock shelves shoving their sharp edges into the current.[29]

Contrary to popular belief, the Missouri was not muddy. In the early nineteenth century, prairie topsoil did not yet saturate its water and the river never appeared black or dark brown. Rather, the stream took on a milky, light-brown coloration or a shade of gray.[30] Nineteenth-century explorers and adventurers appreciated the beauty of this seemingly dirty

Fig. 3.3. Old Vermillion, Dakota Territory, spring 1881. This
photograph shows the destruction wrought by the flood in the town's
business district. (Courtesy of the W. H. Over Museum, Vermillion,
South Dakota)

water, especially when the sun's light struck the river at a particular angle.
Hiram Chittenden, a Corps of Engineers officer assigned to the Missouri
in the late nineteenth century, claimed that the Missouri's water took
on a "crimson hue or silver glimmer" in the mornings and before sunset (Fig. 3.4).[31] The river acquired its color from the sands, clays, gravels, and limestone that washed into the stream from the great short-grass
plains that extend to the Rocky Mountains. These materials formed a
concoction known as silt, which was constantly in motion in the river's
current. Silt was picked up, dropped down, moved from side to side, and
rolled along the riverbed. When it settled down, it formed sandbars,
which littered the river from bank to bank, especially during low-flow
periods. At times, the bars became so numerous that early river navigators had difficulty discerning the location of the thalweg. Sandbars made
the lives of keelboatmen and steamboat pilots hellish. Lewis and Clark,
traveling upstream by keelboat, described their predicament on 12 September 1804: "We with great difficulty were enabled to struggle through
the sand-bars, the water being very rapid and shallow, so that we were
several hours in making a mile. Several times the boat wheeled on a bar,
when the men were obliged to jump out and prevent her from upset-

ting; at others, after making a way up one channel, the shoalness of the water forced us back to seek the deep channel. We advanced only four miles in the whole day and camped on the south."[32] Audubon, traveling by steamboat nearly forty years later, wrote about a similar experience near Fort Pierre. His entry for 31 May 1843 stated that his boat had been moored the previous night only nine miles southeast of Fort Pierre and that the boat had departed for the fort at 3:30 A.M. but had not reached the fort until 4:00 P.M. It took twelve and one-half hours to travel nine miles because the boat kept getting hung up on sandbars. Audubon would have been better off to have walked to Fort Pierre that day.[33]

Islands formed in the Missouri River when the thalweg changed course and separated a piece of land from the main shore or when the river's water no longer inundated a sandbar, which allowed for the growth of vegetation. The Missouri did not possess as many islands as sandbars because the river's erosive action prevented the formation

Fig. 3.4. The Missouri River near the Platte River confluence. The color of the Missouri's water appeared light yellow or at times an ashen gray. The clearer water of the Platte *(to the right)* did not immediately mix with the silt-laden Missouri. (Karl Bodmer watercolor, 1833. Courtesy of the Joslyn Art Museum)

of stable landforms within the channel area. However, the islands that did form in the river supported stands of trees, which in turn anchored the island and prevented its destruction. Two of the largest and most documented islands in the Missouri existed in present-day southeast South Dakota, Bon Homme Island (west of Yankton, South Dakota) and Cedar Island (approximately forty-two miles upstream from Fort Randall Dam).[34] Steamboat travelers noted the attractiveness of these two islands, including their excessive size and the splendor of their trees and meadows.

Sand flats existed on the perimeter of the channel area, especially on the inside edge of bends or at the foot of the bank line. The river frequently scoured or inundated the flats and rendered the establishment of vegetation impossible (Fig. 3.5). Sand dunes formed near the river as the wind blew across the sand flats, picked up dry, fine silt, and dropped it in front of an obstacle, such as a log or a tree. Dunes located near Bon Homme Island so impressed Lewis and Clark with their height that the explorers mistook the formation for an ancient fortress.[35] In

Fig. 3.5. Sand flats below the mouth of the Big Sioux River. The Missouri River channel area in the nineteenth century was wide and divided by numerous sandbars. Extensive sand flats existed along the river's edge, formed during high flows through deposition of silt and the scouring action of the river's current. In this illustration, sand flats are visible at the foot of the Loess Hills. (Karl Bodmer watercolor, 1833. Courtesy of the Joslyn Art Museum)

western Iowa, dunes around trees reached twenty feet in height.[36] The extensive sand flats, dunes, and sandbars in the channel area contributed to vicious sandstorms that tore through the valley.

The Missouri eroded its banks endlessly, shifting its channel and frequently cutting off bends to form oxbow lakes. Thaddeus Culbertson, who traveled up the Missouri Valley to Fort Pierre in 1850, wrote, "I have noticed several lakes within the last two days, all of a peculiar shape, that of a half moon and having wood on the inner side. I am told these lakes are filled with fish which are left there from the high waters of the Missouri."[37] Oxbow lakes formed during high-flow periods, when the river's greater volume and increased current velocity contributed to channel straightening. The river also created oxbow lakes through prolonged erosion of a bend's neck, regardless of increased water volumes descending the channel.

When the Missouri River eroded its banks, it undermined trees and brush. During floods, when the river's erosive powers were greatest, the river channel filled with downed trees, which eventually settled to the river bottom, becoming snags. Over time, rushing water stripped all the bark, leaves, and small branches from the snags. These white barkless snags extended above the murky water and during foggy mornings appeared like ghosts seeking to rise from their watery graves (Fig. 3.6).[38] Floating trees and brush, which collected behind embedded snags, formed what pioneers referred to as an embarras. A French trader wrote, "The first [snags deposited in the river] serve as a stay for the others, which serve in turn for those which follow, and all being entwined and gathered together become a solid mass and form an immovable bridge, all bristling with branches and stumps, which extends far out into the water."[39] Occasionally, embarrases reached stupendous sizes, covering hundreds of square feet and extending all the way across the river channel. When a steamboat or keelboat rounded a bend and its crew sighted the impenetrable ramparts of an embarras blocking the path of the boat, fear and utter dread gripped the men. In order for a boat to pass beyond a massive embarras, an opening had to be sawed through the jumbled mess. During this procedure, there was the constant risk that men wielding axes and saws, standing on top of the unstable pile, would slip or stumble and then vanish under the obstruction, pulled down by the current and kept down until they drowned (Fig. 3.7).

The Missouri possessed, or was possessed by, whirlpools. Hiram Chittenden told the story of the steamboat *Miner*, which narrowly es-

Figs. 3.6 and 3.7. Snags in the Missouri River (*top*). An embarras on the Missouri River (*bottom*). (Karl Bodmer watercolors, 1833. Courtesy of the Joslyn Art Museum)

caped being sunk in a whirlpool just south of Sioux City in 1867. Witnesses claimed the center of the whirlpool descended twelve feet below its outside edge. As the *Miner* tried to pass safely by the swirling mass of water, it was caught in the spiraling current; two men slipped off the deck and drowned in the turbulent water. Fortunately, the whirlpool tossed the *Miner* into calmer water, where it mustered enough steam to proceed onward.[40] A whirlpool near Vermillion menaced that town and its residents from 1875 to 1881. The whirlpool undermined the railroad tracks south of town, threatened the lives of boaters, and in the great flood of 1881 became the depository of many of the town's buildings.[41]

Although the river often shifted course, cut away its banks, and carried trees, brush, and buffalo downstream, it actually accreted more land than it eroded. The wide alluvial valley floor in western Iowa had been aggregating since the last glaciation. And when the Missouri eroded one side of its channel area, it rebuilt the other side; one area's loss was always another area's gain. The Missouri redistributed soils, working in concert with geological and climatic forces to move soils off the plains and prairies, deposit sediments along its entire length, and dump a portion of its silt load into the Mississippi.

The silt deposited by the river along the valley was fertile. Rich in minerals and organic matter, it contributed to the growth of thick underbrush, tall prairie grasses, and forests. Lewis and Clark, while camped near present-day Homer, Nebraska, noted the underbrush and the difficulties of travel along the valley floor: "The walk [to a nearby Indian village] was very fatiguing, as [the men] were forced to break their way through grass, sunflowers, and thistles, all above ten feet high and interspersed with wild pea."[42] The forests lining the river were truly impressive. Lewis and Clark noted that the Missouri "nourishes the willow-islands, the scattered cottonwood, elm, sycamore, linden, and ash, and the groves are interspersed with hickory, walnut, coffee-nut, and oak."[43] Cottonwoods along the river grew to astounding sizes, fed constantly by the river's water. Brackenridge, in 1811, claimed to have measured a river's-edge cottonwood thirty-six feet in diameter at its base.[44] In a more believable depiction, John Bradbury, who also traveled up the Missouri in 1811, measured cottonwoods seven feet in diameter, which maintained that thickness eighty or ninety feet above the ground (Fig. 3.8).[45]

At the start of the nineteenth century, the Missouri River Valley remained lightly touched by the human presence. The river (with its whirlpools, shifting currents, deep holes, side channels, sandbars, rapids, and

Fig. 3.8. Underbrush along the Missouri Valley. The fertility of the river valley's soil fostered the growth of expansive forests, thick underbrush, and tall prairie grasses. Swiss artist Karl Bodmer painted this scene along the riverbank below the grave of Blackbird, former chief of the Mahas. The grave is located in east-central Nebraska. (Karl Bodmer watercolor, 1833. Courtesy of the Joslyn Art Museum)

silt-laden water) and valley (with its marshy bogs, oxbow lakes, tangled underbrush, and overflowed lowlands) had been shaped and changed almost exclusively by geological and climatic forces. Indian peoples did divert water from the river to irrigate small plots of maize or beans. They also burned the valley's prairie grass in the spring to encourage plant growth. They even extracted timber from the valley forestlands for furnishings and fuel. But the Indians only minimally affected the environmental character of the river and valley because their numbers remained low and their population groupings lived in widely separated locations.

Beginning in the early 1800s and continuing through the 1870s, however, large numbers of American settlers entered the Missouri River Valley. They flocked to the valley because its environment, and its concomitant biodiversity, offered many of the raw materials necessary for the maintenance of life in a rudimentary agricultural society, including game animals, fish, fresh water, wood, and rich soil. The river also provided settlers with a transportation route between their peripheral communities and eastern U.S. and European markets. Thus, in its undammed and unchannelized state, the Missouri River played a crucial role in the successful American agricultural settlement of the Missouri Valley and the adjacent uplands.

4 | The Missouri Valley and American Settlement, 1803–1880

From 1803 to 1880 American military personnel, fur traders, and agriculturists settled in the Missouri Valley. The valley's timber, easily accessible drinking water, wild game animals, flat land surface, and lush prairie grasses furnished these pioneers with the resources they needed to survive in a frontier region. The pioneers also relied on the Missouri River transportation route to maintain a communications link with the outside world, supply them with manufactured goods, and carry their agricultural commodities downstream. Thus, for the early settlers, the establishment of homes, farms, and towns in the bottomlands, or along the river's banks, made economic sense. They needed to be close to the resources and transportation artery that allowed them to live there in the first place. Their reliance on the river led directly to efforts to improve the stream for navigation purposes through a program of snag removal. When the railroad arrived in the valley, however, residents abandoned the river route. By the 1880s the railroads had firmly established a monopoly over the transportation system of the upper Midwest. Missouri Valley inhabitants perceived this monopoly as exploitative and sought to revive commerce on the Missouri. But instead of advocating snag removal and the reestablishment of steamboat traffic, the public wanted nothing less than the complete remaking of the stream to facilitate barge traffic.

American agricultural settlers advanced up the Missouri Valley after 1803, spurred on by favorable environmental conditions. In 1804 Meriwether Lewis and William Clark recorded that the most distant white settlement up the valley sat at the mouth of the Osage Woman River, approximately forty-four river miles above the confluence of the Missouri and Mississippi Rivers. West of this village lived a handful of French trappers, a few antisocial American farmers, and several nomadic Indian tribes.[1] On their descent of the river in 1806, the two explorers saw established farmers, raising cattle and hogs, living in the valley as far west as the Gasconade River, ninety miles above the Missouri's mouth. The line of settlement moved fifty miles in only two years.[2] In 1811 Henry Brackenridge witnessed plantations and sizable towns along the banks of the Missouri 200 miles from the river's mouth. Five years later the federal census estimated the presence of 500 whites along the bottomlands in central Missouri. By 1820 the number of whites living in the valley and nearby uplands increased to 17,629.[3] The town of Franklin became central Missouri's commercial hub. A decade later a string of communities lined the Missouri Valley through central and western Missouri, including Osage, Jefferson City, Rocheport, Boonville, Arrow Rock, Glasgow, and Independence, the last over 350 miles above the Missouri's mouth.

Settlers continued to concentrate in the lower valley in the 1840s and 1850s. An editorial in the *St. Louis Post-Dispatch* in 1843 argued that less than a quarter section of land remained unclaimed in the Missouri Valley from the river's mouth to the Missouri-Iowa border. The U.S. Census of 1850 confirmed that 225,000 Americans lived in or immediately adjacent to the Missouri Valley in the state of Missouri. By that same year, the town of St. Joseph, located along the river in northwest Missouri, had become a well-established community, serving as an outfitting center for prospectors headed to the California gold mines. Agricultural settlers occupied the bottomlands in west-central Iowa as early as 1855; and a group of Council Bluffs–based investors founded Sioux City in 1856, an estimated 900 river miles above the Missouri's mouth. By spring and summer 1859, over 1,000 people waited in the Sioux City area for federal authorization to colonize the former Indian lands of southeast Dakota Territory. When that authorization came in July 1859, Americans hurriedly occupied the river valley northwest of Sioux City.[4] During the 1860s and 1870s, the line of settlement moved north-northwest along the river through Dakota Territory. Settlement in the Missouri Valley occurred before the occupation of all the lands to the east of the river. The valley served as both a magnet and a conduit for American entrepreneurs and settlers (Fig. 4.1).

The Missouri Valley contained fresh, easily accessible drinking water for military personnel, traders, and agricultural settlers and their stock animals. Pioneers actually considered the Missouri's silt-laden water to be excellent for drinking because of its coolness and taste. When thirsty, the men of the Lewis and Clark expedition dipped their cups into the

Fig. 4.1. The Loess Hills and the Missouri Valley. Windborne silt formed the Loess Hills during the last glaciation episode between 31,000 and 12,500 years ago. (Karl Bodmer watercolor, 1833. Courtesy of the Joslyn Art Museum)

river, making sure to take only the water near the surface because the water lower down contained the silt. Fur traders in posts up and down the Missouri went to the stream with buckets for their water, as did the passengers on steamboats. Farmers drew water from the river for a number of uses. Stock animals waded into the river to cool off during hot summer days and to quench their thirst year-round.[5] Persons living in the Missouri Valley did not have to dig deep water wells. The elevation of the river in relation to the valley floor kept the water table close to the surface.

In the 1800s extensive timber tracts existed along the valley in the state of Missouri and in western Iowa. Pioneers used bottomland timber to build dugout canoes, rafts, and mackinaws (large, flat-bottomed boats). Crewmen used wood to repair damaged keelboats and steamboats. They replaced a broken mast or a punctured hull with bottomland timber.[6] Moreover, wood fueled the engines of the steamboats. Steamboats stopped two or three times daily to load wood, the crew spending as many as three hours a day gathering the material, either by scouring the countryside or by purchasing it at a wood yard.[7] The furnaces of the boats burned an average of twenty to twenty-five cords in a twenty-four-hour period (Fig. 4.2). On every trip, crewmen became obsessed with obtaining kindling. When steamboat crews found any structure along the river's banks not clearly occupied or in use, they tore it down and carted it off. Cabins, deserted military forts, barns, and fences eventually found their way into the furnaces of the steamers.[8] Furthermore, settlers cut wood for the construction of tools, storage containers, furniture, and dwellings.[9]

Often, the first industry erected in a new river town was a sawmill. Sioux City businessmen constructed a sawmill in summer 1856 at the juncture of Perry Creek and the Missouri River, which supplied Sioux

Fig. 4.2. The steamer *Antelope* and a fuelwood supply at Sioux City, circa 1868. In the photograph, a stack of wood equaling twenty cords (a single day's supply) is visible in the foreground. The wood to fuel the steamboats came exclusively from the valley bottomlands. (Courtesy of the Sioux City Public Museum)

City pioneers with several types of cut lumber, including maple, walnut, oak, and cottonwood. The timber fed to the sawmill came predominantly from the Missouri River Valley, although residents also took trees from the bottomlands along the Missouri's tributaries, including Floyd's River, Perry Creek, and the Big Sioux River. Early settlers used cottonwood more than any other timber because of its availability. A settler who reached Sioux City in summer 1857 admitted that when he built his first house, "All the material used, except some oak and walnut for door and window frames, was green cottonwood, right from the log." He recounted that the other settlers built their habitations with the same material taken from the Missouri River bottomlands. He asserted, "The buildings were in nearly all cases mere frames, covered with a single coat of cottonwood siding." Moreover, wood served as the primary fuel to heat cabins and homes and to cook food. In Sioux City, during the fierce winter of 1856 and 1857, "The only fuel was that obtained from the timber along the Missouri River."[10] And valley forestland provided shelter for stock animals during inclement weather, as settlers guided their cattle into the trees before approaching storms.[11] In the nineteenth century, wood's multiple uses made it the wonder material, the historical equivalent of today's plastic. Without the bottomland timber, human life in the Missouri Valley could not have been sustained.

The river valley from the Yellowstone confluence south provided habitat for a host of game animals, including deer, elk, buffalo, black bears, coyotes, wolves, and beaver. Explorers, traders, and settlers hunted and trapped these animals for food, furs, and oils. The men of the Lewis and Clark expedition ate a variety of meats during their journey, the three primary staples of the expedition including buffalo, deer, and elk, with beaver tail as a delicious appetizer. Hiram Chittenden, in *History of Early Steamboat Navigation on the Missouri River* (1903), wrote that when a steamboat went beyond the last civilian settlement, the crew and passengers relied on hunting to procure meat. Each steamboat had men on board hired specifically to hunt during the journey, and they often left the boat at midnight to pursue their prey in the valley bottomlands. After killing an animal, they hung its carcass in a highly visible spot next to the bank, so the boat could pick it up as it moved upstream.[12] Other steamboat travelers remarked that hapless buffalo were shot from the boats while they sluggishly swam across the river. Men hauled their rigid carcasses on board, skinned and roasted each creature, and then feasted on everything from the brimming entrails to the tongue (Fig. 4.3).[13] Wild

Fig. 4.3. Buffalo along the upper Missouri Valley. The Missouri Valley, because of its habitat diversity, served as home to a wide array of animal species. Above the mouth of the Yellowstone River, early nineteenth-century explorers and adventurers observed great numbers of buffalo. (Karl Bodmer watercolor, 1833. Courtesy of the Joslyn Art Museum)

turkeys, prairie chickens, and waterfowl of various sorts (abundant in the woods and grasslands of the valley) afforded an additional source of food. Settlers in western Iowa in the 1850s ate these birds on a regular basis. Describing Thanksgiving dinner in 1857, Sioux Citian Gertrude Henderson said she ate "turkey, prairie chicken, venison, and rabbit."[14]

Military personnel, fur traders, adventurers, and settlers also caught and ate fish from the Missouri; the river and its feeder streams teemed with them. Lewis and Clark wrote of fishing in a small stream referred to as Maha Creek, near present-day Homer, Nebraska. Several expedition members built a crude net, then dragged it through the creek. The two explorers recounted that "the first company [of men] brought 318 fish, the second upward of 800, consisting of pike, bass, fish resembling salmon-trout, redhorse, buffalo-fish, rockfish, one flat-back, perch, catfish, a small species of perch called on the Ohio silver-fish, [and] a shrimp of the same size."[15] In 1843 Audubon recalled that "we caught seven catfish at the river near [Fort Union at the mouth of the Yellowstone River], and most excellent eating they are, though quite small compared with the monsters of this species on the Missouri below."[16] Audubon acknowledged that the lower Missouri River (below the Big Sioux River) contained the largest catfish; there, the river's deeper thalweg and an abundance of side channels and oxbow lakes provided riverine habitat conducive to the growth of bigger fish. Channel, blue, and flathead catfish either were the most abundant fish species in the river in the early nineteenth century or appeared to be because they received all the attention of journal writers. Nonetheless, their numbers must have been stupendous, and catching catfish took little effort and even less skill or knowledge. Lewis and Clark repeatedly mention men catching catfish, the size of some of these creatures bewildering the men of the expedition. On 25 August 1804, as the expedition approached the mouth of the Whitestone River (the present-day Vermillion River in southeast South Dakota), Sgt. Patrick Gass wrote, "Two of our men last night caught nine catfish, that would together weigh three hundred pounds. The large catfish are caught in the Missouri with hook and line."[17]

The river valley also provided Americans with fruits and vegetables that added variety to their diet. Wild grapes, buffaloberries, strawberries, currants, gooseberries, and plums grew in the brush adjacent to the river, as did mouse beans, wild peas, and tubers of various sorts.[18] American accounts detailed how delicious and refreshing the wild fruit tasted, especially after a grueling day of travel in the valley. Saw grass that grew near the water reached heights of five to ten feet. According to Orville Rowland of Turin, Iowa, one of the first settlers to arrive in the Monona County area in the mid-nineteenth century, farmers used the bottomlands principally for the production of hay. Homesteaders cut the saw grass, which Rowland called "ripgut" or "slough grass," to feed to their cattle during the winter and early spring.[19] In addition to cutting the saw grass, stockmen led their cattle to the ripgut before the advent of a winter storm. Mary Fischer, another early settler from Turin, Iowa, reported that farmers kept cattle in the ripgut near the marshes until late in winter. Henry V. Bingham, who traveled to the Missouri Valley in 1818, asserted, "When the winter sets in [farmers] drive their cattle into the bottoms where in a number of places is a quantity of cane."[20] Ripgut also served as a fuel: pioneers gathered the grass into bundles, twisted it, and then tossed it into the fireplace.

The valley's topography invited American exploration, trade, and settlement. The flat alluvial plain facilitated the establishment of farmsteads. Farmers and their draft animals expended less energy planting, cultivating, and harvesting crops along the valley floor than those who farmed the hilly uplands. Furthermore, the valley's soil, nourished with nutrients from the Missouri's annual floods, produced more corn per acre than the uplands. According to Henry V. Bingham, farmers in the valley produced 80 to 100 bushels of corn per acre. When the bottomlands dried out in late summer, the flat surface expedited overland transportation. Wagons and horses moved faster across the valley floor than through the hill country so that farmers saved time and money when marketing their agricultural produce.[21]

Keelboat and steamboat navigation contributed to the concentration of people in the Missouri Valley, and an ever-increasing population in turn facilitated the expansion of river navigation. Before hard-surfaced roads and railroads, the Missouri River represented the only viable route to the lands west and northwest of St. Louis and the only means for valley settlers to ship their surplus production downstream to eastern U.S. and European markets.[22]

American-owned keelboats plied the Missouri River from 1804 into the 1830s. The majority of them were built in the eastern United States, either in Pittsburgh, Pennsylvania, or Louisville, Kentucky. Their builders designed the boats specifically for navigating on the Missouri. The average keelboat had a length of fifty-five to seventy feet, a width of eight to twelve feet, and a depth of hold between five and six feet.[23] The hull had a flat bottom to accommodate the river's shallow water. When fully loaded, most keelboats drew a mere thirty-six inches of water. On the bow stood a forecastle; the stern held a cabin, averaging ten feet long, four feet high above the deck, and eight feet wide. The hold was approximately thirty to forty feet long. A mast rose skyward from the deck and held a large square sail. On each side of the boat ran a narrow plankway, the *passe avant*, roughly fifteen inches wide. Crews occasionally placed a brass swivel cannon, or blunderbuss, on the bow of each boat for use against Indians.[24]

The keelboat possessed four primary means of motive power. It moved forward either under sail, by a method known as cordelling, by oaring, or with the crew poling. The only method that did not require strenuous physical effort entailed the use of a sail. Keelboatmen unfurled the sail when the winds were favorable, which was not very often on the crooked Missouri. One instant, the thalweg would be flowing directly out of the north and the boat would be under sail from a strong south wind; around the next bend the thalweg would be flowing from the south to the north and the boat would be facing directly into the wind. Occasionally, the river and the winds might cooperate with the keelboatmen, and a boat could travel upstream from twenty to twenty-five river miles in a day.[25]

Keelboatmen tied the cordell (a hemp rope, two to three inches in diameter, that had a length of from 500 to 1,000 feet) to the top of the sailing mast. It then ran from the top of the mast through a looped piece of rope attached to the bow and from there to the bank, where a crew of from twenty to forty men waited to tug on the rope. Each member of the cordelling crew grabbed a section of the rope, and under the supervision of a foreman they were ordered forward. While pulling the rope, the men moved through almost impenetrable vines and brush along the riverbank, stepped into concealed holes, tumbled down stream banks, disentangled the rope from tree branches, forded small streams and rivers, fell into the Missouri as the riverbank caved in under their feet, thrashed through inordinately high elephant grass, tried to keep the blowing sand out of their eyes, nose, and ears, and, worst, fought off incessant attacks from the hordes of mosquitoes that descended on their ravaged bodies, all the while sweating profusely under the summer sun. A cordeller had a tough job.

When the winds died down and the keelboat sat too far from the shore to be cordelled, the crew took out the poles. These were solid pieces of hardwood, usually ash, and were manufactured with a round knob on the top and a sort of shoe on the bottom. Roughly ten men lined up on each side of the front of the boat along the narrow *passe avant*. The crew lowered the poles in unison into the river and placed the round knob under their armpits. Once the poles struck the river bottom, the foreman ordered the men to push. The men then walked in marching step toward the back of the boat. Once the poling crew reached the rear of the boat, the foreman commanded the men to raise the poles, return to the front, and repeat the procedure.[26] Poling, like cordelling, did not win many enthusiasts. The process required great physical exertion, especially when the boat became lodged on a sandbar and the only way off was to pole. Keelboatmen lowered the oars into the river as the need arose, usually as a last resort, when sailing, cordelling, or poling failed.

Not surprisingly, given the difficulties of navigating the Missouri River by keelboat, the boats did not make good time moving up the river. For example, the Lewis and Clark expedition departed St. Charles (twenty-one miles above the mouth of the Missouri) on 21 May 1804 and reached the Big Sioux River on 21 August. The expedition traveled approximately 900 miles, averaging a little more than nine and one-half miles a day. Both Henry Brackenridge and John Bradbury traveled up the Missouri seven years later on separate keelboats. Brackenridge's party left St. Charles on 2 April and arrived at the mouth of the Big Sioux River forty-nine days later, averaging eighteen miles a day. Bradbury's group left St. Charles on 14 March and arrived sixty-three days later at the mouth of the Big Sioux, averaging fourteen miles a day.[27] Considering that the average adult can walk four miles per hour over open terrain, keelboats traveled upstream at a snail's pace. On the trip downstream, the boats made better time, traveling at the speed of the current or faster, anywhere from two to six miles per hour or more. Traveling downriver, boats could cover from 60 to 100 miles a day.

Keelboats supplied fur-trading posts, military forts, and settlements with gunpowder, blankets, tools, and that staff of life—coffee. Keelboats also carried immigrants up the Missouri to recently opened lands and hauled their produce to markets at St. Charles and St. Louis. They shipped tons of agricultural produce downstream in the 1820s, especially tobacco and hemp from the Boonslick country of central Missouri. Although cumbersome, slow, and difficult to cordell, keelboats represented the most efficient means of transporting cargo up and down the Missouri Valley at the time. A wagon pulled by a team of oxen or horses over poor, or nonexistent, roads carried less freight, traveled slower, and cost more.

But the difficulties of keelboat travel led directly to the rapid adoption of the steamboat for use on the Missouri River.[28] In the 1820s the lower river between St. Louis and Westport Landing (now located within the Kansas City metropolitan area) experienced the increasing use of steamboats. Built for the deeper rivers of the eastern United States, these early steamboats navigated the lower Missouri because of its increased water volume, especially during the spring and summer rises. Regular steamboat navigation on the upper Missouri waited until 1831.

That year, the American Fur Company had the steamer *Yellowstone* constructed in Louisville, Kentucky. The boat was a side-wheeler, 130 feet long and 19 feet wide, with a 6-foot-deep hull. Although the *Yellow-*

stone possessed a hull deeper than advisable for the Missouri, two company officials, Kenneth McKenzie and Pierre Chouteau, believed the boat would be able to ride upstream during the annual rises. These two men also thought the steamboat would be faster than the keelboat and would carry more freight, thereby cutting costs and increasing company profits. The boat ascended the Missouri in late April, its crew hoping to reach the company's post at Fort Union before the river began falling in July and August. The *Yellowstone* only reached Fort Tecumseh (near present-day Pierre, South Dakota) on its maiden voyage. McKenzie and Chouteau did not give up their attempt to reach Fort Union, however. In 1832 the *Yellowstone* set off nearly a month earlier and reached the fort on 17 June, demonstrating that 2,000 miles of the Missouri River could be navigated by steamboat (Fig. 4.4).

The number of steamboats on the Missouri increased in the 1830s, 1840s, and 1850s, and their uses expanded in proportion to their num-

Fig. 4.4. The steamer *Assiniboine* on the upper Missouri River. In 1833 Karl Bodmer and Prince Maximilian of Wied traveled to the upper Missouri River region on board the steamer *Yellowstone*. In this painting another early steamboat, the *Assiniboine*, moves past hills located in central South Dakota. By the 1850s large numbers of steamers plied the waters of the Missouri. (Karl Bodmer watercolor, 1833. Courtesy of the Joslyn Art Museum)

bers. Steamboats contributed to settlement by carrying farm products downstream to St. Louis and beyond. In June 1843 two steamers, the *Mary Tompkins* and the *John Aull,* docked at St. Louis with freight hauled from the Missouri Valley settlements. A partial list of the cargo of these two boats illustrates the direct contribution of steamboats to agricultural settlement and the indirect contribution of the Missouri River. The *Mary Tompkins* carried 311 hogsheads of tobacco, 24 bales of hemp, 14 casks of bacon, 11 kegs of lard, 49 barrels of wheat, 45 barrels of flour, 1 keg of butter, 1 pack of peltries, 1 sack of feathers, and a number of miscellaneous items. The *John Aull* carried 234 hogsheads of tobacco, 647 bales of hemp, 38 casks of bacon, 653 sacks of wheat, 6 barrels of beef and lard, beeswax, tallow, and furs (Fig. 4.5).[29] The boats also carried annuities and Indians to reservations in Dakota Territory, hauled troops into battle and weapons and ammunition to military forts in Montana Terri-

Fig. 4.5. The steamboat *General Meade* on the Missouri River, circa 1880. A crew of African-American roustabouts loads cargo onto the steamer *General Meade* while their European-American overseers watch from the upper deck. The height of the sand flats on the far right bank indicates the annual variation in water level along this reach. Note the cut bank and stands of cottonwood on the left side of the Missouri. (Courtesy of the Sioux City Public Museum)

tory, transported immigrants and personal items to new settlements, and moved prospectors to jumping-off points for the California and Montana gold mines. An impressive increase in steamboat numbers and use occurred during this same period, the decade of the 1850s being the height of steamboat travel on the Missouri River south of Sioux City. Only one steamer plied the Missouri River above the mouth of the Platte in 1832; by 1857 the port of Sioux City had twenty-eight steamboat arrivals (Fig. 4.6).[30] In 1858 fifty-nine steamboats operated on the river below the Platte, and twenty-three boats serviced the river north of Sioux City. In that same year, the port of Leavenworth logged 306 steamboat arrivals during the eight-month-long navigation season, and in 1859 Omaha recorded 174 arrivals.[31] The statistics reveal that the bulk of the steamboat traffic moved on the Missouri River from Omaha to the south (Fig. 4.7).

Fig. 4.6. The port of Sioux City, circa 1868. A string of towns and cities appeared along the Missouri's banks after 1803. Before the arrival of the railroad in the Missouri Valley, Sioux City, founded in 1856 at the juncture of the Big Sioux and Missouri Rivers, served as a jumping-off point for settlers headed to the Dakota and Montana Territories. (Courtesy of the Sioux City Public Museum)

Fig. 4.7. The stern-wheeler steamboat *Josephine* plies the waters of the Missouri River. Stern-wheelers were well adapted for navigation on the upper Missouri because they drew only a few feet of water and pilots could steer the boats through the river's narrow chutes and side channels. (Courtesy of the Sioux City Public Museum)

As the demand for the transportation services provided by steamboats increased, the packet companies invested money in designing and building boats adapted to the Missouri River. Better boats meant more reliable delivery, which often resulted in a further increase in demand and higher profits. In 1859 Pierre Chouteau Jr. (son of the Pierre Chouteau of the *Yellowstone* venture) of Pierre Chouteau Jr. and Company received a government contract to deliver Indian annuities to Fort Union, Fort Sarpy, and Fort Benton on the upper Missouri. Company officials also signed a contract to move a military reconnaissance party to the region. In order to fulfill this contract, Chouteau had a special boat built, known as a mountain boat. He christened it the *Chippewa*.

The *Chippewa* had a length of 165 feet, a width of 30 feet, and a cargo capacity of 350 tons; it drew only 31 inches when loaded at over half capacity.[32] Other features included a stern paddle wheel, a new high-pressure steam engine, the use of light woods in the construction of the hull and deck, and a low overall profile. The wider hull of the boat meant the *Chippewa* could be loaded more heavily without drawing as much water as a narrower, V-bottom craft. The stern paddle wheel provided the boat's pilot with greater maneuverability through the Missouri's winding, thin thalweg. On the Missouri, side-wheelers experienced more groundings and more damage than stern-wheelers. The high-pressure engine gave the boat greater horsepower to push through the river's chutes and the accompanying strong currents. The use of lighter woods and building materials lessened the draft of the boat, and the lower profile of the *Chippewa* aided in steering under windy conditions. The strong winds that constantly swept across the Missouri Valley tossed high-profile steamers against sandbars and snags.[33] The *Chippewa* represented the best in steamboat technology, materials, and construction, but it still failed to reach Fort Benton in 1859; it had to stop twelve miles below the fort and unload its cargo. The river was simply too low to support the mountain boat.

Although steamboat technology advanced to new heights in the 1860s and 1870s, and the packet companies learned to time their scheduled trips during the river's annual rises, steamboat navigation of the Missouri River remained fraught with danger and delays. The dangers existed in the form of snags, ice, rocks, and boiler explosions. Snags formed in the Missouri after the river eroded its bank line. Once a tree had been undermined by the river, it fell into the channel, and its root structure and trunk, because of their heavier weight, sunk to the bottom and became securely fastened to the riverbed with the accumulation of sand and gravel around its edges (Fig. 4.8). As the river's current tore away the snag's bark, leaves, and smaller branches, only the trunk and largest branches remained grounded in the river; and these pointed downstream, directly at the hulls of steamboats moving up the river. When the river's level rose and covered the snags with water, steamboat pilots had difficulty discerning their location. Often, the only indication to a steamboat pilot that a snag lurked in the depths was the small break in the surface as water bubbled up after striking the snag. Thus, pilots referred to underwater snags as "breaks."[34] But when the wind ruffled the water, the rain blanketed the thalweg's surface, or fog or darkness descended on the Missouri and reduced visibility, even the most astute pilot had difficulty avoiding striking one of the breaks. Steamboats thus sank with alarming regularity on the Missouri River in the nineteenth century.

Fig. 4.8. The Missouri River at Sioux Point, southeast South Dakota, 1910. This photograph, taken a few miles northwest of Sioux City, Iowa, shows the Missouri eroding its banks, dropping trees into its channel. (Courtesy of the Sioux City Public Museum)

A partial list of the boats that hit snags and went down in the river in western Iowa and southeast South Dakota included *Helena No. 1, Katy P. Kountz, Mollie Dozier, Nora,* and *Carrie.*[35] Other boats sank, including the *Alabama of the North,* a stern-wheeler 160 feet long and 32 feet wide, owned and operated by the Northwestern Transportation Company of Sioux City. On 27 October 1870 the *Alabama* struck a snag near the mouth of the Vermillion River. The boat, and its consignment of whiskey and flour, valued at $12,000, was a total loss. To make matters worse for the boat's owners, the *Alabama* and its cargo were not insured.[36] The *Miner,* which in 1867 had narrowly escaped being sucked into a whirlpool south of Sioux City, ran out of luck in 1874. The boat hit a snag at the mouth of the Niobrara River. Fortunately, the pilot and crew steered the boat to shore and removed its freight (Fig. 4.9).[37]

Fig. 4.9. A steamer sinks in the Missouri River. In the nineteenth century, the Missouri claimed hundreds of steamboats, many of them sinking after striking submerged snags. (Courtesy of the Sioux City Public Museum)

Interests in St. Louis, including the editors of the *St. Louis Post-Dispatch,* petitioned the federal government to lower the risk to steamboats through a program of snag and tree removal along the river and its banks. Congress recognized as early as 1832 that the Missouri needed improvement for navigation purposes, the same year Chouteau traveled on the *Yellowstone* to Fort Union. Congress did not deem snag removal necessary on the river during the keelboat era since they rarely risked destruction by striking snags. Keelboats did not travel fast, perhaps two miles per hour, hardly enough to impale themselves on an underwater snag.[38] Steamboats, on the other hand, traveled two or three times as fast as keelboats, the increase in speed making the former more vulnerable to snags.

From 1838 until the late 1870s the federal government's primary role on the Missouri River involved the removal of snags, trees, and other obstructions to steamboat navigation. The Corps of Engineers cleared the channel of impediments. In 1838 two government snagboats began operation on the Missouri. The *Heliopolis* and *Archimedes* traveled up the river over 300 miles above the mouth and removed 2,245 snags and cut 1,710 overhanging trees that appeared on the verge of dropping into the river. Snagboat crews also engaged in the destruction of the embarrases that cluttered the stream.[39] Over the years, the Corps pulled an enormous number of snags from the Missouri; in one thirteen-year period, snagboat crews removed a total of 17,676 threatening snags. The Corps took the majority of these snags from the lower river, between Kansas City and the Missouri's mouth, focusing its efforts on this section because it carried the heaviest steamboat traffic.[40]

The Corps' snagboats varied in their technological sophistication. The more advanced ones were modified steamboats with a split pontoon bow and a machine-operated pulley system of cables and chain. The less sophisticated snaggers were two flat-bottomed mackinaws attached side to side with a block and tackle mounted on the front.[41] Regardless of the boat, the procedure for removing a snag was the same. The snagboat approached the obstruction from the downstream side in order to use the force of the current to aid in extraction. After anchoring below the snag, the cables or ropes were run out from the pulley and wrapped around the trunk. The boat's crew then used the pulley system to drag the snag out of the water. If the snag was deeply embedded, crewmen wrapped the cable around the trunk a second time, but at a lower point, and used the pulley again.

Snagboats, channel-clearing operations, and bank line tree removal only marginally decreased the threat that snags posed to steamboats. Two factors worked against the success of these procedures. First, the river continually replenished the supply of snags through bank erosion, especially during the high flows of spring and early summer. Second, snagboats operated after the end of the annual rises, when the river level was lower and snag removal safer. Thus, snag removal occurred after the end of the high-traffic season on the river, when boats took advantage of the high flows. Ironically, just at the time steamboat traffic reached its height and the river filled with snags, the snagboats sat in port, a circumstance that contributed to sinkings (Fig. 4.10).[42]

Hiram Chittenden, a Corps of Engineers officer in the nineteenth century, calculated that 273 steamboats sank in the river between 1830 and 1902.[43] Annalies Corbin at the University of Idaho concluded that nearly 1,000 steamers, ferries, and snagboats went down in the Missouri in the nineteenth century. According to another estimate, the number

Fig. 4.10. Giant snags pulled from the Missouri. The Corps of Engineers extracted snags from the Missouri River to facilitate steamboat navigation, costing the federal government thousands of dollars each year. A government snagboat and its African-American crew pull a gigantic snag from the channel *(top photograph)*. A man is dwarfed by a colossal snag, probably a mature cottonwood that had toppled into the stream *(bottom photograph)*. (Courtesy of the Sioux City Public Museum)

of boats lost equaled three of every seven boats that navigated the Missouri during this period.[44] Along the river reach in western Iowa, at least thirty-nine steamboats sank or sustained severe damage during the steamboat era.[45] In one short stretch of river a few miles west of Onawa, Iowa, the Missouri claimed nine boats.[46] Chittenden estimated that snags caused 70 percent of the wrecks; ice, sandbars, rocks, fire, and boiler explosions accounted for the remaining 30 percent. Corbin believes that only 26 percent of the boats sank after striking snags. But she admits that snags accounted for more sinkings than any other cause.[47] When a Missouri River steamer hit a snag and sank, it very rarely disappeared beneath the waves. Instead, the boat just dropped, rather unceremoniously, a few feet to the bottom. The upper deck, pilothouse, and smokestacks usually protruded above the waterline. People seldom drowned during these sinkings. More often than not, passengers and crew hurriedly gathered their personal belongings, stepped off the crippled boat into the river, and waded to shore. Depending on the depth of the thalweg at the point of the sinking, the extent of the damage, and the strength of the current against the faltering steamer, crews might attempt to salvage either the cargo or the boat and cargo. If the crewmen deemed salvage impossible, they abandoned the steamer to the river. Over time, the Missouri would either shred the boat to pieces or bury it under tons of sand and gravel.

Because of the high probability of a boat's destruction in the river, steamboat companies paid exorbitant rates for insurance. According to William Lass, author of *A History of Steamboating on the Upper Missouri River*, boat and cargo insurance cost from 6 to 10 percent of the value of the product.[48] The high costs of insurance translated into high passenger fares and expensive cargo rates.

In addition to the dangers, steamboat passengers endured constant delays. The most common one occurred when the boats became stuck on a sandbar. Crews worked anywhere from a few minutes to several hours or even days to lift the boats off the sandbars. More delays occurred when the boats had to be "wooded." As if the dangers and delays of Missouri River steamboat travel were not enough, the boats made deafening noises, smelt of urine, rotten carrion, and filthy passengers, and were often overloaded with deck passengers and cargo.[49]

Not surprisingly, residents of the Missouri Valley welcomed the arrival of the railroad. Trains offered cheaper passenger fares, lower cargo rates, greater efficiency and reliability, and far more comfort than the steamboats. Most important, the railroad provided farmers with more direct access to markets in the eastern United States and Europe. Commodities did not have to be shipped down the winding river; instead, harvested crops could be placed in railcars moving along straight lines to Chicago.

As soon as the railroad reached the river, profitable steamboat operations were significantly curtailed below that point. Railroad companies extended tracks to the river beginning in 1859, when the Hannibal and St. Joseph line reached St. Joseph, Missouri. The trend continued when tracks reached Council Bluffs (1867), Sioux City (1868), Bismarck, Dakota Territory (1872), Yankton, Dakota Territory (1873), Pierre, Dakota Territory (1880), and Chamberlain, Dakota Territory (1881).[50] The railroad dissected the Missouri River transportation route, cutting

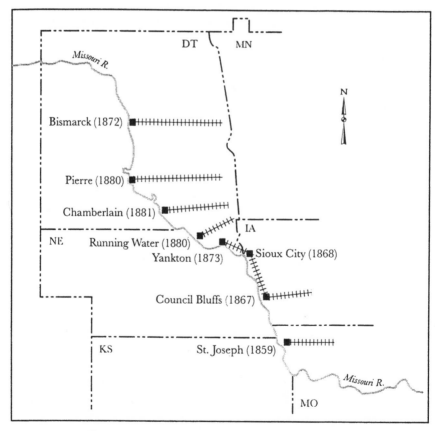

Fig. 4.11. The railroad reaches the Missouri Valley.

the river into smaller and smaller stretches available to steamboat operators (Fig. 4.11).

Missouri River steamboats, with all their drawbacks, gave way to railroads. By 1880 steamboat operations closed down below Yankton. Yankton and Bismarck remained the two largest ports on the river. In 1887, when the Great Northern Railroad reached Helena, Montana Territory, through-steamboat navigation on the Missouri came to an end.[51] Only small packets operated between river towns not serviced by the railroad. The end of steamboat navigation meant that the Missouri's primary role in the settlement of the Missouri Valley also came to an end. Missouri Valley residents no longer needed the river to bring people and supplies to the settlements. The river was no longer the only connection Americans in the valley had with the outside world.

Besides eliminating the river as a transportation route, the railroad also eliminated it as a supplier of food, timber, and provisions. The railroad provided everything imaginable: prefabricated houses, farm implements, cut timber from the forests of Minnesota, furniture, toys, canned foods, and the U.S. mail. Americans quickly replaced their dependence on the river and the valley's resources with a dependence on the railroad.

As that dependence increased, the perception of the river changed. Valley residents began to consider the Missouri as a threat to agriculture and a wasted natural resource in need of improvement. This new perception of the river, along with the belief that the once-welcomed railroad companies charged usurious rates, led directly to efforts by valley residents to redesign the Missouri to carry barge traffic.

5 | The River Abandoned

Competition from railroad companies led to a sharp decline in the number of steamboats operating on the Missouri River. By the early 1880s only a few boats worked the river in Montana and Dakota, and most of these steamers hauled goods between Bismarck and Fort Benton.[1] As the steamboat era came to an end, Missouri Valley residents organized associations to lobby Congress for funding to improve the river. These lobbyists did not seek the reestablishment of steamboat commerce, recognizing that the steamers would never return to the lower Missouri as freight carriers. Instead, they wanted the federal government to channelize the Missouri to inaugurate deep-draft barge traffic. Only these barges, with their large cargo-carrying capacities, could conceivably compete against the railroads.

From the late 1870s to the mid-1890s, people from Sioux City, Council Bluffs, Omaha, Nebraska City, St. Joseph, Leavenworth, and Kansas City requested appropriations from Congress to channelize the Missouri. Citizens from Kansas City, Missouri, represented by the Kansas City Commercial Club, led this organizational movement. These local proponents of river development confronted a reluctant federal government. Members of Congress did not readily finance channelization; instead, they needed to be convinced repeatedly that construction of a Missouri River barge channel represented a justifiable investment of federal dollars. Had it not been for the persistent lobbying efforts of Missouri Valley residents, Congress would not have financed channelization; and even after the start of construction on the barge channel, Congress did not remain committed to its completion. In 1896 federal officials slashed funding for work on the Missouri, and in 1902 Congress abolished the organization charged with construction of the navigation channel. Federal reluctance to pay for channelization, and eventual abandonment of the work altogether, indicates that federal authorities did not impose river development on the residents of the Missouri Valley; rather, valley inhabitants pushed Congress to develop the Missouri.

Attempts to channelize the Missouri began as early as mid-December 1875 when Cong. John B. Clark Jr., from Fayette, Missouri, introduced a bill in the U.S. House (H.R. 267) that sought "to appropriate $1,000,000 to be expended in deepening and permanently locating the channel of the Missouri River with a view of securing a navigable depth of five feet during low water from Sioux City to the mouth."[2] Passage of the bill would have benefited the congressman's constituents living near the river in central Missouri and would have enhanced his political standing. But Clark's bill did not pass the House. Instead, Congress appropriated a much smaller amount in that year's general Rivers and Harbors Act for bank stabilization work at St. Joseph and Nebraska City.[3]

A little over a year later, in January 1877, Cong. Clark Buckner, from St. Charles, Missouri, introduced another bill in the House "to appropriate money to improve the Missouri River between the city of St. Charles and [the Missouri's] mouth."[4] Buckner wanted to ensure that at least St. Charles, a key population center within his district, would be accessible to deep-draft boats that plied the Mississippi River. Buckner, like Clark, failed in his bid to channelize the Missouri.

Although these two Missouri Valley congressmen did not obtain federal backing for channelization, interest in improving the river remained strong, especially within the Corps of Engineers. In February 1881 the secretary of war submitted a report to Congress written by Maj. Charles Suter, Corps of Engineers, Office of Western River Improvements, St. Louis, Missouri, the division that directed Corps work on the Missouri. In his report, Suter examined the feasibility of improving the river for barge traffic. Suter viewed the Missouri in relation to the Mississippi and to a larger system of inland waterways, writing, "The subject of [the Missouri River's] improvement, therefore, is not only of local interest, but is of the greatest general importance now that the improvement of the Mississippi is receiving serious consideration. . . . The cost of this improvement, which if carried out on a large scale and with liberal appropriations, will not probably exceed $10,000 per mile. This would put the cost for the whole 800 miles under consideration [from the mouth to Sioux City] at $8,000,000, and from Kansas City to the mouth of the river at $3,750,000."[5]

Suter, relying on only two years of continuous, daily stream-flow data for the Missouri, calculated that the river south of Sioux City could be deepened to a dependable twelve feet at low water. He asserted, "The benefits attendant on such an improvement can hardly be overestimated. With a guarantee that at lowest navigable stages, a safe and permanent channel, having nowhere a depth less than 12 feet, will be available, boats and barges as large as any now used on the Lower Mississippi could be built and safely navigated."[6] Suter's engineering report provided Congress, and interests within the Missouri Valley, with a blueprint for future action.

One month after the presentation of Suter's report to Congress, the Missouri River overflowed its banks and engulfed the lowlands in Dakota Territory. The flood of 1881 actually began in mid-October 1880, when winter storms, accompanied by snow, sleet, and high winds, buffeted the northern Great Plains and Missouri Valley. Record-breaking cold temperatures followed. By late November the Missouri drifted silently through Dakota Territory under a mantle of ice. An uninterrupted cold spell in December, January, and February then entombed the river beneath four feet of translucent crystal. Heavy snows fell in late February and early March 1881, adding inches to a snowpack that had been steadily growing since the previous October. At some locations in Dakota, four feet of snow lay on the ground.

In the first weeks of March 1881, warm southerly winds blew across western Dakota Territory, freeing the encased Missouri near Fort Buford, although solid ice still covered the river to the east and south of the fort. Once unleashed, the Missouri plowed downstream, bulldozing the ice sheet in front of it, pulling up blocks of ice like shingles from a roof and then throwing the fragments to the sides (Fig. 5.1). The river literally rumbled as it descended the valley, gaining momentum below Bismarck when sudden warm temperatures and rain dissolved the heavy snow cover, feeding water into the swelling stream. The high water, ice, and flotsam formed a particularly destructive mixture.

The river pounded Pierre, Fort Pierre, and Niobrara. The worst devastation occurred at Yankton, Green Island, Gayville, Meckling, Vermillion, Burbank, and Elk Point, Dakota Territory. In Yankton and its environs, where the last few steamboat companies still operating on the upper Missouri docked their boats during the off-season, the river destroyed or damaged several steamers. Ice and floodwaters crushed the steamboats *Western* and *Butte,* punched holes in the *Helena* and *Black Hills,* sent the *Peninah, Nellie Peck, Rosebud,* and *Big Horn* downstream without crews, and ditched the *General Meade* in a grove of trees. The Missouri

Fig. 5.1. Signs of the great flood of 1881 near Vermillion, Dakota Territory. A man stands amid ice blocks thrown by the river against the bluffs. (Courtesy of the W. H. Over Museum, Vermillion, South Dakota)

then spilled its waters into low-lying sections of Yankton's business district (Figs. 5.2 and 5.3).

The community of Green Island with its 150 inhabitants occupied the bottomlands due west of Yankton on the Nebraska shore. Over a period of days in late March and early April 1881, the Missouri lifted the town's buildings from their moorings and carted them off downstream one by one. In Yankton, people climbed to their rooftops to watch the ongoing spectacle across the river. When the Missouri scooped up Green Island's church, a hush fell over the Yankton crowd. All eyes fixed on the church's prominent steeple, which danced across the boiling water as the Missouri hauled it away. After a minute or two, this ballet came to an end as the river pushed the church down and then smashed it against a stand of cottonwoods. Only one building in Green Island survived the flood of 1881 (Fig. 5.4).

In the valley south of Yankton, the rapid rise in the river caught hundreds of farmers in their homes, unable or unwilling to escape across the rising currents. Near Meckling, 150 people ran through the lowlands, eventually taking refuge in a mill, where they sheltered until the river backed away. Most farmers fled to their attics, praying that their houses would not collapse under the weight of the water. High winds, a spring blizzard, and cold slowed attempts to evacuate the hundreds of people stranded in the valley. The winds stopped boats dead in the water. On several occasions, the winds forced crews sent out from Yankton, Elk Point, or Sioux City to turn around or risk being capsized. One witness saw waves over six feet high in the river. A blizzard in early April reduced visibility, froze the Missouri's slush and jumbled ice together, and kept the recovery boats out of the water. Cold temperatures made it difficult for rescuers to stay long on the river because numbing windchills and mist froze their fingers, faces, and feet. Yet the majority of farmers in the bottoms south of Yankton made it to safety.

People died in the flood of 1881 although the exact number of fatalities is unknown. In an era before federal involvement in disaster relief, no one kept comprehensive records of those killed by floodwaters in a predominantly frontier region. From the available information, the number of deaths appears low, approximately fifteen people killed in the valley from Yankton to Sioux City. Great numbers of hogs and cattle perished, however. The *Sioux City Journal* speculated that 50,000 cattle died along the valley from Pierre to Sioux City. Such high losses can be attributed to two factors. First, farmers drove their animals into the river

Fig. 5.2. The steamboat landing at Yankton, Dakota Territory, April 1881. Steamboat companies wintered their boats at the Yankton docks. During the flood of 1881, the Missouri damaged or destroyed several steamers. Visible in the photograph is the ruined hull of the steamer *Western,* almost entirely buried under tons of ice. Two other damaged boats rest in the background. (Courtesy of the W. H. Over Museum, Vermillion, South Dakota)

Fig. 5.3. Yankton, Dakota Territory, April 1881. Low-lying sections of Yankton sustained water damage during the flood of 1881. Beyond the buildings, the Missouri is brimming with ice. (Courtesy of the W. H. Over Museum, Vermillion, South Dakota)

Fig. 5.4. The Missouri Valley in the aftermath of the flood of 1881. Here, two houses have been torn apart and deposited in a grove of trees. Note the effect of the water on the trees. Stagnant pools remained in the bottomlands into June 1881, keeping farmers from their fields. (Courtesy of the W. H. Over Museum, Vermillion, South Dakota)

bottoms to winter in the ripgut and among the cottonwoods, where the inclement weather of March and early April kept them. Then, the speed and force of the freshet trapped the animals beside the river and killed them. Nearly every farmer living in the valley in Yankton County, Dakota Territory, lost cattle and hogs. To illustrate, "Joe Volin lost fifty-six head of cattle, several hogs and other property worth $2,500." "B. M Semple lost forty head of cattle, four horses, fifteen hogs, all his stables, sheds, granary, farming implements, etc., making him a total loser of over $1,800." And "John A. Giggey lost everything, stock, house and barn, chickens, agricultural implements, wagon, household goods and clothing." To add to the calamity, the Missouri ran high through the month of June, and pools of stagnant water lay everywhere across the bottomlands, slowing overland transportation and keeping farmers out of their waterlogged fields during the planting season.[7]

The flood of 1881 affected the burgeoning movement to improve the Missouri River, the disaster reinforcing the public's belief that the river no longer contributed to civilization. It not only jeopardized agriculture (the foundation of a supposedly healthy and wealthy society), but it also challenged notions of prosperity and material progress. As floodwaters focused the attention of valley residents on the seemingly wild, unused river, they became acutely aware of the need to protect their communities from the Missouri's annual rises. Channelization or the Corps' bank-protection works might keep the Missouri from encroaching on valuable urban real estate. Steamboat company executives, who watched their fleets torn to pieces by the river and who already faced stiff competition from the railroads, began to think of Missouri River improvement as a means of recouping their mounting financial losses.

The same year that Suter presented his findings to Congress and the Missouri inundated its valley through Dakota Territory and points south, a group of individuals wishing to revive its navigation held the Missouri River Improvement Convention in St. Joseph. Organizers of the convention had a twofold purpose: to generate popular support for channelization of the river and to use any public endorsement to pressure Congress into adopting the channelization program outlined in Suter's report. Before adjourning, delegates elected a committee to petition Congress for appropriations. In early 1882 this committee sent a letter to Congress, stating, "Could we successfully employ barges on the Missouri River, between Kansas City and St. Louis alone, so as to realize this saving in the cost of marketing our crops, it would make a vast difference to the people of the Missouri Valley."[8] The petition also informed Congress that the shipment of agricultural commodities by barge rather than by rail would save farmers in the upper Midwest over $14 million per year in transportation costs. This amount equaled nearly twice the estimated total expense of improving the river between Sioux City and the mouth.[9] Advocates of a Missouri River barge channel believed it would benefit agriculture and the region's rural population. Even more promising, the channel would pay for itself in saved transportation costs after only six or seven months of operation.

Congress responded to the pleas of the Missouri River Improvement Convention on 2 August 1882 when it passed the Act for the General Improvement of the Missouri River and also designated $850,000 for channelization of the stream. The act and appropriation represented a notable shift in the federal role. Never before had Congress allocated such a large sum of money for work on the river. Previously, it had made only small, yearly appropriations for the Missouri in the Annual Rivers and Harbors bill. In the five-year period ending in 1881, Congress had financed Missouri River work amounting to $861,000; the appropriation of 1882 nearly equaled all the money spent on the Missouri in the preceding five years.[10]

Furthermore, in 1882 Congress endorsed a new type of construction work along the stream. Previously, Congress had ordered the Corps of Engineers to remove snags from the channel area and to stabilize the riverbank in the vicinity of towns. The Corps built revetments (structures designed to prevent bank erosion) adjacent to thirteen towns in the Missouri Valley between 1876 and 1881, including St. Charles, Lexington, Glasgow, Kansas City, Fort Leavenworth, St. Joseph, Nebraska City, Omaha, and Sioux City.[11] But in 1882 Congress embarked on a new path, abandoning piecemeal work for the systematic, continuous improvement of an 800-mile reach of river.[12] This shift in congressional priorities reflected the popular support for channelization that had been cultivated during and immediately after the 1881 Missouri River Improvement Convention.

Major Charles Suter received the responsibility to oversee the construction of the Missouri River barge channel. He used the first $850,000 appropriation to purchase the physical plant needed to build channelization structures. Suter bought and outfitted a fleet of 188 boats, including mattress boats, barges, snagboats, hydraulic graders, hydraulic pile drivers, quarterboats, yawls, skiffs, and a floating machine shop.[13] But

Suter and his engineers did not actually initiate any construction on the barge channel in 1882 or 1883. Suter spent the total allocation (one-tenth of the estimated cost of the entire channelization project from Sioux City to the mouth) on this massive fleet instead of beginning at least partial construction of the barge channel. He had the finances, according to his own calculations, to build a fleet half that size and still channelize forty or fifty miles of river. The reasoning behind Suter's spending decision is not readily apparent. He may have believed that Congress would provide the money needed to complete the barge channel to Sioux City in the next few years; therefore, he wanted to have the boats on hand when Congress made the anticipated appropriations. Another plausible explanation is that Suter wanted to use the presence of the large fleet to procure funding for channelization from a hesitant Congress. The fleet had to be used on channelization work or else the taxpaying public would never get a return on this sizable initial investment. Suter gambled with the first appropriation, confident that Congress would find it hard to reject future allocations for the Missouri River barge channel once such a significant amount had been spent on boats and machinery.

Suter's hope for additional federal money, and the hopes of Missouri River improvement advocates, soared in 1884 when Congress reinforced its commitment to systematic improvement with the establishment of the five-member Missouri River Commission. Federal authorities created the commission because they believed it would be less politicized, less likely to bend to the will of a local constituency seeking bank-protection work, and more resolute in the expenditure of federal funds for the channelization of continuous stretches of the stream. Congress appointed Suter as president of the commission and appropriated an additional $.5 million for channelization work below Sioux City.[14]

The legislature approved the creation of the commission and the accompanying appropriation because they firmly believed establishment of a barge channel along the Missouri would benefit agriculture. In its report to the House, recommending adoption of the Missouri River Commission, the Committee on Commerce argued, "[The Missouri River] is located where it is most needed and where it can perform the greatest service in the shape of transportation. With the great natural advantages possessed by this waterway it should be the main dependence for the bulky freights of an agricultural valley."[15]

With so much apparent congressional and local enthusiasm for Missouri River channelization, Suter made definite engineering plans to transform the stream. He anticipated first channelizing the river at Kansas City, Missouri, and then advancing downstream toward the mouth. According to the *Annual Report of the Chief of Engineers*, "Engineering necessities require that the work should progress downstream. The initial point must, therefore, be at some distance above the mouth. The [Missouri River Commission] have selected Kansas City, 386 miles above the mouth, because it is the first important commercial center to be met with in proceeding upstream."[16] Only Kansas City and its environs could furnish the shipping tonnage to warrant construction of the barge channel. Suter and his colleagues determined that building channelization structures from the mouth to Kansas City would be more costly because the recently completed structures would face the full onslaught of the unchannelized Missouri River just upstream. The unchannelized and unregulated Missouri would continue to shift the direction of its channel and outflank sections of river already channelized. By building from Kansas City to the mouth, Suter hoped to avoid this possibility since the river immediately above sections under construction would have been previously stabilized.

Suter and his engineers had to wait to implement their construction plans. In 1885 Congress overrode the authority it had earlier given to Suter and the commission and ordered him to spend his federal monies on bank-protection work at Kansas City and St. Joseph, where the river threatened to destroy hundreds of thousands of dollars of earlier revetment work. Later that same year, Congress failed to appropriate any funds for channelization of the Missouri in the next fiscal year.[17]

Although stymied, advocates of Missouri River improvement continued to organize and publicize their cause. In September 1885 the city of St. Paul hosted a River and Harbor Convention to discuss strategies for developing the Mississippi River for navigation; approximately fifty disciples of river improvement from the Missouri Valley attended the meeting. Missouri Valley delegates created an executive committee "charged with the prosecution of all matters looking to the improvement of the Missouri River." Two Kansas City men sat on the executive committee, T. B. Bullene and H. M. Kirkpatrick. Other noteworthy members included John H. King of Chamberlain, Dakota Territory, and Thomas C. Power of Helena, Montana Territory. King served as an executive officer of the Missouri River Transportation Company, which ran steamboats in Dakota. Power oversaw the operation of the Benton Transportation Company, another steamboat company that hauled merchandise and passengers on the river above Bismarck. Isaac P. Baker of the Benton Transportation Company joined the movement a few months later. These three executives sought river improvement as a means of lessening their business risks, lowering their insurance costs for freight and company boats, and increasing their competitiveness in relation to the railroads.[18] They also hoped that government construction contracts to improve the stream would provide their flagging businesses with sorely needed capital. Their steamboats, dry docks, and machinery could be employed in the channelization work. Finally, King, Power, and Baker hoped that federal government construction contracts would replace the losses in revenue that resulted from the diminishing military supply contracts. The end of army campaigns on the northern Great Plains had reduced the profits of the steamboat companies.[19]

On 18 November 1885, Power, King, and the other members of the hurriedly established executive committee sent invitations to Missouri basin governors, senators, congressional representatives, and other "distinguished citizens" to attend another convention on Missouri River navigation. Although participants received notification of the event only one month in advance, and the convention occurred during the holiday season, 200 prominent men attended the meeting in Kansas City, Missouri, on 29 and 30 December 1885. Such a high number of participants, at such an inopportune time, indicated the level of interest in river improvement that existed throughout the Missouri basin. Kansas City men constituted the largest single delegation in attendance; of course, holding the convention in Kansas City encouraged hometown participation. Citizens from Missouri represented the largest state contingent. Dakota Territory, Iowa, Montana Territory, and Minnesota sent small delegations, only two or three individuals from each state. The participants came exclusively from the professional classes, with a number of business executives, judges, lawyers, and local government officials present. Few, if any, farmers or laborers attended. A list of names and professions indicates the class of men who led the early movement to transform the Missouri River: Gen. W. H. Beadle (retired); Judge William T. Woods; Winslow Judson, St. Joseph Board of Trade; and Joseph S. Nanson, St. Louis Merchants Exchange.[20]

For two days, these men discussed the federal government's seemingly inherent responsibility for developing the nation's inland waterways and for improving the Missouri River for barge traffic. A sampling of these December 1885 discussions suggests how the men viewed Missouri River improvement and what they wanted from the federal government. The mayor of Sioux City, D. A. Magee, asserted, "We [members of the convention] earnestly recommend and urge the present and permanent improvement of the navigation of the Missouri River upon a general and systematic plan to prepare it for commerce by steamers and barges, and we urge the policy of large and continuous appropriations by Congress therefor[e]."[21] E. H. Allen of the Kansas City Board of Trade stated, "We are making a plain business proposition. It is our purpose to improve the Missouri River from its source to its mouth, to make it thoroughly available for navigation. This, if accomplished, would be an exceedingly valuable thing to the commercial, manufacturing, and agricultural interests of this section of the country."[22] James Craig of St. Joseph told the assembled delegates that if the Senate and House did not provide the necessary money to finance river channelization, then the government officials should be booted from office. Craig insisted, "Whenever you unite, you will make the earth quake underneath your Congressmen and Senators. Their commissions will not be very safe unless they help you with all their might. If they don't do their duty, I would do the same with them as I would with a farm hand; find some one else to do the work."[23] One of the last speakers at the convention, Purd Wright of St. Joseph, spoke about the need for unity among all the river interests. Towns and cities in the valley had to present a united front to Congress in order to secure money for improvement. Once the money had been allocated, the Missouri River Commission and the Corps of Engineers should be allowed to spend it as they deemed necessary for the establishment of barge navigation. Wright also warned that localities must not go to Congress alone to seek money for their own pet projects, such as bank-stabilization work; otherwise, the channelization of the whole river would never be achieved. The convention ended with a resolution to hold another river convention in Omaha in 1886 and to send several men to Washington, DC, to lobby in the halls of the Capitol.[24]

The campaign of the Missouri River Improvement Convention to win federal financing succeeded. On 30 June 1886 Congress allocated

$375,000 to the Missouri River and in 1888 appropriated an impressive $1 million. But the Missouri River Commission, under pressure from local officials and congressional representatives from towns in the Missouri Valley, spent the federal money on bank-protection structures adjacent to several river towns and not on the proposed barge channel.

Although Missouri Valley residents spoke of systematic improvement, they undermined efforts to channelize the river by seeking bank protection near their own localities. Widely dispersed bank-protection work did nothing to foster barge navigation on the stream. Barges required consistent, reliable depths in order to move up- and downstream. An unchannelized stretch of river between two communities, with its sandbars, shoals, and shallow thalweg, would irreversibly ground deep-draft barges, preventing the through shipment of commodities. The fact that localities received the federal appropriations instead of the channelization project indicates the level of local control over the direction of river development. Two federal agencies, the Missouri River Commission and the Corps of Engineers, responded to the orders of Congress, which, in turn, reacted to the demands made by residents in towns throughout the Missouri Valley, especially the citizens of Kansas City and St. Joseph. Local groups possessed more influence over Missouri River development than either the Corps of Engineers or the Missouri River Commission.

Consequently, continuous, systematic improvement of the Missouri did not occur. Of the $2,015,000 appropriated to the Missouri River Commission between 1884 and 1890, $279,951 was used for revetment work at Kansas City and another $97,983 for work at St. Joseph, proof of the political clout of these two urban centers. None of the $2 million was spent to channelize the river below Kansas City.[25]

The decade of the 1890s witnessed greater unity among Missouri Valley towns, and the type of work performed on the river between 1891 and 1896 reflected it. On 19 September 1890 Congress appropriated $800,000 for the Missouri River Commission and ordered the secretary of war to expend the funds for channelization work, not for bank protection.[26] In 1891 Suter and the engineers under his charge finally began channelizing the Missouri River along what they referred to as the first reach. Suter divided the river from the mouth to Sioux City into six reaches, and the first reach extended 137 miles from the mouth to the Osage River confluence.[27] The commission meanwhile reversed its earlier decision to build from Kansas City to the mouth; instead, it determined to extend the navigation channel from the mouth to the west and north, progressively opening more of the Missouri River Valley to the commerce of the Mississippi River and beyond. This political decision, which contradicted Suter's engineering recommendation, would subject the newly completed channelization structures to the full erosive power of the unchannelized river just upstream (Fig. 5.5).

Nonetheless, Suter forged ahead with his engineering plans. The major clarified the principle that would guide construction of the barge channel: "By utilizing the natural forces at work, we hope to avoid any direct conflict with the river, as in such a conflict we would in all probability be worsted."[28] Suter planned on using the river's heavy silt load to facilitate channelization. The Missouri River carried an immense amount of silt to the Mississippi each year. The quantity varied depending on flow volumes. Corps officials estimated the ratio between maximum monthly silt load and minimum monthly load at 166 to 1. Stated another way, the Missouri could carry 166 times more silt in a given month than the lowest load ever carried in a month. Even more astonishing, the river's highest daily silt discharge past Kansas City equaled 2,086 times the lowest daily discharge.[29] Another study carried out by the Corps placed the average annual amount of silt moving past Kansas City at 397,700,000 tons. A lower estimate put the average silt load past Omaha at 275,000 tons per day, or 100,375,000 tons per year, still enough sediment to fill 5,500 railroad cars (with fifty-ton capacities) every single

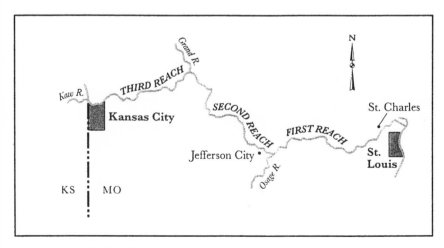

Fig. 5.5. The Missouri River between Kansas City and the mouth.

day.[30] The Missouri exhibited the consistency of a chocolate milkshake. Suter wanted to use this awesome silt load for channelization purposes. Channelization would be accomplished through the use of hydraulic pile drivers, piles, and pile dikes.

A hydraulic pile driver consisted of a small steamer or diesel-powered boat with a hydraulic jack attached to its bow (Fig. 5.6). The piles used by the Corps were actually long poles of white oak or cypress, with head diameters of eight to ten inches and butt diameters of thirteen to nineteen-and-one-half inches. Piles ranged from thirty to over fifty feet long, roughly the same size as a telephone pole.[31] The Corps' hydraulic pile drivers pounded piles into the riverbed, through layers of sand and gravel and into a layer of clay, which securely anchored the pile and prevented it from being washed out by the river's current. The hydraulic pile drivers did not hammer the piles into the bedrock underlying the river; clay served as an adequate foundation material. But pounding a pile through layers of sand and gravel and then into the clay required plenty of time and energy. Occasionally, 600 to 700 blows of the jack were needed to

Fig. 5.6. A hydraulic pile driver in operation on the Missouri River. (Courtesy of the Sioux City Public Museum)

drive one pile deep into the subsurface clay deposits. According to Corps officials, between two and one-half to thirty feet of the pile remained above the surface of the riverbed.

Corps officials placed the piles at ten-foot intervals in a row extending from the natural bank line into the stream. Ten feet on either side of the original row, another row of piles was driven, extending the same distance into the river. At particular locations, the force of the Missouri's current required that a three- or four-row set of piles be driven. These piles served as the base for the pile dike. With the piles embedded deeply in the clay, laborers bolted pine boards along the entire length and width of the pile dike. These boards served as braces, giving greater strength to the structure. Finally, men placed a series of small willow saplings, trimmed of their branches, along the length of the dike, running from the top of the structure down into the sand and gravel of the riverbed. The placement of the willows formed a willow curtain, which served the purpose of further slowing the river's current. As the current slowed on the downstream side of the willow curtain, the water no longer had the momentum to carry its silt load, so it dropped the silt on the downstream side of the pile dike.[32] Over time, the deposited silt accumulated behind the entire length of the dike, forming a solid landmass and pushing the thalweg out beyond the downstream end of the structure (Fig. 5.7). By using two-, three-, or four-row pile dikes, each spaced at intervals of several hundred feet perpendicular to the natural riverbank, engineers created a new bank line, redirected the flow of the river, narrowed the river's channel area, deepened and stabilized the thalweg, and improved the stream's navigability. Thus, the engineers worked within the existing environment to channelize the Missouri.[33]

The commission and its construction engineers considered a number of factors while building pile dikes. First, each pile dike had to extend above the natural bank line a sufficient distance to prevent the river from flanking the structure during high flows. Second, the dike had to reach far enough beyond the river's low-waterline to remain effective during low flows. Third, the piles and willow curtain had to be driven into the riverbed the proper depth. If they went too deep, the river at flood stage could overtop the structure, reducing its effectiveness. If driven too high, the river would flow past the structure without depositing the requisite silt. A fourth consideration was that pile dikes could not be too long. If the dikes on either side of the stream constricted the Missouri's channel too much, the river's current velocity would increase

Fig. 5.7. A three-row pile dike along the Missouri River, circa 1895. The pile dike in the foreground has a willow curtain running down the center of the structure. (Courtesy of the Sioux City Public Museum)

proportionately, thereby making upstream navigation by barges and steamers difficult or even impossible. Furthermore, excessive narrowing of the channel would induce greater downstream scouring and erosion, which would threaten downstream pile dikes. A final design feature related to the thickness of the piles. They had to be thick enough to withstand the full force of the river's current and to resist destruction from floating debris and ice. Thin wooden piles could be smashed to splinters by ice flows, but thick piles cost more to purchase, transport, and place. The engineers strained to discover the proper balance between pile diameter, strength, and cost.

The commission and the Corps also used revetments in their work along the first reach. Federal engineers usually built these structures on the outside edge of bends, where the river's slashing current habitually peeled off strips of land.[34] During this early period, engineers relied almost exclusively on the woven willow mattress and stone revetment. Its construction involved certain procedures. First, engineers waited until the river dropped to low-water stage so that the bank line needing improvement became exposed; thus, construction of revetments most often occurred in fall or winter.[35] Laborers next graded, or smoothed out, the original bank line, giving the bank a forty-five-degree angle. Corps engineers then supervised the cutting of thousands of small willow trees, which grew on sandbars and sand flats near the water's edge, using them to weave a mattress. Men wove the mattress by hand, monotonously intersecting the willows over and under each other, eventually forming a mat. Constructing a willow mattress required considerable time and patience. Men built the mattresses either at the location of the bank needing improvement or at the location of the willows, where the completed mattress was loaded on a mattress boat and carried to the graded bank. The men then laid the mattress on top of the graded bank, with a portion of the mattress extending several feet above the river's high-water line and several feet below the low-water line. Mattresses extended beyond these two waterlines to prevent them from being undermined by persistent low flows or from being eroded from above by excessive high flows. Water either seeping under the mattress or behind it could destroy the revetment in a few hours. Because the difference between the annual high waterline and low waterline could be over 35 feet along the river below Kansas City, the commission and Corps built immense mattresses, some 40 or 50 feet wide and over 100 feet long. After laying the mattress on the bank, men placed stones on top of it, which kept the mat in place and protected the bank line.[36]

The commission and Corps built a modified revetment just below the mouth of the Osage River. Here the river had long been the bane of steamboat pilots, with its braided channel, sandbars, and fast currents. In order to narrow the channel and deepen the thalweg, the engineers had to close off side channels and concentrate the river's flow. One notorious side channel, known as the Osage Chute, needed to be sealed from the barge channel. Forty-five percent of the river's flow moved through the chute, taking needed water away from the proposed navigation channel. The Corps built a sophisticated and costly willow mattress and stone revetment across the upstream end of this chute. Laborers placed willow and stone in seven consecutive layers over its entrance, laying the lowest mattress and stone on the riverbed itself. The structure stretched 1,525 feet and rose 14.5 feet above the riverbed. This unique revetment cost $25,329, a prohibitive amount compared with the $10,000 Suter originally believed would be necessary to construct one mile of channelized river. After the revetment's completion, the volume of the water through the chute dwindled to 5 percent of the total; the remainder moved through the barge channel. The revetment accomplished its design purpose.[37]

Suter and his engineers did not know how narrow or deep they could build the barge channel. In the early 1880s Suter estimated that the Missouri contained enough water to sustain a twelve-foot-deep channel from Sioux City south, even during low-flow periods. In 1891 Samuel Yonge (who supervised the actual channelization work along the first reach) relied on only twelve years of daily stream-flow data to calculate that the Missouri at its lowest stage possessed enough water to maintain an eight-foot depth downstream from Kansas City. Yonge told a crowd of river boosters in Kansas City, "From an extended series of measurements made in the Missouri River at Kansas City and at other points, it has been ascertained that the probable volume of water at Kansas City will seldom be less at any time than 20,000 cubic feet per second. . . . It is, therefore self-evident that if the volume of water given above flows at the velocity stated in a channel 850 feet wide, the average depth of the channel must be about eight feet."[38]

The Corps' work on the Missouri River had no precedent; it would be experimental, trial and error. Pile thickness, dike length and height, distance between adjacent dikes, and the proper channel width would have to be determined as the project moved forward. Suter's men field-tested new techniques and technologies on the river. The engineers did not have the fail-proof channelization structure; instead, they built structures and modified them until they found the ones suited for the stream and its local characteristics. But the willow mattress and stone revetment, along with the pile dike, remained the standard construction technique for channelizing the Missouri River until the mid-twentieth century.[39]

Although channelization work began along the first reach in 1891, the project's future remained uncertain. Congress did not automatically finance the continuance of construction on the barge channel. Instead, Missouri Valley residents had to keep soliciting Congress for funds. To ensure continued federal backing, a group of Kansas City men organized yet another Missouri River Improvement Convention in 1891.

At a meeting of the Kansas City Commercial Club on 21 October 1891, its president, G. F. Putnam, and its members expressed their fear that Congress would cut funding for Missouri River improvement unless Missouri Valley interests organized and lobbied for additional appropriations.[40] Ohio and Mississippi Valley residents had already taken the initiative to push Congress for appropriations for their streams. The people of the Missouri Valley needed to organize or face the possibility of no future subsidies. To prevent that scenario, Putnam invited the Boards of Trade of Kansas City, Kansas; Leavenworth, Kansas; Atchison, Kansas; and St. Joseph, Missouri, to attend a meeting on 27 October 1891 to discuss means of gathering the people of the valley into a unified river improvement movement. At that meeting, the attendees created an executive committee to lead the tentative movement. Kansas City, Missouri, men dominated the committee's membership, holding fifteen of its thirty-one seats. Other locales, including St. Louis, Omaha, St. Joseph, and Sioux City, were also represented. As with the 1885 convention, the men leading the movement came from the commercial and professional classes. The new executive committee represented only lower valley interests; no one from the Dakotas or Montana had membership in the assemblage. The committee extended invitations to individuals and commercial clubs throughout the valley for a convention to be held 15 and 16 December 1891 in Kansas City, Missouri.[41]

Over 400 individuals from throughout the Missouri Valley and beyond attended the Kansas City convention. Men from Memphis, Tennessee; New Orleans, Louisiana; Rosedale, Mississippi; Denver, Colorado, and from Ohio, North Dakota, South Dakota, and Iowa participated in the conference. The large number of participants and their geographical origins indicated the groundswell of support that existed for Missouri River improvement, and for inland waterways development, across the United States.[42]

G. F. Putnam opened the convention with an address that focused on the reasons he and his colleagues wanted the Missouri River improved for barge traffic; "The Commercial Club does not claim to be above the inspiration of selfish motives, neither do the people of Kansas City claim to be too magnanimous to be mindful of their own interests. They expect to be benefited, and largely benefited, by the improvement of the Missouri River."[43] He continued, "The business of the Commercial Club is to promote whatever it believes to be for the best interests of the people of Kansas City and the country tributary to it."[44] Putnam hoped establishment of a barge channel along the Missouri River would substantially lower the cost of shipping agricultural commodities, raw materials, and manufactured goods into and out of the Missouri Valley, with the result that valley farmers and Kansas City businessmen would save millions each year that would otherwise go to the railroads. Any transportation savings could then be reinvested in the region, including Kansas City proper, spurring further economic development.[45] Putnam even asserted, "Deepen the channel of the Missouri River and you confine its water to much narrower limits, excepting in times of great overflows—and consequently render more valuable every acre of land now subject to tillage in the valley, besides adding to the tillable area of our country."[46] Channelization would allow valley farmers to reclaim thousands of acres of bottomland formerly occupied by the river channel, enable them to drain oxbow lakes and swampland into the deeper river, and increase property values by reducing the threat of erosion. These changes would have a multiplier effect. The new acres put under the plow would contribute to increases in agricultural productivity and larger farm incomes, which would result in more business orders for Kansas City firms.[47] A rise in property values would increase the tax base of the valley counties and at the same time permit farmers to borrow more money for capital improvements on their farms.

But Col. G. C. Broadhead of the Corps of Engineers saw the situation in another light. He explained to the assembled crowd that his organization was not intended to improve the Missouri River to increase the value of farmland in the valley. Broadhead said, "The law says, [the] primary object [of the Corps is] to protect commerce and navigation, but nothing is said about protection of private property from washing." The purpose of the channelization project was to establish barge traffic on the Missouri, not to safeguard the river's banks and adjacent agricultural land from erosion.[48]

The convention ended with the passage of a series of resolutions and plans for further action. The delegates resolved to name their permanent organization the Missouri River Improvement Association. Its primary purpose was to seek congressional funding for the channelization of the entire Missouri River (even into the Dakotas and Montana) and the Mississippi River below the Missouri's mouth. The river boosters recognized the interdependence of the proposed Mississippi and Missouri River barge channels. Specifically, the Mississippi had to be deepened before the Missouri River barge channel could be used at all. Barge operators on the Missouri would need access to St. Louis, Memphis, New Orleans, and the Gulf of Mexico in order to market their cargoes profitably; it would not be enough to channelize only the Missouri. According to another of the convention's resolutions, the association's total membership consisted of anyone from the states of Montana, North Dakota, South Dakota, Minnesota, Nebraska, Iowa, Kansas, Colorado, Missouri, Illinois, Kentucky, Tennessee, Arkansas, Mississippi, and Louisiana willing to work for the promotion of its agenda.[49] Convention delegates wanted their association to be a broad-based, democratic body, not an elitist, exclusive organization.

The Missouri River Improvement Association did not have a hard time selling its program to residents of the basin. In 1891 few people in the Missouri Valley or in surrounding states objected to river channelization; they believed that everyone but the railroad companies would benefit from the construction of a barge channel. Farmers, businessmen, industrialists, realtors, bankers, and shippers assumed they would profit from the project.[50]

With so much public fervor for channelization, Congress granted large appropriations for work on the Missouri between 1890 and 1895. But by late 1895 and early 1896, Suter and his subordinates had finished only forty-five miles of the barge channel between Kansas City and the mouth at a cost of approximately $2.6 million, or roughly $58,000 per river mile. The cost per river mile was over five times greater than the original estimate Suter had made in 1881. Furthermore, the engineers merely achieved a low-water depth of six feet in the barge channel, not Suter's twelve feet or even Yonge's eight feet. The Missouri River simply did not have the water to sustain those greater depths. Corps administrators in St. Louis recognized the hard facts. Constructing a barge channel to Sioux City, or even to Kansas City, would cost considerably more and take far longer than anyone had originally planned. Any future project would be gargantuan in scale and complexity.[51]

Considering the tremendous costs of improving such a small stretch of river, the embarrassing absence of any traffic on the Missouri, the slow progress of construction, the fact that the river continually undermined completed structures, and the eventual disbanding of the Missouri River Improvement Association, it came as no surprise to anyone when Congress curtailed appropriations for channelization in 1896. The navigation project had become too costly and its results too uncertain. Furthermore, the panic of 1893 had passed, the national economy had improved, and the need for federal expenditures for public works and indirect unemployment relief did not appear as pressing in 1896 as it had during the previous years.[52]

Between 1896 and 1902 work on the Missouri River diminished to little more than snag-removal operations and small-scale bank-protection projects.[53] During these years, the engineers seemed to believe that if they removed enough downed trees from the channel, they would somehow resurrect navigation on the stream. In 1902 there still remained 324 miles of free-flowing river between Kansas City and the mouth. That same year, Congress passed an act abolishing the Missouri River Commission.[54] As 1902 ended, federal appropriations for the Missouri River were at levels barely high enough to maintain even snagging operations. Congress, state and local entities, and the general public abandoned the Missouri River.

6 | The River Rediscovered

Not long after federal funding for Missouri River improvement had dropped to its lowest level since the 1870s, a series of events prompted a resurgence of interest in developing the stream. The first of these events, the 100-year flood of 1903, rekindled interest in river channelization only one year after the dissolution of the Missouri River Commission.[1] Thus, the river itself had a direct effect on the conceptualization and implementation of development plans.

The great flood of 1903 resulted from the convergence of two natural forces. From five to fifteen inches of rain fell in May 1903 in the Kaw River basin west of Kansas City and in an area to the north of it encompassing southeastern Nebraska, southwestern Iowa, northeastern Kansas, and northwestern Missouri. Most of the rain came in an eleven-day period, from 21 to 31 May.[2] Much of it drained into the Kaw River, filling its banks to the second-highest level recorded by European-Americans.[3] The Kaw flows nearly due east through east central Kansas, past Topeka and Lawrence, and on toward Kansas City, entering the Missouri River only a mile northwest of downtown Kansas City, Missouri. As the high water descended the Kaw, it ran directly into an engorged Missouri, experiencing its annual June rise. Because the floodwaters of the Missouri blocked the flow of the Kaw, the Kaw had nowhere else to go but onto the streets of the two Kansas Cities. Of seventeen bridges across the Kaw in the Kansas City area, sixteen washed downstream. The flooding rendered 22,000 people homeless and covered the city's business district with several feet of water.[4] At the height of the flood on 1 June, the Missouri's flow measured 548,000 cubic feet per second at Kansas City, the equivalent of nearly three and one-half times the mean monthly flow of the river at that point for that month.[5]

Once the Missouri's floodwaters passed the Kansas City metropolitan area, they spread across the entire width of the valley, inundating hundreds of thousands of acres of the best agricultural land in the state of Missouri. Although the great flood of 1903 remained confined to the Kansas City district and regions to the east, it cost more in monetary terms than any other Missouri River flood to that date; population numbers and property values in the valley had soared since the last great flood in 1844.[6] The 650,000 acres inundated cost valley farmers a total of $9.78 million in lost earnings and property. Damage within the two Kansas Cities equaled $1 million.

The disaster emphasized the need for Missouri River improvement to control flooding. Both engineers and valley residents believed the winding channel of the Missouri had slowed the movement of flood-waters past Kansas City, thereby forcing the Kaw's waters into the city's business and industrial zones. A completed navigation channel, the engineers argued, would deepen the Missouri's channel, straighten it, and increase its current velocity—changes that would allow future floods to move more quickly past the city and through the state.

In mid-June, only days after the flood had subsided, Capt. Hiram Chittenden of the Corps of Engineers, who had been assigned to work on the river at the Corps' Sioux City office, wrote a letter to the mayor of Kansas City, Missouri, James A. Reed, recommending that Kansas City officials ask Congress to restore the Missouri River Commission. According to Chittenden, the reconstituted commission would work not to improve the Missouri River for barge traffic but to protect private property and lower the risk of future floods.[7]

Mayor Reed followed Chittenden's advice. Along with members of the Kansas City Commercial Club, Reed organized a River Congress in early October 1903. The event's sponsors wanted to bring together officials from towns along the Missouri and Kaw Valleys to discuss means of preventing a repeat of that year's disastrous spring flood and to form an organization to persuade Congress to finance a series of flood-control projects.

Over 200 individuals attended the congress, including Sen. J. Ralph Burton of Kansas, Sen. Francis Cockrell of Missouri, and Congressmen W. S. Cowherd, W. W. Rucker, and John Dougherty of Missouri. The delegates concluded that sufficient flood protection for Kansas City could be provided by the placement of a system of dams and reservoirs along the upper Kaw River (in the vicinity of Topeka), the building of a line of levees adjacent to the Missouri and Kaw Rivers, and the straightening of both streams.[8] Before the close of the congress, the delegates formed a permanent river commission made up almost entirely of Kansas City, Missouri, men to try to acquire federal financing for its proposed flood-control projects. Unfortunately for the Kansas Citians, the U.S.

House Committee on Rivers and Harbors rejected all the proposals for flood control, pointing out that such action was outside the jurisdiction of the federal government. The Congress and the Corps only had constitutional authority to improve the Missouri for navigation. Thus, the Kansas City River Congress and its river commission failed to achieve their grand design.[9]

Floods that descended the Missouri River in 1904 and 1905 again influenced the formulation of development plans and focused the attention of valley residents on the river. Since the federal government would not implement a flood-control program for the Missouri, Kansas Citians attempted to obtain congressional aid for the moribund barge channel, the construction of which would supposedly lessen the likelihood of floods. In summer 1906, Lawrence M. Jones of the Kansas City Commercial Club and a group of forty Kansas City businessmen established the Missouri Valley River Improvement Association.

Jones and his colleagues sought Missouri River improvement for many of the same reasons advocated by past river boosters, including flood control, land reclamation along the valley, and the ever-illusive dream of fostering barge traffic. Creation of a barge channel remained this group's supreme objective. Demographic and economic trends also affected the ideas of Jones and his partners. The Kansas City metropolitan area had been experiencing an economic boom since 1900. The settlement of the Great Plains to the west, along with the expansion of the city's meatpacking industry, led to an increase in population and wealth in the city. By the end of the decade, Kansas City's population increased 51 percent over the previous decade, from 163,752 in 1900 to 248,381 in 1910.[10] Members of the Commercial Club hoped Missouri River improvement would sustain this economic boom by lowering transportation costs, increasing the value of real estate, and developing new avenues of trade.[11]

Jones contrived a strategy to achieve the association's principal aim. First, he would prove the Missouri navigable with either deep-draft barges or steamers. Once he had illustrated the plausibility of navigation on the impetuous river, he would argue before Congress, and any federal official willing to listen, that the Missouri and its fledging commerce deserved federal funds for channelization. Then, possibly before but more likely after the Missouri had been realigned and deepened, he and other Kansas City businessmen would invest their own capital in a barge line to inaugurate routine traffic on the river. Given the failures of the past twenty-five years to spawn barge traffic on the Missouri, Jones and his colleagues held lofty intentions.[12]

To prove the river navigable, Jones and A. G. Ellet of the Commercial Club's river committee in July and August 1906 chartered the steamboats *Lora* and *Thomas H. Benton* and the barges *Louise* and *America* in St. Louis and loaded each with freight for Kansas City. When the boats and barges arrived in Kansas City on 23 September 1906, a crowd estimated at anywhere between 10,000 and 15,000 celebrated the supposed reopening of Missouri River navigation. That winter, Congress, impressed with the movement of cargo on the river, voted a modest appropriation for the removal of snags from the Missouri.[13]

Possessing the evangelical fervor of a recent convert to a religious cult, Jones, in spring 1907, boarded a train to Washington to exhort congressmen to join him in promoting Missouri River navigation. He educated congressional representatives on the situation in the Missouri Valley but accomplished nothing substantive. Later in the year, Jones, with sixty followers from Kansas City, attended the Lakes-to-the-Gulf Deep Waterway Association meeting in Memphis, Tennessee (Fig. 6.1). President Theodore Roosevelt also attended, displaying his own devotion to the development of the nation's inland waterways. Jones announced in a speech in Memphis that the Missouri River must be key to any planned national system of inland waterways. According to Jones's own testimony, he put the Missouri River "on the map," making federal officials aware of the river's importance to the future prosperity of commercial and agricultural interests in the valley.[14]

Roosevelt's appearance and the hundreds of individuals present at the Memphis meeting illustrated the level of private and federal interest in internal-waterways development that emerged during the first decade of the twentieth century as part of the progressive conservation movement. The progressive conservationists, who included Roosevelt and Gifford Pinchot, head of the Forest Service, believed the federal government should use its authority to conserve the nation's natural resources for sustained-yield production. Initially, the progressives focused on the conservation and wise use of the nation's timber, oil, and mineral reserves. But by 1907 the progressives believed the nation's rivers needed to be developed to the fullest extent possible for hydroelectric generation, irrigation, navigation, or all three.[15] To progressives like

USE THE RIVERS—THE ALL WATER ROUTE

KANSAS CITY TO THE SEA

Compiled for W. S Dickey, President of Kansas City Missouri River
Navigation Company, by Tuttle & Pike, Civil Engineers

Fig. 6.1. The Lakes-to-the-Gulf Deep Waterway. Missouri River navigation boosters tried to gain federal support for Missouri River channelization by linking their project to a proposed system of inland waterways that included the Great Lakes and the Illinois, Mississippi, and Ohio Rivers. (Map by Tuttle and Pike)

Roosevelt, failure to develop the rivers of the United States constituted the waste of a valuable resource.

Progressives viewed the Missouri River as only one part of a much larger transportation system that included the Great Lakes, Mississippi River, Ohio River, and the soon-to-be-completed Panama Canal. These various waterways would be linked together, with each maintaining the same reliable depth, thus providing the United States with the means to ship agricultural commodities directly from the bountiful Midwest to virtually any port in the world without breaking bulk (the expensive and time-consuming process of transferring cargo from a deep-draft barge to a shallow-draft barge or vice versa). Moreover, such an integrated waterways system would accomplish two major policy objectives for the progressives: it would increase the competitiveness of the United States within global markets and decrease the menacing and monopolistic economic and political power of the railroad companies. As a first step toward the wise use of the nation's rivers and the creation of a system of connected deep waterways, President Roosevelt in 1907 established the Inland Waterways Commission; its mission was to take an inventory of the nation's water resources and to establish guidelines for their development.[16]

At the close of the Lakes-to-the-Gulf Deep Waterway Association meeting, members of Roosevelt's Inland Waterways Commission, at the invitation of Jones and Edgar C. Ellis, a congressman from Kansas City, traveled to Kansas City aboard the Commercial Club's luxurious private train car. After they arrived, the Commercial Club held a series of meetings with their federal guests, including prominent conservationists Gifford Pinchot, Sen. Francis P. Newlands, author of the Reclamation Act of 1902, and Frederick H. Newell, chief of the recently created Reclamation Service. After treating them to a sumptuous breakfast, the Commercial Club gave the federal entourage a motor tour of the city and then hosted a lunch in their honor, where Jones spoke of the necessity for Missouri River channelization along the reach between Kansas City and the mouth. He did not mention channelization between Kansas City and Sioux City. For the first time, the Kansas Citians decoupled their own agenda for the river from that of their valley compatriots to the north and west. This apparent shift in policy may have been made inadvertently. The nervous excitement induced while speaking with such influential officials possibly caused Jones to forget to address the river north of Kansas City. But more likely, he wanted his audience to know that Kansas City would accept a federally sponsored barge channel half the length of the one originally envisioned by the Missouri River Commission and Maj. Charles Suter. Jones employed a standard marketing ploy: if you cannot sell all your inventory, at least try to sell a portion of it. An accomplished businessman (he owned and operated the Jones Dry Goods Company), he recognized that if he could not peddle the concept of an 800-mile, already discredited, Missouri River barge channel to the federal government perhaps federal officials would buy a less lengthy channel.

Following the luncheon, the Kansas Citians and their guests boarded the Corps of Engineers' snagboat *Suter,* named in the major's honor, for a tour of the Missouri River. Once on the water, Col. E. H. Shulz of the Corps explained the techniques and technologies that would channelize the river, while the Kansas City men described how the resumption of river traffic would save their citizens and region millions of dollars in reduced shipping costs each year. After lengthy conversations with members of the Inland Waterways Commission, Jones, Ellis, and the others spoke to the press with confidence that federal officials, including the president, would support Missouri River improvement.[17] The close of these discussions made it apparent that the Kansas City Commercial Club had effectively tied their movement for river channelization to the larger national crusade for inland-waterways development advocated by the progressive conservationists.

An indication of renewed federal interest in the improvement of the Missouri came in 1907 when the Corps of Engineers formed the Kansas City District Office to oversee work on the river. Previously, the Missouri had been under the jurisdiction of the division office in St. Louis; creation of a separate office for the Missouri illustrated the increased importance placed on the stream by the federal bureaucracy. The founding of the Kansas City District gave further impetus to Jones's efforts and those of the Missouri Valley River Improvement Association. Members of the Kansas City Commercial Club would now be able to articulate their demands for river work directly to the Corps of Engineers. They could also cooperate more fully with Corps officials to secure funding from the Congress. The Kansas Citians would no longer need to travel to St. Louis to speak with Corps officials; instead they simply could travel across town.

Establishment of the Kansas City District also meant the careers of the Corps' military officers and civilian engineers became intertwined with Missouri River improvement. In St. Louis, Corps officials did not possess any great loyalty to the development of a particular stream because the office supervised numerous projects. But the institutional survival of the Kansas City District and the careers of Corps personnel assigned to it depended solely on the improvement of the Missouri River. Indeed the district needed Missouri River work to justify its existence. Thus, the Missouri Valley River Improvement Association gained a major ally in its struggle to acquire federal financing for Missouri River channelization.[18]

In 1907 the association published a pamphlet to engender public and congressional support for Missouri River channelization. *The Missouri: A Deep Waterway* set forth the association's motives for seeking a twelve- or even a fourteen-foot channel from Kansas City to the mouth. The pamphlet reiterated some familiar arguments for channelization while espousing a few new justifications:

1. Barge traffic would relieve the transportation bottleneck caused by insufficient railroad trackage.
2. Water-borne freight rates for bulk agricultural commodities were one-sixth that of railroad rates.
3. River transportation would end the railroad monopoly over the nation's transportation system.
4. Missouri River channelization would aid the development of the Great Plains region to the west and south of Kansas City.
5. Missouri River navigation would aid in U.S. competition with other world powers, especially grain producers such as Argentina and Australia.
6. Full use of the Panama Canal would result from the development of the nation's waterways, including the Missouri.
7. A twelve- or fourteen-foot channel would avoid any break-in-bulk between the Missouri River ports and ports along the Mississippi, Ohio, or proposed Lakes-to-Gulf Deep Waterway.[19]

The revival of interest in Missouri River channelization spread northward from Kansas City to other Missouri Valley towns, spurred by the promotional campaigns of the Kansas Citians. In November 1907 the Real Estate Association of Sioux City met and decided to host a Missouri River improvement convention. George C. Call, A. B. Beall, and J. L. Kennedy coordinated the event. On 22 and 23 January 1908, 600 Missouri River improvement advocates from throughout the Missouri basin and the United States gathered in Sioux City, Iowa, for the First Annual Convention of the Missouri River Navigation Congress. It represented the largest single meeting ever convened for the purposes of Missouri River improvement. The number of dignitaries alone lent an air of importance. Governor Coe I. Crawford of South Dakota; Joseph Ransdell, president of the National Rivers and Harbors Congress; Mayor Henry M. Beardsley of Kansas City, Missouri; Gov. John Burke of North Dakota; Gov. George L. Sheldon of Nebraska; and Gov. A. B. Cummins of Iowa attended and spoke in favor of federal improvement of the stream that flowed only a few blocks from the conference site.

Both Lawrence Jones and Edgar Ellis gave presentations in Sioux City. Predictably, Jones spoke of the benefits to agriculture from channelization of the Missouri River. He anticipated a substantial reduction in shipment costs for agricultural commodities as farmers placed their produce on barges instead of in railcars. Jones also spoke of the likely increase in the value of valley farmland as the Corps stabilized the river's banks. Ellis talked of the difficulties inherent in convincing Congress to finance river channelization: "To induce the national government to take hold of this great project, to approve it, and to provide the money for it, is incomparably the greatest legislative undertaking that any community or section of our country has ever attempted. That is the point I am trying to make. The favor we seek is not going to be conferred as a compliment."[20] The federal government would not readily commit to improving the Missouri River; furthermore, other river associations vied for the same federal dollars for improvement of their streams. Only the people of the Missouri Valley could put the political pressure on Congress to make channelization possible. According to Ellis,

The first work, you will readily perceive, will be to shape public sentiment right here at home. In doing this there will be work for commercial organizations in all our towns and cities, there will be work for our press, for our city press, and our country press. The public will have to be educated to true conceptions and to sufficient conceptions of what is proposed, what it will be worth, and how it is to be brought about. . . . It must be demonstrated that benefits are to be general; that advantages are to [i]nure to all classes and to all communities. We must have a public sentiment that will prompt the people to support with some constancy and consistency their representatives in Congress who must front this fight.[21]

At the close of the Missouri River Navigation Congress, the delegates elected Ellis as its president and Jones as vice-president.

The congress represented a notable moment in the history of efforts to channelize the Missouri River. Never before had so many people gathered in support of the cause. Although the active proponents of river improvement came from the business and professional classes, the group stands as an example of democracy in action, of private citizens taking the initiative to develop a major natural resource to benefit themselves. Federal authorities played a minor if not nonexistent role in the congress.

Later in 1908 the Missouri Valley River Improvement Association published another pamphlet to instruct the public and Congress. *The Deep Water Project for the Missouri River* contended that a twelve-foot channel between Sioux City and the mouth would not only be possible but that it also would cost only $50,000 per mile, or $42.5 million, including the physical plant, for the entire 800 river miles. Colonel E. H. Shulz of the Kansas City District made this assertion, either ignoring or forgetting years of experience gained along the first reach by Suter and his men, who attained only a six-foot depth in their navigation channel and spent $58,000 per mile doing it. The association even claimed that a fourteen-foot navigation channel might be maintained along the river during years of above-average precipitation. The pamphlet mentioned that channelization of the stream would result in the reclamation of 210,365 acres of bottomland between Sioux City and the mouth; the value of this reclaimed land alone would pay the total cost of channelization.[22]

Meanwhile, association members continued to charter steamboats and barges to carry goods between St. Louis and Kansas City. The financial backers of these endeavors cared less about the profitability of barge and steamer service and more about its propaganda value. Hauling freight on the river, even if at a loss, allowed association members to argue with federal officials that carriers would use the river even more frequently if Congress would channelize the stream. Barge and steamer service had been revived on the river, and the volume of traffic would jump substantially once the federal government deepened the Missouri. Thus barges and steamers traveled up and down the river between Kansas City and its mouth in 1906, 1907, and 1908.[23] The freighting companies either loaded these boats lightly or scheduled their trips during the spring and summer rises, which were the only means of ensuring the delivery of the goods on the still-unchannelized Missouri.

In spring 1908 another major flood descended the Missouri River. Only two previous floods exceeded the magnitude of the high flows of 1908—those of 1903 and 1844. For farmers in the valley, the deluge of 1908 may have been the worst ever; the water remained high longer than during any previous summer rise and prevented valley farmers from planting even a marginal crop that season.[24] The promotion of Missouri River channelization thus took on an added urgency. Although no one affiliated with the movement dared speak publicly of channelization for flood control and property protection because of congressional opposition, river development devotees silently wished for channelization to reduce the flood threat.[25]

After his election to the presidency of the Missouri River Navigation Congress, Cong. Edgar Ellis took the initiative to organize the people of the valley. He believed that if more people actively supported channelization, Congress would be more likely to provide funds for the work. On 23 July 1908 Ellis wrote a letter to Louis Benecke of Brunswick, Missouri, a lawyer and longtime ally of Missouri River improvement: "Permit me to suggest, . . . that you form a local organization at Br[u]nswick, even if you can get no more than a dozen or a score of members. . . . Such a local group would be a nucleus for cooperative effort. I could then furnish you with bulletins showing progress, plans, and prospects, and the help you could afford would be very substantial and gratifying. It has been my plan to invite just this sort of cooperation in every town between [Kansas City] and St. Louis."[26]

Benecke responded quickly to the request for a local organization of the Missouri River Navigation Congress. In early September he reported to Ellis that he had organized a "local group" with twelve members. The resolution forming the Brunswick branch of the Navigation Congress stated, "It will be the object of the local group to secure much needed river work at points near Brunswick."[27] Thus Ellis, with the assistance of men such as Benecke, organized the valley towns between Kansas City and St. Louis. Support for river improvement readily increased in the river towns, especially with the flood of 1908 still fresh in everyone's mind.[28]

With central Missouri squarely in support of the Missouri Valley River Improvement Association and the Navigation Congress, Ellis presented a decisive argument to his Washington colleagues for appropriations for channelization. In January 1909 Congress appropriated $655,000 for the resumption of channelization work along the Missouri River. According to the *Kansas City Times,* "Much credit is due to Representative Ellis for the appropriation for the Missouri River. Mr. Ellis has worked long, continuously, industriously, and effectively for this provision."[29] The allocation signaled the first substantial appropriation for channelization since 1895. After passage of this bill, Ellis confidently claimed that Congress would authorize some type of channelization project for the Missouri River in 1910, which would tacitly commit the federal government to the completion of any project.

Of the $655,000 approved in 1909 for the Missouri River, Congress earmarked $450,000 for river work between Kansas City and the mouth. Such a large appropriation for this reach illustrated the political influence of Ellis, the Kansas City Commercial Club, and the river towns of central Missouri. A further indication of their political power became apparent in spring 1909 when the Corps of Engineers, rather than arbitrarily deciding where to spend the $455,000, held a series of public meetings to determine the most politically acceptable location for immediate river improvement.

Ellis continued to pursue larger federal appropriations for the channelization of the Missouri. He suggested to several Kansas City businessmen that they form a barge line and establish routine freight service between Kansas City and St. Louis. The infrequently chartered barge and steamer trips between 1906 and 1908 no longer had any propaganda value. According to Ellis, a legitimate barge company regularly moving freight on the Missouri would convince congressional skeptics that people in the valley wanted to use the river. Such a company would also send a signal to Congress that commerce could flourish on the stream if only the Corps deepened the channel. The Kansas City Commercial Club followed Ellis's advice. In fall 1909 club members organized the Kansas City Missouri River Navigation Company and named Walter S. Dickey of Kansas City as its president. Dickey then sold stock in the new company to members of the Missouri River Navigation Congress, the Missouri Valley River Improvement Association, and the Commercial Club. In a letter to members of the Navigation Congress, Dickey asserted, "When you join this movement to start freight cargoes up and down the Missouri, you will be making an investment that will prove profitable to yourself, your property, and your county." Over 4,000 persons invested in company stock, and with that financial support Dickey incorporated the company in late 1909. This public endorsement of Missouri River barge navigation did impress Congress. The chair of the House Rivers and Harbors Committee, Theodore Burton, remarked, "Those who have to do with river and harbor improvements [in Congress] are watching the situation [in the Missouri Valley] very closely, with the thought that provision should be made for the traffic that is being developed along the Missouri River."[30]

In February 1910 Burton and his committee conducted a hearing to consider whether the Missouri River channelization project should receive any more federal monies. Numerous members of the Kansas City

Commercial Club traveled to Washington to attend the hearing, including W. T. Bland, E. M. Clendening, J. C. Swift, H. G. Wilson, and Walter S. Dickey. Dickey voiced the same arguments his Kansas City predecessors had used since the 1880s, claiming that Missouri River channelization would benefit the rapidly growing population of the Missouri Valley and upper Midwest through an eventual lowering of freight rates. W. T. Bland, using undocumented statistics, informed the committee members that farmers and industrialists along the valley would save five cents per ton on their freight costs, an amount that would equal a total savings of $5 million per year once the barge channel was completed. The committee members wanted to know whether the Kansas City men would use the Missouri River as a transportation route. Dickey replied with a brash assertion: Kansas Citians would use the river even without a federal channelization project. As proof, he noted that valley residents had already formed a navigation company to move cargoes on the un-channelized stream. Dickey and his colleagues actually made such a favorable impression on the Rivers and Harbors Committee that its members recommended to the full House that the Missouri River channelization project receive a $1 million appropriation that year. The House and Senate concurred, and the channelization project received the money. But the bill did not contain Ellis's hoped-for project authorization. In the same Rivers and Harbors bill, Congress appropriated money for the construction of a six-foot channel along the Mississippi from St. Louis north to St. Paul and for a nine-foot channel below St. Louis. Large-scale construction of a national waterways system had begun in earnest.[31]

The momentum for channelization remained strong through 1911 and early 1912, when Congress authorized the construction of a six-foot-deep channel between Kansas City and the mouth. The river above Kansas City had been excluded from this legislation. A six-foot channel would be significantly shallower than the original twelve- and eight-foot channels recommended by Charles Suter and Samuel Yonge. However, by 1912 Corps studies of river-flow volumes indicated that only a six-foot channel would be attainable below Kansas City. The river did not have the water to sustain deeper channels.[32] Although the lobbying efforts of Missouri Valley towns and their commercial interests played a vital role in securing the federal appropriation in 1910 and authorization in 1912, the sympathies of the progressive conservation movement and the widespread public enthusiasm for development of the nation's rivers for navigation made federal officials receptive to the promotional efforts of Ellis, Dickey, the Commercial Club, and the Missouri Valley River Improvement Association.[33]

Before World War I, the federal government provided money on a regular basis to channelize the Missouri. In July 1912 Congress allocated $800,000 to the project. One month later, the project received an additional $600,000. Then in March 1913 Congress purveyed another $2 million.[34] The Corps estimated that it needed $2 million per year to complete the project in ten years. Congress, although not furnishing that much money each year, did provide the Corps with enough to construct long stretches of the barge channel. The technologies and techniques used in river channelization after 1910 resembled those first used by Suter during the 1890s. The willow mattress and stone revetment, along with the pile dike, remained the two predominant methods.[35]

Ironically, just as Missouri River channelization received its greatest appropriations and congressional endorsement, it came under its sharpest attack. In March 1915 Congress ordered the Corps of Engineers' Board of Engineers for Rivers and Harbors to review the cost-effectiveness of a number of navigation projects, including the Missouri River barge channel. (Congress had formed the Board of Engineers in 1902 to investigate, endorse, or reject proposed or existing federal navigation projects and to serve in an advisory role.) This reexamination occurred after $6.25 million had been spent on additional construction below Kansas City in the preceding five years.[36] The board gave Kansas City District engineer Lt. Col. Herbert Deakyne the task of overseeing the study, and he submitted his report to the board in August 1915.[37] His conclusions shocked not only his superiors but also Missouri Valley residents, especially the Kansas City contingent who had worked so many years to win appropriations for channelization.

Deakyne insisted that Missouri River barge traffic would never reach levels necessary to justify the expense of constructing the navigation channel. Furthermore, railroad rates could be lowered through the enactment of regulatory laws, rendering the expenditure of $20 million on a barge channel dubious. Valley residents did not need a six-foot channel to ship their agricultural commodities downstream. Instead, they could continue to use the rail lines that paralleled both banks of the river between Kansas City and St. Louis. Deakyne ended his report by proposing that the federal government abandon Missouri River channelization altogether and that future river work be restricted to snagging operations.[38] The free-thinking lieutenant colonel stated, "I recommend that the present project be modified so as to provide for snagging alone at an estimate[d] cost of $40,000 per year, and that all other work be stopped."[39]

Missouri Valley residents reacted quickly to Deakyne's report. Learning of the submission of the study to the Board of Engineers on 5 August 1915, Kansas City Commercial Club president C. S. Keith responded, "We will get busy at once to prepare to make an appeal [to the board]. No stone will be left unturned. I will call a meeting of the board of directors of the Commercial Club the very first thing tomorrow morning."[40] Keith and his colleagues decided to rally the people of the Missouri and Mississippi Valleys against Deakyne and his supporters in Congress and the Corps. Members of the Commercial Club promptly sent telegrams to senators, representatives, state and local officials, farm organizations, and commercial clubs from Sioux City to St. Louis and from St. Paul to Memphis, urging them to contact the Board of Engineers and express their support for Missouri River channelization. The public response to the Commercial Club's call for action was breathtaking in scope. A group of fifty-six farmers from Norborne, Missouri, signed a petition that declared, "We the undersigned farmers, residing in the Missouri River Valley . . . hereby petition the federal government to continue appropriations that the river service may be continued." The Glasgow, Missouri, Commercial Club wrote to their Kansas City collaborators, "The business men of Glasgow are for river improvement and deplore the adverse recommendation made by Colonel Deakyne." The people of Chamois, Missouri, angrily declared, "Our Commercial League and citizens of this community are unanimous in opposing the abandonment of the improvement of the Missouri River." Up and down the valley the response was the same; valley residents adamantly rejected Deakyne's recommendations. Residents of St. Charles, Hermann, Jefferson City, Hardin, Boonville, Brunswick, Washington, Bonnots Mill, Carrolltown, and New Haven, Missouri, pledged to support the Kansas City Commercial Club in its campaign to influence the Board of Engineers and to defeat Deakyne's proposals.[41]

Under pressure from Missouri Valley residents and their congressional representatives, the Board of Engineers convened a hearing on the Missouri River channelization project in October 1915 in Kansas City, Missouri, to determine whether Congress should continue to finance the work. For two days, businessmen and potential shippers from throughout the valley urged federal completion of the barge channel.

O. V. Wilson of the Commercial Club made the familiar assertion that
the savings in the price farmers paid to ship their grain on the barge
channel would be so great that the project from Kansas City to the mouth
would pay for itself in one year, even though by then the cost exceeded
$20 million.[42] Because of the public support for channelization, the
Board of Engineers rejected Deakyne's conclusions. In April 1916 Col.
W. M. Black, chairman of the Board of Engineers, submitted a report to
his colleagues that unequivocally endorsed the future channelization
of the Missouri. Black urged Congress to continue to underwrite the
project. Deakyne's superiors then quietly ordered his transfer from the
Kansas City District Office. The Kansas City Commercial Club could not
work with a man who advocated the abandonment of their pet project.[43]

During the Deakyne affair, private interests overrode the authority and
recommendations of the Corps of Engineers and determined the direction of Missouri River development. The incident illustrated the power
of local groups in the promotion, planning, and implementation of
channelization work. The events surrounding the submission of Deakyne's
report also indicated the level of cooperation needed between local organizations and federal entities to bring about development.[44]

The success of Missouri Valley residents in defeating Deakyne's recommendations enraged Sen. Theodore Burton of Ohio and Cong. James
Frear of Wisconsin. Burton believed the Missouri River project represented a "pure, bald, unmitigated waste" of federal dollars.[45] Of course,
Burton's constituents wanted to improve the Ohio River with the same
federal funds expended along the Missouri. Frear, whose district bordered the Upper Mississippi River, another river being channeled by
the Corps at that very moment, called for the House of Representatives
Judiciary Committee to investigate the "river lobby," especially the "Missouri River lobby," requesting "that [the judiciary] committee shall further investigate the activities of the Missouri River lobby that is alleged
to have active interest in securing appropriations for the reclaiming at
government expense of ½ million acres of private land along the Missouri River valued, according to official reports, at 60 million dollars."[46]
Frear argued that the navigation project was a sham, that the real purpose of the project had been and continued to be the stabilization of
the Missouri's banks so that bottomland farmers could acquire the land
that either accreted behind the pile dikes or remained free from inundation as the channel deepened itself. Congressman W. P. Borland from
Kansas City challenged Frear's assessment of the situation: "I invite you

here and now to Kansas City to show what that city is doing toward navigating the river. I want you to come there, and I invite you to come to convince you that many of the statements you make here today are untrue."[47] The Kansas Citian argued that the purpose of the channelization project had always been to establish barge traffic on the river. Bank stabilization remained an incidental benefit of the project, not its sole purpose. Frear then yelled across the House floor, "Pork, Pork! . . . These statistics [on the amount of freight carried by water] invite the services of a lunacy commission in order to determine where the responsibility rests for such unmitigated waste put over Congress by waterways lobbies and army engineers."[48] Nothing came of Burton's and Frear's threats, however; Congress preserved the Missouri River channelization project.

World War I forced reductions in expenditures for federal waterways projects, and after 1916 work on the Missouri River navigation channel slowed to a standstill. A further indication of the poor state of the project along the river occurred in 1918 when the Kansas City Missouri River Navigation Company sold its last remaining boats to the federal government, which in turn transferred the steamers to the Mississippi River for service during the war.

Following World War I, work along the Missouri River did not resume. Between 1916 and 1922, the Corps spent just a little more than $1 million on the project, not even enough money to maintain the integrity of the existing channelization structures, which deteriorated under the constant assault of the river's ice flows, floating debris, and annual floods. By 1922 only 35 percent of the river reach from the mouth to Kansas City had been channelized. The cost of channelizing a mere 135 miles of river was $55,000 per river mile, or $5,000 higher than the estimate made by E. H. Shulz to justify the project.[49] Not surprisingly, with the channel incomplete, deep-draft steamers and barges remained confined to the Mississippi River. The Kansas City Missouri River Navigation Company never returned boats to the Missouri. The noise of barges and steamers remained absent from the valley; the only sound that could be heard was that of flowing water moving against the bank, over rocks, and around the aging pile dikes.[50]

The inactivity along the river worried members of the Kansas City Commercial Club, who by 1923 had become desperate to establish barge traffic on the river.[51] At a meeting in November of that year, the club's executive secretary, E. M. Clendening, argued that proponents of Missouri River barge navigation had to go it alone and assume the federal government would not finance the completion of the channelization project. Clendening stated that new methods had to be discovered by which barges could be moved up and down an unchannelized river. One idea tossed around at the Commercial Club envisioned a barge with two tanklike treads extending along the bottom of the hull on each side. When the barge hit a sandbar, which would occur often, the tank tread would be activated and the barge driven over the obstruction.[52] The mastermind of this idea failed to realize that a barge drawing six feet of water would have to be driven all the way from the mouth to Kansas City through a thalweg averaging only between three and four feet. This outrageous notion remained confined to a few overactive imaginations. No one came up with any other miracle plan to foster barge traffic on the shallow Missouri.

J. C. Nichols, a Harvard-educated Kansas City real estate mogul and member of the Commercial Club, knew that the only hope for navigation of the Missouri rested with channelization of the stream under federal auspices and that the government had to be persuaded to improve the river. Toward that end, Nichols attended a meeting of the Mississippi Valley Association sometime in 1923 or 1924. The association, formed in 1919, consisted of river development advocates from twenty states within the Mississippi basin. New Orleans, St. Louis, St. Paul, Cincinnati, and Pittsburgh businessmen represented the bulk of its membership and dominated its executive offices. They organized the association to coordinate the efforts of navigation promoters throughout the basin, to ensure that river boosters did not work at cross-purposes, and to lobby Congress for funding of river improvement projects (Fig. 6.2).[53]

When Nichols attended the conference, he expressed amazement that the Missouri River was not mentioned in any of the presentations. Instead, discussions centered on the development of the Mississippi and Ohio Rivers. At the close of the conference, Nichols decided to create an organization to lobby Congress on behalf of the Missouri River. In fall 1924 and spring 1925, Nichols, working in concert with longtime river developer Lawrence Jones, met with members of the commercial clubs of Omaha, St. Joseph, and Sioux City to discuss means of organizing the entire valley.[54] From these meetings and from subsequent correspondence Nichols concluded that interest in Missouri River improvement had not diminished since the war and that with proper

Fig. 6.2. Jesse Clyde (J. C.) Nichols. Nichols played an important role in Missouri River development during the 1920s and 1930s. (Courtesy of the J. C. Nichols Company, Kansas City, Missouri)

organization the federal government could be induced to finance the completion of the project below Kansas City. To perfect an organization, Nichols, Jones, and the new Kansas City Chamber of Commerce invited businessmen, industrialists, agriculturists, and educators from states in the Midwest to a conference on Missouri River navigation to be held 19 and 20 October 1925 in Kansas City.[55]

The response to the invitation surprised the Kansas City men; approximately 750 individuals attended the conference. These numbers surpassed attendance at any previous Missouri River navigation meeting, even the one at Sioux City in 1908, which had 600 delegates. Herbert Hoover, secretary of commerce, gave the keynote address. Hoover advocated the completion of a system of internal waterways that embraced the Great Lakes, the Mississippi and Ohio Rivers, and the Missouri River from its mouth to Kansas City. This system had been known as the Lakes-to-the-Gulf Deep Waterway but had acquired the title the Cross of Commerce. By thus naming their waterways project, navigation enthusiasts gave their movement an overtly religious tone. Besides being sanctioned by the Creator, who formed the nation's rivers and lakes for human benefit, the Cross of Commerce would include a deep channel running from Chicago south to New Orleans along the Illinois and Mississippi Rivers and another channel running from Pittsburgh down the Ohio to its mouth and from the confluence of the Mississippi and Missouri Rivers west to Kansas City. Hoover believed that this vast waterways system would serve American agriculture by reducing the cost of transporting bulk commodities: "Water-borne traffic and its cheaper cost is peculiarly adapted to primary agriculture products."[56] He also claimed, "Modern forms of development have made water carriage the cheapest of all transportation for many types of goods. Broadly, 1,000 bushels of wheat can be transported 1,000 miles . . . by our modern equipped Mississippi barge service for $60 to $70, and by railroads for $150 to $200. These estimates are based not on hypothetical calculation, but on the actual going freight rates."[57]

Hoover countered the arguments of those people who believed waterways development to be a waste of federal dollars, contending that commerce had not developed on the nation's rivers because river improvement had been piecemeal. The nation's major rivers had to be linked in order for the people to reap any benefits. He compared the contemporary waterways system of the United States to a railroad that remained unfinished: no railroad could possibly turn a profit if its trains had to stop every few miles because of obstacles.[58]

Before closing his speech, Hoover committed himself and the Department of Commerce to the development of a connected national waterways system that embraced the Missouri River to Kansas City. "We know what we should do. We know [river development's] vast benefits; we know [development] can be accomplished by a comparatively trivial cost compared to these benefits. We should go to it and have [the Cross of Commerce] completed within the next decade. And it is my hope that we shall see not only the steady completion of the Ohio

River section, but also of the Chicago and Kansas City lines."[59] Hoover's speech gave the cause of Missouri River channelization an incredible boost.

Capitalizing on Hoover's support, the conference delegates resolved to form the Missouri River Navigation Association, with two primary goals: to induce Congress to complete the navigation channel between Kansas City and the mouth and to convince Congress to authorize the extension of the navigation channel north of Kansas City, to a point yet to be specified. Membership in the association remained open to anyone, but it consisted mostly of bankers, lawyers, businessmen, heads of farm organizations, presidents of commercial clubs, and state and local government officials. The governors of the ten states of the Missouri basin served as board members, and individuals affiliated with various professional organizations held the bulk of administrative positions. The conference attendees elected Arthur J. Weaver, a banker from Falls City, Nebraska, as president. Nichols explained why Weaver was chosen: "To prevent it from being regarded as too much of a Kansas City affair, Arthur J. Weaver of Falls City, Nebraska, was selected as President of the Association."[60] Nichols and the Kansas Citians wanted to form a broad coalition. The choice of Weaver could not have been more fortuitous; he proved his worth to the movement again and again during the next decade.[61] A list of other officials in the association included Stewart Gilman, mayor of Sioux City, Iowa; Ballard Dunn, editor of the *Omaha Bee;* Dr. C. M. Pugsley, president of the South Dakota State College of Agriculture, Brookings; P. F. Walker, dean of the College of Engineering, University of Kansas, Lawrence; and Harry L. Keefe, president of the Nebraska State Farm Bureau Federation, Walthill. A few farmers served as officers, including Dr. Frederick Roost, Sioux City, Iowa; W. C. Children, Council Bluffs, Iowa; and R. W. Brown, Carrollton, Missouri (Fig. 6.3).[62]

Weaver, Nichols, and other members of the association wasted no time in working toward their two goals. According to a statement by Weaver, the group effectively lobbied Congress in December 1925 to increase the appropriation for rivers and harbors from $40 million to $50 million, the additional $10 million slated for the Mississippi River basin. Weaver and Nichols understood that money for the Mississippi or its tributaries would contribute to the eventual channelization of the Missouri. More specifically, the Mississippi had to be deepened before the Missouri could ever be used for barge traffic.

Fig. 6.3. Arthur J. Weaver, Falls City, Nebraska. Weaver worked tirelessly with his friend Nichols to promote Missouri River channelization among federal officials. (Courtesy of Mrs. Philip [Jane] Weaver, Arthur J. Weaver Estate, Falls City, Nebraska)

Also during December 1925, the Missouri River Navigation Association formed the Upper River Committee, whose purpose was to determine the economic feasibility of channelizing the Missouri as far north as Sioux City. By early 1926 the Upper River Committee had concluded that future annual barge tonnage between Kansas City and Sioux City would justify the expenditures necessary to construct the navigation channel along this reach. The long-term savings in transportation costs to valley residents would surpass the costs of any future project. The committee then submitted a detailed report to the Kansas City District of the Corps of Engineers and its head, Maj. C. C. Gee. Gee and his subordinates initially disapproved of the construction of the channel to Sioux City, believing any extension should wait until the river below Kansas City had been opened to barge traffic. But the Upper River Committee's report, along with public clamoring for the extension, convinced the district engineer's office to abandon its opposition and to endorse the immediate improvement of the stream to Sioux City.[63] Top officials within the Corps of Engineers held other opinions toward the Upper River Project. Chief of Engineers Harry Taylor and members of the Board of Engineers vehemently objected to any extension of the channel, and they refused to take the project before Congress. Taylor and the board wanted first to see if the Kansas City–to–mouth reach would carry enough barge traffic to justify a further investment.[64]

Blocked by high officials within the Corps, Weaver and the association stayed active on other fronts. In January 1926 Weaver and Nichols personally contacted Chief of Engineers Taylor to see whether the federal government would purchase the assets of the inactive Kansas City Missouri River Navigation Company in order to start a federal barge line on the Missouri River. Weaver and Nichols believed that federal sponsorship of a barge line would further commit the government to a program of improvement and that the barge line's profitability would induce private investors to start their own companies.[65] Taylor, suspicious of Weaver and Nichols, replied that the matter needed further study.

Weaver and Nichols held meetings in towns along the river in early 1926 to keep the residents of the Missouri Valley organized and interested in the cause of channelization. In Yankton in late February the men conferred with South Dakota governor Carl Gunderson, who reiterated his support for the six-foot-channel extension north of Kansas City. In Sioux City, before members of the Chamber of Commerce,

Weaver said, "This river project needs the united action of farmers, industrial organizations and consumers. It is a common cause imperative to the welfare of our section and our nation."[66] The two men worked diligently to generate and to sustain mass public support for the proposed navigation channel.

The lobbying and organizational work of the Missouri River Navigation Association between October 1925 and April 1926 bore fruit when Congress, in late April 1926, appropriated $2 million for channelization work below Kansas City from the total $50 million appropriation for rivers and harbors for that fiscal year. Unfortunately for river boosters along the upper river, Congress did not allocate money for channelization of that reach.

Although only $2 million had been directed toward the lower river project, the money had symbolic importance; for many river boosters it marked a turning point in the efforts for channelization of the river. Members of the Kansas City Chamber of Commerce, along with officials of the Missouri River Navigation Association, spoke with confidence that the Kansas City District of the Corps of Engineers would receive enough federal dollars to complete the six-foot channel. The reasoning that supported this conviction was that Pres. Calvin Coolidge, the secretary of commerce, the secretary of war, and the chief of engineers had given the Kansas City men every indication that their project would be carried through to completion. O. V. Wilson of the chamber of commerce predicted, "We have been working many years for river navigation, and it begins to appear as if we actually will have it in a few years." T. J. Brodnax, another member of the chamber, proclaimed, "If everything proceeds as it should, I believe it will be possible for [barges] to be in operation on the Missouri River in about three years."[67] Convinced that they had nearly achieved their first goal, completing the channel below Kansas City, the association's leadership shifted their focus to the north, to secure congressional authorization for the extension of the six-foot channel to Sioux City.

In late April 1926 a delegation of river boosters from Omaha met with members of the Missouri River Navigation Association in Kansas City to discuss how to win congressional approval for that extension, referred to as the Upper River Project. Attendees agreed that they should immediately push Congress for its authorization. The climate in Washington appeared to be favorable for approval of river projects, however dubious they might be. And considering the support for Missouri River channelization shown by Congress in the past few months, the river boosters believed they had the momentum to push the extension through.

The association kicked off its congressional lobbying campaign in spring 1926 by sending a large delegation to Washington to meet with congressional representatives from the Missouri Valley states. After laying out a legislative strategy, the Missouri Valley contingent agreed that an amendment to the Annual Rivers and Harbors bill would be introduced on the floor of the House. It would contain an authorization to construct a six-foot-deep barge channel from Kansas City to Sioux City. The reason for using this procedure was simple: an amendment would bypass the traditional route that navigation-project proposals followed through the bureaucracy of the Corps of Engineers and Congress on their way toward passage in the Annual Rivers and Harbors bill. There would be no review of the project by the chief of engineers, the Board of Engineers, or the House Rivers and Harbors Committee. Weaver and his partners did not want the Upper River Project scrutinized by these bodies because they rightly feared opposition, which had been publicly stated earlier in the year. The House passed the Rivers and Harbors bill, with the amendment, by a vote of 219 to 127 in June 1926. Weaver, obviously defending his actions, said, "This legislation was passed on its own merits. It was supported almost unanimously by the West and South as a matter of economic justice, because of the high transportation charges upon agricultural products and manufactured articles made in the Middle West." He also acknowledged that Missouri Valley congressmen voted as a solid bloc, putting aside party politics and embracing bipartisanship.[68]

After clearing the House the Rivers and Harbors bill went to the Senate Commerce Committee, which held hearings in June on the Upper River Project (Fig. 6.4). Once again the Missouri River Navigation Association sent a delegation to Washington to participate in these hearings to try to convince the Senate of the project's importance.

One of the first association members to testify before the Senate Commerce Committee, C. E. Childe of the Omaha Chamber of Commerce, argued that the river valley north of Kansas City needed water transportation to provide rate relief to farmers and business interests. According to Childe, the region north of Kansas City sat on the periphery of numerous markets; thus, its residents had to import and export commodities and finished products over great distances, which in turn

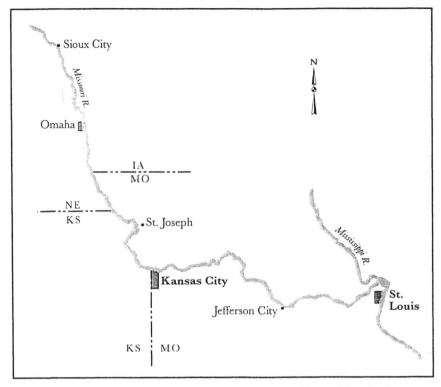

Fig. 6.4. The Kansas City–to–mouth reach and the Upper River Project.

lowered the region's competitiveness compared with other regions of the United States.

To add to the economic hardships of the area, Childe continued, railroads had arbitrarily raised their rates 60 to 100 percent since the end of World War I. The railroads could dictate freight rates because no other form of transportation existed in the area. The increase in these rates, combined with the region's disadvantageous market location, had worsened the agricultural depression that had gripped the Midwest since the early 1920s. Childe claimed that barge traffic on the Missouri River would allow the region to compete more effectively in national and world markets. He concluded his analysis by insisting, "All the people of the Missouri Valley are united in demanding this improvement and they want action. . . . Our people are not radical, but they want relief, and they are voicing their demand that something be done."[69] Mayor Stewart

Gilman of Sioux City told the committee, "Both businessmen and farmers looked to improvement of the upper river as the only means of lowering freight rates from that section." And continued, "About all the river is good for now is for a despondent farmer to commit suicide in." In response to this point, a committee member asked, "And you have lots of despondent farmers?" Gilman answered, "Too many of them, and they are expecting the government to devote some attention to their condition."[70] But the Commerce Committee did not report favorably on the Upper River Project to the full Senate, which struck it from the bill. The project appeared headed for defeat.

The action of the Senate Commerce Committee dismayed Weaver and Nichols, but they still did not give up hope. On 9 November 1926 the association met again in Omaha to discuss how to reintroduce the Upper River Project into the Senate Rivers and Harbors bill. At the close of this meeting, the men agreed to send a resolution to the full Senate, urging it to authorize channelization north of Kansas City. They also planned to send another large lobbying delegation to Washington in mid-December, when the Rivers and Harbors bill went before the Senate for a final time. Moreover, Weaver and his colleagues decided that Missouri basin senators should reintroduce the Upper River Project on the floor of the Senate as an amendment to the original Rivers and Harbors bill, in the same fashion that the House amendment had been introduced that past June.

During the final push for authorization of the Upper River Project in the Senate, Sioux City men, rather than the Kansas Citians, played the pivotal role. Two residents, Mayor Stewart Gilman and Iowa senator David W. Stewart, organized a Missouri Valley bloc in the Senate, which aligned with senators from the northeastern United States, who wanted a canal constructed across Cape Cod, to secure passage of the Upper River Project as an amendment to the Rivers and Harbors bill. According to George R. Call, another Sioux Citian, Senator Stewart displayed incredible political astuteness by maneuvering enough votes for acceptance of the amendment.[71] The Upper River Project became law on 21 January 1927 with President Coolidge's signature.[72] After this tremendous legislative victory, Weaver remarked, "Men who have been identified with the river navigation movement for many years and have watched the long struggle made for approval of various projects say that the approval of the Upper River [Project], without the recommendation of the Chief of Engineers and in such a short time, was a very unusual victory."[73] He also said, "The bill as it stands is the most constructive piece of legislation to come to the Middle West, as eventually it means a much larger population and prosperity."[74] But Weaver and his accomplices did not rest; they wanted more.

In that same Rivers and Harbors bill, Congress authorized the Corps of Engineers to conduct a survey of the river below Kansas City to determine the feasibility of constructing a nine-foot navigation channel. Weaver and the other Missouri River navigation interests recognized that the six-foot channel would become obsolete the instant the Mississippi River had been deepened to nine feet below St. Louis because barges that drew seven or eight feet of water would not enter the shallower channel of the Missouri. Barges would be forced to break bulk in St. Louis before traveling to Kansas City. Any break-in-bulk would increase the cost of transporting cargo on the Missouri River and consequently lower its usefulness. The channel had to be the same depth as the Mississippi's navigation channel or risk being forever neglected by barge operators.

7 | The Dry Years, 1927–1942

After congressional and presidential approval of the Upper River Project in January 1927, members of the Missouri River Navigation Association, along with businessmen, politicians, and farmers living in the territory north of Kansas City, pressed Congress, the War Department, and presidents Calvin Coolidge and Herbert Hoover for the money needed to start construction on the channel extension to Sioux City. Defenders of the Upper River Project believed that it would benefit the agricultural economy and the rural population by reducing freight rates and providing relief to the increasing number of men thrown out of work by the worsening economic depression. But the lobbying efforts of these Missouri Valley navigation boosters did not immediately succeed. For six years, federal authorities rejected local appeals to start large-scale construction on the Upper River Project.

Franklin D. Roosevelt adopted a different approach toward Missouri River development. By late 1933 FDR and his administration pledged themselves to the extension of the six-foot channel to Sioux City, the construction of the world's largest earthen dam at Fort Peck, Montana, and the eventual deepening of the navigation channel to nine feet. The shift in policy evident during the Roosevelt administration occurred for a number of reasons, including political, social, and economic concerns. But the river itself also affected development during the 1930s. The low-river levels that lasted from 1929 into the late 1930s forced local and federal officials to expand the navigation project to include the construction of a storage reservoir.

Between 1927 and 1942 the Missouri River underwent recognizable changes. By 1932 the Corps had confined the river below Kansas City into a single channel. From 1932 to 1940 it channelized most of the 385 miles of river between Kansas City and Sioux City. At the same time that the channelization project progressed along the lower river, federal engineers built Fort Peck Dam. In summer 1937 the Corps closed the massive dam and its reservoir began to fill with water, eventually creating a man-made lake 134 miles long. By the end of 1942, 750 miles of the lower river and 134 miles of the upper river barely resembled the Missouri's former character.

In spring 1927, only months after its authorization, Congress appropriated a mere $45,000 for work on the Upper River Project; this minuscule sum did not even allow the Corps to conduct studies necessary for future construction. On the other hand, the reach from Kansas City to the mouth received $2 million.[1] Again in 1928 Congress provided money for channelization below Kansas City but completely neglected the Kansas City–to–Sioux City reach. A Nebraska senator, whose constituents would profit from the Upper River Project, expressed his frustration with the lack of congressional support: "No section has suffered more in an economic way than the West. If we are to reduce the river funds even more, what are we of the West to hope for? If I did what my inclination prompts me to do I would offer an amendment [to the Annual Rivers and Harbors bill] increasing the appropriation 12 million for the upper Missouri alone. But I know it would only delay matters and would not be approved at this time."[2]

In November 1928, when Herbert Hoover was elected president, champions of the Upper River Project believed they would soon have a major ally in the White House. Three years earlier at the Missouri River Navigation Conference, Hoover had vowed to develop the nation's inland waterways. During his Kansas City address, Hoover had outlined a plan to create a north-south barge channel from Chicago to New Orleans and an east-west route from Pittsburgh to Kansas City and possibly beyond. With his election, members of the Missouri River Navigation Association expected Hoover to submit budget requests to Congress that included large appropriations for the completion of the Cross of Commerce, the six-foot channel to Kansas City, and the Upper River Project.

But Hoover and his new secretary of war, James W. Good, did not fully sanction the Upper River Project. In March 1929, only days after being sworn into office, Good, who possessed discretionary power over the dispersal of congressional funds allocated to the Missouri River, ordered the expenditure of $6 million for work on the Kansas City–to–mouth reach. As a concession to upper valley interests, Good directed that the remaining $1 million of that year's appropriation be spent on work between Kansas City and St. Joseph (located approximately 100 river miles above Kansas City). Good's action represented the first allocation of money for construction purposes to the Upper River Project.

However, $1 million would cover the cost of channelizing only about 20 miles of stream, an insignificant length considering that 385 miles of river flowed between Kansas City and Sioux City.[3]

Rather than placate local interests, Good's spending decision angered residents of eastern Nebraska and western Iowa who wanted channelization work started in their locales. In mid-May 1929 a group of congressional representatives from this area met with the secretary of war to persuade him to direct more money to their section of the Missouri. This delegation wanted the original $7 million appropriation dispersed evenly along the entire river from its mouth to Sioux City instead of its being spent almost exclusively in the state of Missouri. The delegates also argued that the federal government should open the upper river to barge traffic simultaneously with the opening of the channel to Kansas City. The upper valley did not want to wait for its six-foot channel. Good listened to the delegation's arguments, then responded that work needed to be concentrated along the Kansas City–to–mouth reach in order to inaugurate barge traffic there as soon as possible. By keeping the Corps' equipment, materials, and manpower along the lowest reaches, the government decreased that barge channel's overall cost. To spread out the Corps' work along the entire river below Sioux City would substantially increase costs by requiring more time to move men and materials into position, boosting the price of transporting piles and rock to isolated sites, and guaranteeing higher maintenance expenses for disconnected pile dikes and revetments destroyed by the river. Good believed that the sooner the navigation channel east of Kansas City carried barges, the sooner the federal government would receive a return on its investment. Good and the War Department wanted to save federal dollars; upper river interests simply wanted those dollars, disregarding issues of efficiency and cost-effectiveness.[4]

In response to the demands of congressional representatives from the Missouri Valley, however, Good directed an additional $1.5 million to the Upper River Project later in 1929. The Corps spent this entire allocation just above Kansas City, with the idea of gradually extending the barge channel northward. The secretary of war also procured another $7 million for work between Kansas City and the mouth, for a total of nearly $13 million for the year.[5] Never before had the federal government provided so much money in a single year for Missouri River improvement. The allocations for the river equaled 25 percent of the federal government's rivers and harbors budget for 1929.[6]

Good ordered such massive expenditures for the Missouri River navigation project because he hoped to tie the Missouri quickly into the larger inland waterways system then taking shape. By 1929 the Corps had already deepened the Mississippi River to nine feet from St. Louis to New Orleans. Another nine-foot channel existed from Cairo, Illinois, to Pittsburgh along the Ohio River. At the same time, work steadily moved forward on the six-foot channel along the Upper Mississippi River from St. Louis to St. Paul. Prompt completion of the six-foot channel to Kansas City would be a substantial step toward the realization of Hoover's Cross of Commerce.[7]

Hoover spoke about the Cross of Commerce in late October 1929 during a visit to Louisville, Kentucky, to commemorate the addition of the Ohio River to the inland waterways system. During a rousing speech, the president reiterated his commitment to the establishment of barge navigation on the nation's rivers: "As a general and broad policy, I favor modernizing of every part of our waterways which will show economic justification in aid of our farmers and industries. Now is river navigation's day of renaissance. Upon deep and regular channels unromantic diesel tugs now tow long trains of steel barges. What the river has lost in romance it has gained in tonnage."[8] He then argued for the construction of a waterways system in which all of the rivers possessed a single, uniform depth of nine feet. Such standardization would eliminate the need to break bulk at any port. A standard nine-foot depth would also enable operators to increase the carrying capacities of their barges, thereby decreasing their shipment costs, and through these savings contribute to general economic development.[9] The president asserted, "While it is desirable that some of the [Mississippi River] tributaries be made accessible to traffic at six or seven feet, yet we should, in the long view, look forward to increasing this latter depth [nine feet] as fast as traffic justifies."[10]

Hoover's Louisville speech thrilled members of the Missouri River Navigation Association. Not only did the president promise to finish the Cross of Commerce, but he also supported the deepening of rivers to nine feet. J. C. Nichols proclaimed, "The President's favorable attitude toward a 9-foot channel wherever justified fits in well with the demand of the Missouri River states for such a channel. We believe that with a 9-foot channel the Missouri River would become a trunk line waterway, earning all those benefits to agriculture and industry the President foresees accruing to the territory of the Ohio River." Although the six-foot channel below Kansas City remained years away from completion, the Missouri River Navigation Association now wanted a nine-foot channel.[11] That same month, the association's executive committee held a hearing in Kansas City to determine the economic feasibility of deepening the channel to nine feet below Kansas City. The association invited the head of the Kansas City District, Maj. Gordon R. Young, to the hearing, along with hundreds of businessmen from the surrounding area. Over the course of four days, Young heard repeated arguments in favor of deepening the channel.[12] Walter S. Dickey of the defunct Kansas City Missouri River Navigation Company unashamedly announced to Young that a "deeper channel would attract such a quantity of freight as to crowd the river with traffic." Other speakers claimed that a nine-foot channel would eliminate the need for operators to break bulk at St. Louis; thus, more companies would use a nine-foot channel. Specific Kansas City area companies pursuing construction of a nine-foot channel included the Sonken-Galamba Corporation (scrap metal dealers); Burnham, Munger, and Root Dry Goods Company (wholesalers); National Cast Iron Pipe Company; Thompson-Hayward Chemical Company; and the Independent Oil and Gas Company. Four hundred Kansas City businesses presented Young with declarations of how they would use a nine-foot channel. Nichols, who presided over the hearing, closed the meeting with a plea to Young, the War Department, and Congress: "Agriculture is at a low ebb in the territory. . . . The deeper river is needed to revive [the farmers]." Nichols then asked Young to recommend the nine-foot channel to his superiors in the Upper Mississippi Valley Division in St. Louis; he also beseeched him to include the nine-foot channel in the next Rivers and Harbors bill, slated for consideration that December.[13]

Young responded to the demands of the Missouri River Navigation Association. During December 1929 and January 1930 the district engineer wrote a report on the proposed nine-foot channel in which he endorsed the project for inclusion in the upcoming Rivers and Harbors bill. Young believed the amount of future barge traffic that would use the proposed channel and the comparatively low cost of deepening the six-foot channel to nine feet justified the project.[14]

Young's endorsement of the nine-foot channel represented a significant coup for Kansas City interests, but it did not guarantee legislative passage of the project. Young's findings still had to be accepted by the Board of Engineers. Brigadier General Herbert Deakyne, who had been caught in a firestorm of controversy fifteen years earlier when he rejected the Missouri River navigation project, served as chairman of the Board of Engineers. When Young's preliminary report favorable to the nine-foot channel went across Deakyne's desk, he rejected it. Deakyne believed the nine-foot channel needed further investigation. In particular, he thought that the Corps should learn more about the river's water-discharge rates. Did the river have enough water to sustain a nine-foot channel? He also wanted to know how the Missouri would behave once it had been narrowed and deepened to nine feet. Would the current's velocity increase to dangerous speeds? These issues had to be addressed before he and his colleagues would even consider submitting the entire nine-foot-channel project to Congress. Deakyne doubted whether the Missouri could ever be engineered to a nine-foot depth.[15]

Deakyne sent the report back to Young in Kansas City. Young, who still wanted to get the nine-foot-channel project included in that year's Rivers and Harbors bill, hurriedly wrote a report on the engineering feasibility of the project. Young claimed that the Missouri could be deepened below Kansas City for an additional investment of $27 million above the cost of completing the present six-foot channel. Moreover, Young believed the deepening of the channel could be accomplished using the same channelization techniques employed during construction of the six-foot channel. The existing channel needed only to be further straightened and confined to achieve the greater depth.

Young sent his report to Lt. Col. George R. Spalding, the division engineer in St. Louis, who looked at the study and then sent it to his superiors in Washington. Spalding disagreed with Young's conclusions and attached an addendum to the report that warned against adopting the nine-foot channel. Spalding wanted the Corps to build an experimental nine-foot-channel section along the Missouri to determine whether the remainder of the river could be engineered to that depth; he advocated a wait-and-see approach.[16] The division engineer did not want to rush construction on a nine-foot channel until the engineers understood more of the Missouri's intricacies.

When Young's engineering report and Spalding's addendum reached Deakyne and the Board of Engineers, the board concurred with Spalding's assessment. Deakyne agreed that Young's report inadequately addressed the engineering feasibility of the nine-foot channel. Deakyne, for the second time in his long career, dealt a blow to the advocates of Missouri River channelization.[17]

By rejecting the nine-foot channel, the Board of Engineers adhered to the fiscally conservative policies of Congress and President Hoover. As political appointees, the Board of Engineers, chief of engineers, and the secretary of war followed the advice and recommendations of President Hoover with regard to river projects. Hoover promoted only the construction of river projects that possessed favorable cost-to-benefit ratios. He also believed each river improvement project should provide a tangible dividend for the American people. Projects must either indirectly or directly return money to the U.S. Treasury. Projects of doubtful value or of a pork-barrel nature did not receive the administration's support. Thus, the Upper River Project and the nine-foot channel below Kansas City did not receive the political or financial backing of the administration or the War Department. Still, the administration deemed the six-foot channel to Kansas City a worthy project, first, because it had been ruled feasible from an engineering standpoint, and second, because it appeared as though it would actually be used as a navigation route. As a result, the six-foot channel project to Kansas City received tremendous appropriations during the years of the Hoover administration.[18]

When Patrick Hurley succeeded James Good as secretary of war in early 1930, he clarified the administration's policy toward river improvement. Hurley stated that the administration would resist pressure from local interests to fund their pet projects and instead focus its efforts on the creation of an integrated system of waterways. According to Hurley, piecemeal appropriations for disconnected river projects would end. Thus, money for the Upper River Project would not be forthcoming at least until after completion of the project below Kansas City.[19] In September 1930 Hurley elucidated the administration's stance: "We have departed from the idea that this is a local matter. The inland waterways are national in scope and national in benefits which they will bestow. There will be no dipping into the pork barrel in connection with appropriation and spending of waterway funds."[20] The Hoover administration had no intention of using either the Upper River Project or the nine-foot channel merely to alleviate unemployment caused by the advent of the Great Depression.[21]

Even with unemployment worsening in the United States throughout 1930, Hoover and the War Department refused to initiate large-scale work on the Upper River Project.[22] In December 1930 Chief of Engineers Lytle Brown requested a scant $800,000 from Congress for work above Kansas City for the following fiscal year. Learning of Brown's small request, Cong. Edward Campbell of the Eleventh Iowa District, which included Sioux City, commented, "The time to make public improvements is in the days of depression. The time to put men to work is in the days when men want work. No American wants to waste our public funds but surely constructive building of needed public improvements is not a form of waste. The flow of money through the wages paid will enliven every avenue of trade, and it looks as if every sensible American citizen should take this view."[23] But Hoover and the War Department held tightly to the federal purse strings.

In order to get a sizable allocation for the Upper River Project, Arthur Weaver requested and received an audience with President Hoover on 8 December 1930. J. C. Nichols of Kansas City; George C. Call, John Kelly, and George F. Silknitter of Sioux City; Rufus E. Lee and C. E. Childe of Omaha; Charles E. Wattles of St. Joseph; W. C. Lusk of Yankton; and Congressman Campbell accompanied Weaver to the White House. Twenty-five Missouri Valley men met with Hoover in the Oval Office, and Weaver served as the group's spokesman. He told the president that the interests above Kansas City wanted a $10 million appropriation for the fiscal year beginning July 1931. He said that this huge sum for the Upper River Project would contribute to unemployment relief and hasten the recovery of the agricultural sector in Nebraska, Missouri, Iowa, South Dakota, and North Dakota.[24] Hoover politely listened to Weaver and the others and expressed sympathy for their aims, but he did not commit to the expenditure of more money along the river reach north of Kansas City.[25]

Through their lobbying efforts, the advocates of the Upper River Project did secure more than the original $800,000 appropriation for the fiscal year 1931. By the end of that year the Corps spent $2,565,619 on the Upper River Project, but this money was spent for work in the vicinity of Kansas City. The region above St. Joseph still did not receive any tangible allotments.[26]

Disappointed that the War Department neglected their region, members of the Missouri River Navigation Association from Nebraska and Iowa again traveled to Washington in fall 1931 to urge Secretary of War Hurley to begin channelization simultaneously at St. Joseph, Omaha, and Sioux City. The group wanted federal money in order to provide work for large numbers of unemployed men in those cities, but War

Department officials rejected their pleas. Instead, the department requested only $1.4 million from Congress for work on the Upper River Project during the fiscal year beginning July 1932, which amounted to less than the amount spent in 1931. Outraged at this apparent disregard for their needs, another group of thirty Missouri Valley residents traveled to Washington in December 1931 to confer with Hoover. Arthur J. Weaver once more served as spokesman. Sioux City, Omaha, and St. Joseph sent numerous representatives. Weaver asked the president to seek $8 million from Congress for the fiscal year 1932 for the Upper River Project instead of the $1.4 million appropriation.[27] Hoover told the Missouri Valley men that he would consider their request, but he did not pursue the larger appropriation. Only $1.1 million went to the Upper River Project in 1932. It became clear to all involved that Sioux City, Omaha, Council Bluffs, and St. Joseph had to do without ample federal waterways funds.[28]

In contrast to the paltry amount granted to the Upper River Project between 1927 and 1932, colossal sums of money were allotted to the Corps for the reach east of Kansas City during this same period. The largest appropriations for this section of the river came during the Hoover administration. The engineers expended $12,825,000 in 1929; $14,041,498 in 1930; $10,916,775 in 1931; and $9,499,153 in 1932 on river work between Kansas City and the mouth.[29] This money paid the wages of thousands of laborers, purchased fuel for boats and machinery, repaired worn-out pieces of equipment, transported men and materials to construction sites, quarried stone, and bought cypress and pine piles. As a result, the Missouri River below Kansas City was transformed in just a few short years.

During these years, the Corps used the pile dike and the willow mattress and stone revetment to channelize the Missouri. The revetment's design remained unchanged since its introduction on the stream in the nineteenth century, but the pile dike used in the late 1920s and early 1930s represented a modification of the original. The engineers recognized that placement of the piles in clusters ensured against the rapid destruction of the dike; therefore, pile drivers hammered two or three piles within inches of each other. Crewmen then wrapped wire around this cluster to keep it together. Next, the pile driver pounded another cluster approximately ten feet away. The engineers placed a series of pile clusters at intervals extending in a straight row from the natural bank line. After completing one row, the pile driver placed one or two more rows of clustered piles adjacent to the original row. Finally, men laid piles horizontally in between the rows, tying them to the vertical piles. This technique gave the dike added strength. The Corps no longer employed the willow curtain; the pile clusters alone slowed the river's current enough to expedite the deposition of silt on the downstream side of the dike.

The scale and intensity of construction activity during this period dwarfed every previous level. At no other time in the history of Missouri River improvement had so many men, machines, and materials been combined in its channelization. From 1929 to 1932 the Corps of Engineers and private contractors annually employed between 10,000 and 13,000 men on the reach below Kansas City. In 1929, the first year of frenzied activity, a total of 12,000 men labored along the river's banks, in the willow groves adjacent to the stream, and on floating platforms tied to pile dikes.[30] In May 1930 the number of men working on the river approached 13,000.[31] By December the number dropped to as few as 2,000.[32] The advent of spring witnessed the hiring of men again. In early March 1931, 3,500 men endeavored to reshape the Missouri River.[33] These numbers rose to approximately 10,000 by that fall, only to drop off again during the winter months. In 1932 another 10,000 men found employment either with the Corps or with one of its private contractors.[34]

The majority of men working on the river came from farms, towns, and cities located along the valley in central Missouri. A large percentage also came from the two Kansas Cities. Many of the private construction firms under contract with the Corps had home offices in Kansas City and thus hired residents.[35] The laborers were usually local men willing to accept temporary employment. They required almost no training; anyone could learn to cut willows, lay rock, quarry stone, or weave willow mattresses. The Corps hired unskilled workers on a short-term basis, laying off the men during the winter months. Skilled laborers, trained engineers, and machine operators often came from outside the valley or from one of its major cities. These men were less likely to be laid off during the winter months and often remained on the Corps' permanent payroll.[36]

The level of channelization work occasionally reached a fever pitch. In 1929 a total of fifty-six pile drivers operated on the river, incessantly hammering the cypress and pine piles into the riverbed, nonstop, twenty-four hours a day, seven days a week, month after month. Crews shut down a pile driver only when it needed oiling or when its parts wore out.[37]

That same year the Corps placed electric lights at thirty-four points along the shoreline so that men could lay mattresses and build stone revetments during the night hours. In 1930 the federal engineers increased the number of pile drivers working below Kansas City to seventy-two and continued to deploy electric lights along the riverbank.[38] During peak construction periods, men worked long hours and took few breaks. Thousands of men slept on government quarterboats that lined the riverbank near each construction site. Since channelization work required the frequent movement of the labor force, quarterboats served the vital purpose of keeping the men close to their work sites. Quarterboats also allowed Corps supervisors to maintain strict discipline, preventing crewmen from drinking or participating in other illicit activities during their off-hours.[39]

Channelization work during these years adhered to a seasonal regime, dictated by the Missouri's water-discharge rates. By following the river's natural ebb and flow cycles, the engineers saved time, money, and effort. During the months of March, April, and May, for example, the engineers pushed the construction of pile dikes, with the goal of having the dikes in place before the start of the June rise.[40] As the June rise descended the valley, its waters carried unmatched amounts of suspended sediment; more silt rode downstream during that month than at any other time of the year. This silt fell behind the completed pile dikes and quickly realigned the river's thalweg. According to Corps officials, "Enough silt can be deposited during a single rise in the river to completely cover the dikes with sand, thus narrowing the channel to a desired width. This seems especially remarkable in view of the fact that the piles are 6 to 8 feet high [above the surface of the riverbed]."[41] Along sections of river where pile dikes and revetments had been in place for years, the high-water levels, moving from five to six miles per hour past the end of the dikes, scoured the sands and gravels from the river bottom and deepened the thalweg to the requisite six-foot depth. And high, fast water kept the new navigation channel free of snags and debris by preventing their deposition in the riverbed. Corps officials referred to the June rise as Santa Claus because of the gifts it bestowed on their navigation channel.[42]

After the river's water level dropped in mid-July, the engineers shifted gears, focusing their efforts on the construction of willow mattresses and stone revetments. This type of work progressed rapidly during low-flow periods when the banks protruded far above the waterline. By waiting

until late summer to build mattresses and stone revetments, the Corps
of Engineers saved time, money, and materials; high flows made mattress placement difficult, time-consuming, and hazardous for the crews.[43]

Each year, during November, December, January, and February, the
pace of channelization work slowed down. Colder temperatures, ice
flows, and the frozen ground led to higher construction costs, frequent
delays, and greater wear and tear on equipment and men. The Corps
thus kept the level of work during these months to a minimum, usually
repairing damaged pile dikes or revetments or reinforcing structures
along strategic points in the river.[44]

Work moved steadily forward after 1927. In that year the Corps had
channelized approximately 40 percent of the Kansas City–to–mouth
reach. By 1929 the reach was almost 70 percent complete; and in 1930,
80 percent of the barge channel had been finished by the engineers. By
1932 only a few miles of the river remained unchannelized, and the
Corps claimed that the barge channel stood 95 percent complete. Near
the end of the Hoover administration a total of 370 miles of the river
had been narrowed and deepened with channelization structures. The
river became noticeably different in just a few years. The previously wide,
shallow, unstable, meandering channel maintained an almost uniform
width and depth; sandbars, side channels, islands, and snags disappeared
from the river.

In June 1932 Secretary of War Hurley, accompanied by Maj. Gen.
T. Q. Ashburn, chairman of the Inland Waterways Corporation, a govern-
ment-subsidized barge line; Col. George R. Spalding, division engineer
of the Upper Mississippi Valley Division; and Capt. Theodore Wyman
Jr., the new district engineer at Kansas City, traveled on board a small
flotilla of government towboats from the mouth of the Missouri to Kansas City to inspect the nearly completed six-foot navigation channel.
Hurley had other motives for making the trip. He wanted to see first-
hand what the government had accomplished along the Missouri and
to campaign for President Hoover, who was seeking reelection that fall.

Just before his departure from St. Louis on 21 June, Hurley told an
assembled crowd, "I am here to redeem a campaign pledge made four
years ago by a candidate for president. Much has been said about making the Missouri River navigable. That job has been completed, as far as
Kansas City."[45] Speaking about the administration's policy toward river
improvement, Hurley proclaimed, "A few days ago we were asked if we
could spend 539 million dollars next year on river improvement. The

Corps of Engineers estimated that with this money it could add 34,000 men to the 30,000 now employed. There are about 8 million men unemployed in the country. To employ 34,000 of them, we would unbalance the budget, throw the country into confusion and employ only a drop in the bucket."[46] Even with the number of unemployed rising, the Hoover administration balked at spending liberal sums of money on river projects.

When Hurley's inspection boats entered the Missouri, they ran squarely into the highest water level to descend the river in three years. Corps officials estimated that the channel depth in the Missouri averaged twenty feet. Along with the high water came a fast current, up to five miles per hour.[47] Although the government boats struggled to move upstream, the high water convinced Hurley that the river could carry barge traffic. He boasted, "The Missouri River between Kansas City and St. Louis has been conquered by the engineers."[48]

Hurley's entourage stopped at a number of towns along the river, including St. Charles, Hermann, Jefferson City, Boonville, Waverly, and Lexington. At each town Hurley gave speeches commending President Hoover for his efforts in developing the Missouri and the other major rivers of the United States.[49] On Monday 27 June the government boats neared Kansas City.[50] A crowd estimated at over 10,000 cheered as the flotilla docked at the Kansas City wharf. Once on land, Hurley shook hands with Arthur Weaver, J. C. Nichols, and George Miller of the Missouri River Navigation Association. A band belted out patriotic music, and 75-mm howitzers blasted a salute that scattered Kansas City's pigeon population in all directions. Weaver, speaking to the throngs under the beaming sun, claimed that the completion of the river channel below Kansas City represented the greatest single achievement in the Missouri Valley in the last twenty-five years: "Transportation is vital. We rejoice with Kansas City in the demonstration of the feasibility of the channel. I feel the opening of the Missouri will bring a rejuvenation to our entire valley."[51]

The rejuvenation of the valley would occur once regular barge traffic moved on the river. Such traffic would create competitive carrier rates, lower transportation costs for farmers and industrialists, and bring prosperity to valley residents. But the rejuvenation of the valley's economy did not occur in 1932. Even though Hurley and his flotilla made it upstream, the six-foot channel remained incomplete. Hurley's trip was a fluke; the government boats had been lucky to avoid grounding on shoals. After the passage of the June rise, barges could not use the river; too many shallow points remained between Kansas City and the mouth. Not surprisingly, the era of prosperity did not arrive. Instead, the economic depression deepened, and the numbers of unemployed soared in late summer and early fall 1932.

In September 1932 a writer for *Fortune* magazine calculated that the number of unemployed in the United States had risen to 10 million. Another 1 million would be out of a job by winter. Taking into consideration the number of persons relying on these 11 million for their livelihood, the author estimated that over 27.5 million Americans had already lost, or would soon lose, their only source of income. Nearly one-fourth the population of the United States would need some kind of relief in the approaching months.[52] The economic crisis had reached ominous dimensions. Hungry, bored, and hopeless people often turned to violence to meet their needs.

In the presidential election of 1932, the American people chose the Democratic Party and Franklin D. Roosevelt to solve the deteriorating economic situation. During the campaign, Roosevelt promised the public that his administration would reverse the failed policies of the Hoover years and would offer the American people a "new deal." Just what Roosevelt's new deal would entail, no one really knew. Most voters just wanted a change and a president who might be able to reverse the depression. Hoover's policies, like much of the country, were bankrupt. Roosevelt was elected by a wide margin, taking 57 percent of the popular vote. The Democrats also captured significant majorities in both the House and the Senate.[53] Roosevelt would have an opportunity to initiate his new deal. But during the months before his inauguration, the unemployment rate continued to spiral out of control. By early 1933 an estimated 12 million former workers did not hold jobs.[54]

Prior to Roosevelt's inauguration, members of the Missouri River Navigation Association tried to determine the president-elect's policy toward their navigation project. Concern arose among valley residents over whether the new president would fund their project or abandon it. Fears subsided somewhat in early February 1933 when Roosevelt, during one of his first "fireside chats" at Warm Springs, Georgia, disclosed his intentions for the Tennessee Valley. Roosevelt planned to employ 200,000 people in the Tennessee basin working on dams, cutting trees and brush, and reseeding eroded areas. The president-elect declared, "If [the Tennessee Valley project] is successful, and I am confident it will be, I think this development will be the forerunner of similar projects in other sections."[55]

While Roosevelt prepared to take office and valley residents wondered what his plans would be for the Missouri River, the Kansas City District Office of the Corps of Engineers made plans of its own for the river. Two events spurred the engineers to consider further development of the river. The first was the opening of the nine-foot channel along the Mississippi below St. Louis and the nine-foot channel on the Ohio. Deeper channels on these two rivers made the Missouri River's six-foot channel obsolete before it was even finished. Corps officials understood that barge operators would shy away from the Missouri because its shallower depth would require the profit-eliminating break-in-bulk at St. Louis. In order to make the Missouri a viable component of the inland waterways system, the river needed to be deepened. Otherwise, the $60 million investment to date would be wasted for navigation purposes.[56]

The second event that led the Corps to envision further development was the drought that had gripped the northern Great Plains and upper Midwest since 1929. It dropped the Missouri to unprecedented levels and raised the serious question of whether the navigation channel would ever be used to carry barges. In the 1920s the Corps calculated that the Missouri River needed to possess a volume of approximately 20,000 cubic feet per second (cfs) below Sioux City in order to maintain the depth needed for a six-foot navigation channel. But during the navigation seasons of 1929, 1930, and 1931, the river below Sioux City did not meet this minimum-depth requirement for a total of 413 days. Each navigation season lasted 246 days, from 15 March to 15 November. Thus, for 56 percent of the time during the previous three navigation seasons, the river remained too shallow for a six-foot channel. The Corps had designed the six-foot channel below Kansas City to hold approximately 23,000 cfs,[57] but during the severest drought periods, the river did not provide that amount of water. In 1931 alone, the river below Kansas City did not have enough water for a six-foot depth for a total of seventy-two days during the navigation season. On 19 September 1931 the river shattered all former low-flow records when it dipped to 10,700 cfs at Kansas City. This amount represented only half the water volume required for the six-foot channel. The Corps of Engineers had made a serious and costly miscalculation by believing the Missouri would never drop below 23,000 cfs at Kansas City.[58] The channel's reliability and usefulness were in serious doubt. If barge companies faced a similar drought in the future and could not navigate the Missouri for over two months during the navigation season, barge service would die on the river. No company could survive on the stream if its equipment, labor force, and barges had to lie idle for months on end.

The Corps quickly concluded that the only solution to the obsolete six-foot navigation channel was the construction of upstream storage reservoirs either on the Missouri main stem or on one of its larger tributaries. Corps officials ruled out any modification of the existing channel to obtain either the six-foot or nine-foot depths with lower volumes of water. Officials concluded that it would be impossible to further restrict the river channel to achieve greater depths with less water. Such a narrowing would result in perilously fast current velocities during high-flow periods. Moreover, narrowing would not guarantee consistent depths, since a future drought could still reduce the river to a trickle. Thus, the only conceivable option to combat droughts and to establish a deeper, nine-foot channel on the river appeared to be the construction of one or more storage reservoirs. Reservoir water would augment flows in the low river. The central question was where to build the dam, or dams.

Engineers in the Kansas City District conducted a survey in the early 1930s to determine the best sites for storage reservoirs and by late 1932 had limited the choice to two. The Corps considered building a large dam across the Kaw River near Topeka, Kansas, a dam at Fort Peck, Montana, across the Missouri, or both (Fig. 7.1). Each of these sites had numerous advantages and disadvantages. A Topeka dam would sharply curtail floods along the Kaw River in the vicinity of Kansas City, provide enough water downstream to maintain a nine-foot channel from Kansas City to the mouth, and provide irrigation water to farms in central Kansas. However, a dam at Topeka would require the relocation of a significant Kaw Valley population, estimated at 5,000 persons. Moreover, a dam there would not contribute any water to the six-foot channel that might eventually be built from Kansas City to Sioux City. Any navigation channel north of Kansas City would remain vulnerable to drought periods. Further, a Topeka reservoir would shrink during drought periods since its primary source of water would be rainfall, which would obviously diminish with any Great Plains drought. A Topeka dam would reduce the threat that droughts posed to the barge channel below Kansas City but not entirely remove it.

A large dam at Fort Peck would provide numerous benefits to the navigation channel. Primarily, the dam's water supply would be more

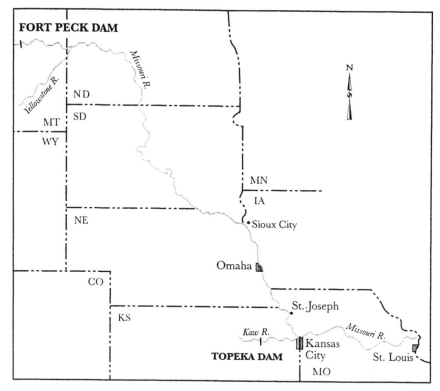

Fig. 7.1. The Topeka and Fort Peck Dams and the navigation channel.

reliable than that stored at Topeka. Above the mouth of the Yellowstone the Missouri maintained a fairly constant water volume because the river received the majority of its runoff from snowmelt. Snowfall amounts in the Rockies did not vary as much as rainfall amounts across the Great Plains or in central Kansas. Downstream from the Yellowstone, the river volume fluctuated greatly each year and over a period of years. The oscillations in water level resulted from the highly variable weather patterns over the northern Great Plains. Corps officials ruled against dams in the Dakotas because they believed reservoir water levels there would be severely affected during drought periods, just as a Topeka reservoir would be. Thus, Dakota reservoirs would be unable to supply reliable flow volumes for the navigation channel downstream. Stable water volumes above the Yellowstone would ensure that the proposed dam at Fort Peck would still be able to supply water to the lower river, even if the Great Plains and middle Missouri endured a severe drought.[59]

Moreover, a dam at Fort Peck would provide the water needed to maintain depths of eight to nine feet in any future barge channel constructed from Kansas City to Sioux City. Another advantage of the Fort Peck site was that a reservoir there would inundate a sparsely settled area with much lower land values than those around Topeka. Only two small communities and several hundred isolated cattle ranches existed in the planned reservoir area. Few people would be forced to relocate, and the inexpensive price of land would lower the overall cost of the dam. Further, a dam at Fort Peck would not block the movement of as much waterborne silt as a dam on the Kaw. Fort Peck reservoir would take a reputed 400 years to fill with silt, guaranteeing it a long life expectancy. But the Fort Peck site had disadvantages. The dam would sit so high up on the Missouri that its contribution to flood control in the lower valley would be negligible. The Missouri's largest plains tributaries would still be able to pour their water into the stream. And the dam site's remoteness increased its cost. Large pieces of machinery, boats, materials, and men would have to travel great distances to get to any future construction site.

Captain Theodore Wyman in Kansas City considered four development options in relation to either the Topeka or the Fort Peck dam. In the first option, he could reject any reservoir projects designed to augment flows in the navigation channel, which would be allowed to remain susceptible to dry cycles. The second option was to build a low dam at Fort Peck and another dam at Topeka, the former having a reservoir storage capacity of 4 million acre-feet, enough storage to provide for a six-foot, drought-resistant channel below Sioux City. A Topeka dam would supplement flows from Fort Peck and provide enough water to maintain a nine-foot navigation channel from Kansas City to the mouth. With this alternative, Wyman and the Kansas City District considered the establishment of a future navigation channel of nine feet from the mouth to Kansas City and a shallower channel from Kansas City to Sioux City.

The third option was to build a higher dam at Fort Peck with a storage capacity of 6 MAF, which would still maintain the six-foot channel between Sioux City and Kansas City and provide a little additional water in case of extremely severe drought conditions. The dam at Topeka would still be built to maintain the nine-foot channel below Kansas City.

The fourth option entailed the construction of a huge dam at Fort Peck with a storage capacity of 17 MAF. It would provide for a regulated flow of 30,000 cfs past Yankton during the eight-month navigation season and would furnish the water necessary to maintain a nine-foot channel from Sioux City to the mouth. A Topeka dam would not be built under this fourth plan.[60]

Wyman and his colleagues in Kansas City were still studying their options when Franklin D. Roosevelt took office in March 1933. The new president did not immediately reveal his position on Missouri River development, which worried residents of the Missouri Valley. Anxiety became acute in late March when Roosevelt ordered the War Department to halt all new work along the nation's rivers, including the Missouri. Administration officials wanted to review existing river projects to ascertain those worthy of continued federal financing. More specifically, the White House planned to initiate a massive unemployment relief program across the United States in the coming months; the review would help officials decide which river projects to include in the relief program. In response to the suspension of work, the *Kansas City Star* reported, "President Roosevelt's policy towards inland waterways continued today to be as much a puzzle as it was before his inauguration March 4."[61]

Arthur Weaver and George Miller spent ten days in Washington in late March consulting with administration officials and members of the War Department in order to discover Roosevelt's attitude toward the Missouri. During the trip, Weaver learned about the Corps' studies on the Topeka and Fort Peck dams. Jubilant at the possibility of securing a reliable volume of water for the navigation channel, Weaver declared, "Navigators could be assured of an 8- or 9-foot channel from the Dakotas to the mouth of the Missouri if the excess water were impounded in Montana."[62] He made it clear that he favored the Fort Peck site over Topeka, not only because of Fort Peck's import for the proposed nine-foot channel below Kansas City but also because a dam there might lead to the completion of the neglected Upper River Project. But Weaver and Miller did not get a firm answer from anyone in the administration regarding the president's disposition toward Missouri River development. The two men left the capital unsure if the Missouri would be included in any economic recovery plan.[63]

In May 1933 the Annual Rivers and Harbors bill went before the House of Representatives. For the first time in a decade, it did not contain any provision for the Missouri River. Without a congressional appropriation, the only hope for continued financing of Missouri River channelization rested with the administration and its future relief program. But Missouri Valley interests still did not know Roosevelt's stance on the Upper River Project, the six-foot channel below Kansas City, or the tentative storage reservoirs at Topeka and Fort Peck. All attempts by members of the Missouri River Navigation Association to learn the president's position met with noncommittal replies from administration officials. To try to get a solid answer, George Miller and Arthur Weaver headed back to Washington in early May, taking J. C. Nichols with them. Nichols, Miller, and Weaver, in their discussions with administration officials, asserted that continued channelization work would employ significant numbers of men. Miller reasoned, "There isn't a project in the country which would put men to work more quickly than the authorization to proceed on the river. Eighty percent of the cost goes for wages."[64] Although no one in the administration agreed to push for appropriations for the Missouri, the three men went home confident that the White House held a favorable opinion toward Missouri River channelization.[65]

In June 1933 Congress passed the National Industrial Recovery Act (NIRA). The act allocated $3.3 billion to a public works fund and established the Public Works Administration (PWA) to disburse the money. Through the NIRA, Congress placed the PWA under the authority of the president and granted the organization the power to initiate federal construction projects without the approval of Congress. In essence, Roosevelt possessed discretionary power over the $3.3 billion. Congress hoped such singular control over funding decisions would result in rapid implementation of construction projects to spur industrial recovery. In order to receive PWA money for its river projects, the War Department would be required to submit its funding requests to a Public Works Board, which would then advance the request to the head of the PWA. Roosevelt named Secretary of the Interior Harold Ickes as PWA chief.[66]

Only three days after the adoption of the NIRA, the Corps of Engineers held hearings in Washington to ascertain whether the War Department should seek funding for the Missouri River from the PWA.[67] At the time of the hearings, the War Department considered two distinct proposals for the future development of the Missouri. One report had been written by Capt. Theodore Wyman in Kansas City and the other by division engineer George Spalding in St. Louis. Wyman recommended to his superiors the continued construction of the six-foot channel from the mouth to Kansas City and the immediate commencement of large-scale operations on the Upper River Project. He also believed work on a dam at Fort Peck should begin as soon as possible. Spalding, on the other hand, argued that work on the six-foot channel should end at or near St. Joseph and that the government should not build either the Fort Peck or the Topeka dam. Instead, federal officials should wait to see whether a significant amount of barge traffic emerged on the river below St. Joseph. If boats began to use the river in justifiable numbers, then the river could be developed farther north and its flows augmented with upstream reservoirs. Spalding wanted to proceed slowly with development because he doubted that barge operators would use the channel. He also harbored misgivings about the rising costs of maintaining the channelization structures already in place. Spalding reasoned that if the Corps moved too quickly upriver with their pile dikes and revetments, the cost of maintaining this extensive system of structures against the ravages of the river might possibly negate the benefits derived from incremental increases in barge traffic.[68]

A large Missouri Valley contingent traveled to Washington to ensure that the army engineers and War Department rejected Spalding's recommendations and adopted Wyman's proposals for a major expansion of the navigation project. C. E. Childe of the Omaha Chamber of Commerce told the army engineers during the hearing that the Missouri River channelization project offered "far more in public benefits and economic potentialities than any other public works under consideration." He then begged federal officials to "give us an outlet to the sea and our population will increase, our industries will expand, our agriculture [will] become profitable."[69] Weaver pleaded with the engineers, "We helped pay for the Panama Canal, seaports, and other waterways. Now we have the right to demand development of our waterway."[70]

Ten days after the hearing, the War Department submitted a request to the Public Works Board for over $17 million for Missouri River channelization. The department had decided against Spalding. From the $17 million request, the Corps planned on spending $3.5 million on the river below Kansas City and another $14.1 million for construction work on the Upper River Project.[71] But the Public Works Board did not immediately agree to fund this request; instead, one of its members, Secretary of War George Dern, traveled to the Missouri Valley to learn about the region's needs. On 7 August, Dern arrived in Omaha and met with Weaver and thirty other river boosters. Businessmen and political officials from Sioux City, Council Bluffs, Omaha, Nebraska City, Lincoln, Blair, and Plattsmouth urged the secretary to push for the start of large-scale work on the Upper River Project. Dern assured the group that he understood their problems. The secretary said he would go back to the capital and press his colleagues on the PWA Board for an allocation for the Upper River Project.

After his Omaha meeting, the secretary of war boarded a plane and flew south above the river to Kansas City, where he met another thirty-five Kansas City businessmen and members of the Missouri River Navigation Association in the Muehlebach Hotel. These men informed the secretary about the importance of the channelization work to their region and its unemployed. Dern told the group, "There was an acute farm problem before other industries had difficulties. For that reason I'm sympathetic to waterways development."[72]

Ten days after Dern's visit to the valley, PWA chief Harold Ickes ordered Chief of Engineers Lytle Brown and Deputy PWA Administrator H. M. Waite to again study the six-foot channel to Sioux City to determine whether the project should receive PWA funds. A few days later, Brown and Waite reported favorably on the project to Ickes. This endorsement, along with Dern's advocacy and the widespread public agitation for the project along the Missouri Valley, convinced Ickes to approve funding for the Upper River Project. On 24 August 1933 Ickes released $14.1 million for immediate expenditure on the river between Kansas City and Sioux City. But he did not release any money for construction along the river below Kansas City or for a dam at Fort Peck.[73]

The allocation of funds for the Upper River Project represented a significant shift in federal policy toward the river. From 1927 to 1933 the Corps of Engineers had resisted the extension of the navigation project north of Kansas City. Concerns about cost-effectiveness, maintenance of installed structures, engineering feasibility, and a desire to finish the reach below Kansas City kept work on the Upper River Project to a minimum. But the $14.1 million PWA allocation exceeded every past allocation for the Kansas City–Sioux City reach. The Roosevelt administration and the War Department reversed earlier policy for a number of reasons.

The single greatest motive for this reversal involved the number of unemployed in the Missouri Valley. In May 1933 the mayor of Sioux City,

W. D. Hayes, declared that 4,000 unemployed families lived in Sioux City. This figure, based on an average family size of four, meant that 16,000 people in that community of 80,000 needed federal assistance. A few months later, L. S. Wernell of the Iowa Emergency Relief Administration and J. D. Mehner of the Nebraska Emergency Relief Administration confirmed that 19,137 families residing in a two-row tier of counties on either side of the Missouri River from Sioux City to Omaha required federal aid. Over 76,000 people along this thin strip of land depended on federal welfare to survive. Local and state officials believed that the river project, if adequately funded, would transfer 13,000 families, or 52,000 inhabitants, from the relief rolls to self-sufficiency. A second and related reason for the allotment stemmed from the fact that work along this reach could start quickly. The Kansas City District had already drawn up design plans for the Upper River Project, the physical plant used on the nearly finished channel below Kansas City could be easily transferred to the north, and a trained cadre of Corps employees existed to supervise the mass of workers who could be hired. Thus, federal money would put men to work within a matter of weeks. Time factored strongly into Ickes's decision; men needed work immediately, before further hardship and the onset of winter.[74]

A third reason for such a large appropriation was that channelization work entailed the execution of labor-intensive tasks. As George Miller had earlier claimed to federal officials, "Eighty percent of the cost goes for wages."[75] Thousands of men could be employed, carrying stone, cutting trees, laying willow mattresses. The project was ideal for employing high numbers of men. A fourth factor was that work on the river below Kansas City was winding down as the channel there neared completion. Not to fund the Upper River Project would have idled an extensive construction fleet whose operation contributed to the health of other industries, including oil, timber, and machine tools. Moreover, the project would contribute to soil conservation, a key component in Roosevelt's plans for other river basins. The stabilization of banks would prevent erosion and increase the value of valley farms. Further, administration officials hoped the work would create a navigation route that would someday contribute to an economic recovery through the reduction of freight rates.

Speed was of the essence in the expenditure of funds. The PWA administrators wanted men employed without delay. In September 1933 the Kansas City District rushed ahead with the letting of construction contracts for work on the Upper River Project. According to District Engineer Wyman, "Every effort will be made to employ the maximum number of men immediately so that the greatest amount of work possible may be accomplished and wages paid before winter." He then explained, "Men will be put to work first in the vicinity of St. Joseph and Nodaway. But the work will be spread out over the whole length of the [upper river] project rapidly." Assistant Secretary of War Harry Woodring proclaimed, "Everything that can be done by hand will be done by hand. We intend to give employment to the greatest number of men possible and to make them once more paying consumers for the products of the country's industry."[76]

Wyman intended on having 8,000 men on the river before the cold set in. He planned on spending the money not only at St. Joseph and Nodaway but also at White Cloud, Rulo, Tarkio, Corning, Nebraska City, Plattsmouth, Omaha, Council Bluffs, Florence, Brownville, Dakota City, and Sioux City. The former policy of concentrating funds along particular reaches of the river had been abandoned in favor of the less efficient and more costly technique of spreading the work out over a number of different locations.[77]

George Miller of the navigation association concluded that the allocation for the Upper River Project could mean only one thing: the Roosevelt administration was leaning toward the adoption of a dam at Fort Peck. Otherwise, according to Miller, it did not make economic or engineering sense for the administration to finance the Upper River Project when future flow volumes along that reach could not be ensured.[78] Miller claimed that the work on the Upper River Project "certainly means that the government is going to finish the job to some such strategic point as Omaha. And it is my opinion that having done that, it will not stop short of the Fort Peck reservoir and the 9-foot channel."[79] Harry H. Woodring agreed with Miller's assessment. Only days later he stated, "We will have first a 6-foot channel. I believe the 6-foot channel must lead inevitably to a 9-foot channel with the development of the reservoir system."[80]

But the administration kept quiet about Fort Peck. Throughout September, members of the Missouri River Navigation Association and residents throughout the valley wondered whether the dam would receive administration approval. Meanwhile, the president and Ickes, unknown to Missouri Valley residents, waited for a final Corps study on the feasibility of the dam.[81] On 29 September 1933 Lytle Brown reported to Harry

Woodring that the Corps of Engineers had concluded its studies of Fort Peck and favored the construction of the dam, using PWA funds. Brown advocated building the largest possible dam, one with a storage capacity of between 17 MAF and 19.5 MAF. This reservoir would supply the river channel below Sioux City with an approximate eight- to nine-foot depth. Brown also recommended the completion of the six-foot channel to Sioux City. The Corps tallied the total cost of the two projects at $145 million.[82] Woodring then sent the Corps study, and the $145 million request, to the Public Works Board for review.

When informed of the War Department's request, Ickes indicated that he might oppose any additional allocation for the Missouri, including the dam at Fort Peck. He blurted, "It's a lot of money. We've already allotted 14 million dollars out there."[83] To avoid any opposition from Ickes, members of the Missouri River Navigation Association and congressional representatives from the Missouri basin states decided to go straight to the president for the money to build Fort Peck. On 5 October Roosevelt met with Weaver, Nichols, Miller, Sen. Bennett C. Clark of Missouri, Sen. Burton Wheeler of Montana, and Sen. Lynn Frazier of North Dakota. A number of other senators accompanied the group to the White House.[84] During this meeting Roosevelt told the group that he favored the completion of the six-foot channel to Sioux City and the construction of a dam at Fort Peck.[85] A dam at Topeka would not be built because of determined local opposition to the project. The president also told Senator Clark to see Ickes about getting money for the channelization project below Kansas City. He and Ickes would discuss funding for Fort Peck later.[86]

Clark met with Ickes on 7 October and received assurances from the secretary of the interior that he would provide $3.5 million for the river below Kansas City. Clark claimed that with this money, "The channel to Kansas City could be completed by spring, ready for opening of navigation, and employment would be provided immediately to several thousand men."[87] Three days later Ickes released the money for the lower river project.[88]

Concerned about the status of the Fort Peck project, Senator Clark again met with the president on 13 October to urge a release of funds to begin construction on the dam. Roosevelt assured the Missouri senator that he would get as much money for it as could be efficiently spent in the upcoming year. The next day Ickes released $15.5 million for the start of construction on the dam at Fort Peck.[89]

The administration supported its construction for many of the same reasons it funded the Upper River Project: work at the dam site could be initiated without delay; construction tasks would be labor-intensive and require the employment of large numbers of men; the dam would be built in the economically depressed region of eastern Montana, thereby aiding that territory's recovery; heavy industrial equipment, machine tools, and extensive amounts of raw materials would be used by the Corps of Engineers during construction; the dam would fit into the president's overall policy of conserving natural resources; and it would support downstream navigation, soil conservation, and flood prevention. Moreover, Roosevelt sanctioned the dam because of the persuasive arguments of Missouri Valley residents who had met with him and Ickes several times during the fall. FDR and Ickes could have given the federal money to numerous other projects, but they decided on Fort Peck because of their contacts with Clark, Wheeler, Weaver, Nichols, and Miller.[90]

By approving the construction of the dam, Roosevelt, Ickes, and the War Department virtually committed the federal government not only to the completion of the six-foot channel to Sioux City but also to the future deepening of the channel to nine feet. The navigation channel south of Sioux City would be useless without the dam, and the dam would be useless without the navigation channel, especially a nine-foot channel. Approval of a dam at Fort Peck tied the federal government to a still larger development program for the Missouri River. J. C. Nichols confirmed this view in mid-October: "The building of the Fort Peck reservoir is of immense importance to the whole Middle West, both from the standpoint of industry and agriculture. It assures a dependable channel for navigation and removes this [channelization] project from a position of doubt." Sioux Citian George Call declared, "The allotment for Ft. Peck will mean the ultimate stabilization of the river, at least as far as Sioux City."[91]

Within days after the PWA allocation of funds for Fort Peck, District Engineer Wyman swung into action; he first established a Corps office in Glasgow, Montana, seventeen miles north of the dam site, to oversee the project. Only nine days after Ickes released the money, Wyman had seventy local men removing brush at the dam site.[92] Brush- and timber-clearing operations continued until mid-December. On 10 January 1934 the crews began construction of dredge boats, which would suck clay from the riverbed and deposit the material on the dam embankment to form the impervious earthen barrier. By early February the Corps employed over 1,000 men at the dam site. The majority of the common laborers came from Valley County, Montana, which bordered the Missouri on the north.[93] The only employees to come from outside the immediate area consisted of heavy-machine operators and Corps personnel; PWA policy required that as many men as possible should be hired locally. On 28 February the engineers began construction of a combination railroad-highway bridge across the Missouri just downstream from the future dam. The bridge would allow work to proceed apace on both banks of the river. In May crews initiated construction on a 287-mile-long power line from the Rainbow Falls Dam near Great Falls, Montana, to the Fort Peck site. Electricity from this upstream dam would power lights, machines, and the employee housing facilities then being built. The Missouri River would be turned against itself, its hydroelectric generating capacity contributing to the further damming of the stream.

Work during the first year involved building the infrastructure necessary to support construction of the dam itself. By June the Corps began burrowing four twenty-eight-foot-diameter tunnels that would eventually carry the Missouri around the earthen dam, through the bluffs, and safely downstream.[94] In July Ickes ordered another $25 million from the PWA fund spent on Fort Peck. The secretary of the interior wanted the work on the project accelerated to relieve the continued economic hardship evident in Montana that summer as the region suffered from another year of severe drought.[95] This big allocation meant the dam would be completed; with so much invested in the project, there would be no turning back. In early August Roosevelt visited Fort Peck. Looking down on the dusty, windswept dam site from the hills above, the president proudly observed 7,000 bronzed men erecting an edifice in his name.[96]

While men perspired under the burning sun at Fort Peck to arrest the flow of the Missouri, thousands more toiled along the river south of Sioux City, attempting to bind the river within a wooden straitjacket. Only a couple of months after Wyman received PWA money for the Upper River Project, the engineer boasted that he had 4,000 men working on the river between St. Joseph and Sioux City.[97] Significant numbers of these men were farmers who needed additional income to supplement their meager earnings from crop and livestock sales. Corps officials had received instructions from the PWA not only to hire local labor but also to ensure that farmers received a better-than-fair consideration for the available construction jobs.[98] With so much money at his disposal, Wyman and his colleagues nearly completed the six-foot channel to St. Joseph by early June 1934. Work above that point had been spread out at different locations, so a continuous navigation channel did not exist north of that city. The $3.6 million PWA allocation for the river reach below Kansas City enabled the Corps to pronounce that reach's six-foot channel complete in fall 1934.

By early 1935 the first PWA allocation had been nearly exhausted, and members of the Missouri River Navigation Association again traveled to Washington to lobby the administration for more money. On 1 February Weaver and several other men from Sioux City and Omaha met with Roosevelt to ask him for $35 million for the Upper River Project so that the engineers could finish the channel to Sioux City within the next couple of years. Weaver reminded the president that the counties bordering the river in western Iowa and eastern Nebraska had severe unemployment. The number of families on relief rolls had increased from a little over 19,000 in late 1933 to 31,362 in fall and winter 1934–1935. The president listened to Weaver's arguments but did not make a definite commitment to dispense the money.[99]

By May 1935 no decision had been made by the administration regarding the Upper River Project. Weaver, apprehensive about its future financial status, again traveled to Washington to meet with Roosevelt. On 6 May Weaver and Nebraska senator Edward Burke requested $40 million from the president to finish the Upper River Project. Weaver also wanted the money so that the Corps could hurry the construction of pile dikes in time to capture the heavy silt load of the approaching June rise.[100] On 17 May Ickes released $10 million; although quite a bit less than the $40 million requested, it would be enough for the Corps to build the channel to Omaha.

Dissatisfied with the small allocation, Weaver urged members of the navigation association to write or send telegrams to the president requesting more money. Key to Weaver's urgency was his belief that the completed Fort Peck Dam would forever end or dramatically reduce the Missouri's annual June rise (Fig. 7.2). Deprived of its high flows and heavy silt content, the Missouri River below Sioux City would be unable to realign itself within the system of pile dikes. Some other possibly prohibitively expensive means of channelizing the river would then have

Fig. 7.2. Fort Peck Dam. (Courtesy of the Corps of Engineers)

to be discovered by the Corps.[101] But Weaver's letter-writing campaign failed to gain more money for the Upper River Project.

Although PWA and Works Progress Administration (WPA) financing for channelization work decreased after 1935, the Missouri River Navigation Association still secured enough incremental allotments from Congress and the president to push work to Omaha and then to Sioux City.[102] The Corps had the river tied down as far as Omaha by winter 1938–1939. The first barge arrived in that city in May 1939, churning upstream on top of spring floodwaters. Then during 1939 and 1940 the Corps concentrated its resources along the Omaha–Sioux City reach.

Corps officials believed that reach of the river to be the most unstable section of the entire river system.[103] Here the valley floor and the river's bed consisted of highly erosive alluvium that facilitated frequent changes in the direction of the channel. Furthermore, the distance between valley walls was greater along this section than anywhere else. The river had a wide path to move through on its way south; hence, the channel not only spread out south of Sioux City but also formed long bends. The average channel area (the area of the river with free-flowing water) below Sioux City was 1,000 to 10,000 feet wide.[104] A river nearly two miles wide with long loops would require extensive alteration in order to develop a navigation channel 6 feet deep with a 200-foot-wide thalweg.

The other major physical challenge confronting the Corps above Omaha was the climate. Wet cycles affected the river here more than to the south or north. High flows exacerbated the inherent instability of the river in western Iowa. During floods, the Missouri jumped all over the place. High flows would make the task of maintaining a permanent navigation channel difficult because the river could outflank the Corps' pile dikes and revetments. The annual flooding posed the most serious risk to the construction and maintenance of the six-foot channel in western Iowa.

In the actual construction of the channel along western Iowa, the Corps relied on the two-clump and three-clump pile dike and on willow mattresses and stone revetments. The only distinction between the methods used along this reach and those employed to the south was the length of the pile dikes; they were longer here to compensate for the greater width of the river.[105] The Corps also used the excruciating "one rock, one man" technique for building revetments because it ensured employment for thousands of men (Figs. 7.3 and 7.4). During this procedure, men lifted one stone at a time from a nearby stockpile and placed it on the graded bank, slowly and painfully fashioning the revetment. Although draglines and bulldozers could have arranged the rock at a lower cost, those technologies did not meet political, social, and economic goals.[106] Men still cut willows near the bank and wove the mattresses by hand (Fig. 7.5). But by the mid-1930s the engineers began to construct wooden mattresses, built with 1 × 4-foot pieces of lumber, replacing the traditional willow mattress.[107]

Innovative technologies employed in the 1930s to channelize the river included hydraulic hoses for bank-leveling, asphalt revetments, and gigantic dredges. The hydraulic hoses were used in place of grading the bank with hand-held shovels, bulldozers, and draglines. The hoses sat on a floating platform, placed adjacent to the bank needing leveling, and then water was pumped directly from the river through the hose and onto the bank, causing the alluvium to melt away. This approach was quick and effective. Asphalt revetments were considered a replace-

Fig. 7.3. A stone revetment under construction along the Missouri, circa 1935. In the photograph, men place one stone at a time on top of a willow mattress. (Courtesy of the Corps of Engineers)

ment for the standard willow mattress and stone revetment, but their performance was dismal on the Missouri, where the majority of them were undermined in short order.[108]

Dredges, a standard feature of channelization work during the 1930s, sucked tons of sand and gravel from the riverbed in just a matter of minutes. By summer 1939 the Corps had nine dredges working continuously between Kansas City and Sioux City.[109] Corps officials named two of the largest dredge boats after the explorers Meriwether Lewis and William Clark; each boat had a length of 260 feet, a width of 50 feet, and a draft of 4 feet. The boats weighed close to 250 tons and mustered the power to pull 3,000 cubic yards of material from the river every hour. Another dredge, the *William S. Mitchell,* could cut a path through alluvium 80 feet wide, 1,300 feet long, and approximately 25 feet deep in a single day.[110] The Corps employed these behemoths to remove sandbars obstructing the thalweg, deepen shallow channel crossings, and cut off long bends. To form a cutoff, the engineers placed a dredge on the downstream end of a bend; from that point, the dredge excavated a

Fig. 7.4. The "one rock, one man" technique of building revetments. Note the three-pile clump dike *(right center),* which replaced the former pile dike and willow curtain. (Courtesy of the Corps of Engineers)

Fig. 7.5. Men weaving a willow mattress along the Missouri in western Iowa, circa 1935. Willow mattress construction was a labor-intensive task that ensured employment for thousands of men during the depression years. (Courtesy of the Corps of Engineers)

narrow channel across the bend's neck. Once the dredge neared the natural river channel on the upstream side of the neck, it "punched through" the remaining alluvium and forced the river south along the cutoff. After a bend had been cut off from the new navigation channel, it filled in with silt, dried up, and became overgrown with vegetation.[111]

The engineers conducted extensive snag removal and timber-clearing operations along the river in western Iowa. The Corps undertook the former not for its contribution to commercial navigation but for the safety of the Corps construction fleet moving up- and downstream. The number of snags pulled from the river equaled or surpassed the number taken from the stream during a given year in the nineteenth century, proof that the erosive Missouri continued to refill its channel with trees. In 1936 and 1937, for example, snagboats extracted 790 snags from the riverbed. Moreover, tree-clearing operations reached impressive levels. Between 1934 and 1937, men cut down a total of 9,097 trees deemed threats to navigation along the Kansas City–Sioux City reach.[112] The majority of these trees were large, mature cottonwoods growing close to the riverbank. The number of trees felled in the 1930s exceeded the quantity cut down by the Corps during the steamboat era of the nineteenth century.

Through the use of dredges, pile drivers, and thousands of men, officials at the Corps of Engineers could assert in 1940 that the river between Omaha and Sioux City "is very much improved and is practically completed, except for six or seven troublesome bends where major corrective action is now in progress."[113] With the navigation channel to Sioux City almost fastened down, a towboat, the *Kansas City Socony,* and two barges owned by a subsidiary of Mobil Oil Corporation ventured toward that city in June 1940. The barges held 400,000 gallons of gasoline, half of their potential capacity, and drew four and one-half feet. As the tow and its barges approached Sioux City on 27 June, a crowd estimated at several thousand waited at the riverfront for their arrival. George R. Call and Lachlan Macleay of the Mississippi Valley Association stood proudly on the bank, convinced they were witnessing the fulfillment of a long-held dream, the arrival of barges at this inland port.[114] Personnel from two radio stations, KSCJ and KTRI, performed the novel task of broadcasting live from the Sioux City dock.[115] As the tow and its barges floated toward the dock and in sight of the anxious crowd, the vessel hit a shoal and abruptly stopped. The tow's captain instantly reversed engines in an attempt to free the boat, but after sputtering and coughing up smoke, the tow and barge sat still, unable to move. At that embarrassing moment, two government boats hastened downstream and dislodged the *Kansas City Socony*. The boat and its crew then sheepishly docked at Sioux City, indiscreetly ushering in what the *Sioux City Journal* proclaimed as the "advent of a new era in Sioux City transportation."[116] The opening of Sioux City to regularly scheduled barge traffic appeared to be within sight.

But even with the completion of Fort Peck Dam and the channel to Sioux City, barge traffic remained absent from the river. Only two private companies operated on the Missouri above Kansas City by 1940, and each of these barge lines possessed only one towboat and a couple of shallow-draft barges. The pathetic showing by barge operators along this reach was graphically illustrated in fall 1940 when the recently incorporated Sioux City–New Orleans Barge Line built the towboat *Sioux City*. It possessed a 110-horsepower engine, barely enough power to push one deep-draft barge designed for service on the Mississippi. Moreover, the *Sioux City* sat so low in the water that the pilot could not see the river in front of the barge.[117] On its maiden voyage, a crew member standing at the head of the barge nervously relayed steering directions to the pilothouse. The *Sioux City* pushed scarcely 200 tons of freight, or the equivalent of one-fourth the carrying capacity of its deep-draft barge. And the barge had to be loaded lightly; otherwise, it would have struck bottom so frequently that it might never have reached its final destination. A Corps launch assisted the *Sioux City* on its voyage upstream, taking soundings along the journey to prevent a grounding.

The Corps also sent launches out to assist every towboat carrying cargo on the lower river. Even though the Corps had certified the river reach below Kansas City open to barge traffic in 1934, private operators did not use the Missouri. Not until 1937 did a private company commence operations on the stream. And the government-owned Inland Waterways Corporation sent barges to Kansas City only on an irregular schedule, staying completely clear of the river north of Kansas City.

Environmental, economic, and political factors combined to keep barges away from the Missouri River. During the 1930s the river below Sioux City repeatedly dipped to record low levels. Low flows hindered the movement of barges, making groundings all too common, requiring a break-in-bulk in St. Louis, and eliminating the profitability of moving goods by water. But even when the river contained enough water to float deep-draft barges, the current running down the barge channel impeded upstream navigation. In 1937 the Corps admitted, "During the periods of high water which usually occur in April and June, drafts of 8 feet or more are possible, but the increased velocity of the current during these periods renders impracticable depths in excess of 5 feet for the type of equipment normally used for navigation." Deep-draft barges could not fight the current.[118] At this early date, the Corps confessed that it had incorrectly engineered the river. The elimination of the river's bends and twisting side channels, along with the cumulative effects of pile dikes and revetments, straightened the Missouri and resulted in a corresponding increase in the river's gradient, or slope. Before the navigation project, the Missouri wound down from the mountains to the Mississippi. The river's sinuosity slowed its current, which in turn permitted steamboats to move upstream. But a straighter, steeper river presented deep-draft barges with an insurmountable obstacle, the very water they needed to float cargo profitably.

Moreover, the Great Depression reduced available investment capital and increased the financial risks of starting barge operations along an unreliable river channel. Further reducing the economic incentives to operators and shippers alike, a highway bordered the river from Kansas City to St. Louis by the mid-1930s. Trucking firms could haul goods between the cities in just eight hours; a towboat and barges took anywhere from five days to a week to travel between the two cities.[119] The other major impediment to the emergence of barge traffic on the Missouri was the approach of war in Europe and Asia. By 1940 and 1941 federal appropriations for Missouri River channelization were decreasing, funds were being spent for defense purposes, and the channel began to deteriorate from lack of maintenance. By 1942 the Corps did not have enough money to keep up with the maintenance of existing structures. Consequently, shoals and sandbars made their dreaded reappearance in numerous locales. Then, the advent of a wet climatic cycle over the northern Great Plains and upper Midwest further threatened the integrity of channelization structures south of Sioux City. Prospects for the establishment of barge traffic on the Missouri did not appear bright.

8 | South Dakota Attempts to Develop the River

After 1910 South Dakota became the center of a movement to construct dams across the main stem of the Missouri River. Although interests in Montana and North Dakota sought river improvement, their level of organizational activity and the scale of their proposed projects did not compare with the grandiose schemes of the South Dakotans. In Montana, the Montana Power Company built a number of hydroelectric dams across the Missouri in the vicinity of Helena and Great Falls during the first decades of the twentieth century. Engineers built Hauser Dam, and other dams rose above the river at Wolf Creek (Holter Dam), Black Eagle Falls, Rainbow Falls, Crooked Falls, and Great Falls. These projects, however, provided only local benefits and had minimal influence on the river's flow rates or its environment outside their immediate vicinity. Near Williston, North Dakota, farmers had sought and received federal sponsorship for the construction of a small-scale water-diversion project along the Missouri River between 1910 and 1920. But this project, like the Montana dams, had little influence on the general environment of the river.[1]

The projects proposed by South Dakotans between 1910 and 1942 had tremendous consequences for navigation proponents based in the lower valley. Residents from Iowa, Nebraska, Kansas, and Missouri, working in conjunction with the Corps of Engineers, thus repeatedly hindered South Dakota's efforts to build dams across the Missouri River. South Dakota residents failed in their dam-building plans largely because lower valley navigation interests had already succeeded with their own development schemes. The inability of the South Dakotans to gain cooperation from the Corps of Engineers for their development proposals illustrates the nature of the Corps' political authority. It did not wield arbitrary power over the inhabitants of the upper and lower valley; indeed, its influence along the Missouri River ultimately depended on the more numerous residents of the lower valley and their greater influence with Congress and the chief executive's office.

South Dakotans had been involved in river improvement efforts since the 1880s. Individuals from the state's various communities participated in the river congresses and conventions held in Kansas City, St. Joseph, and Sioux City between 1881 and 1908. John King from Chamberlain, W. H. Beadle from Yankton, and Coe J. Crawford from Pierre were just a few of the notable residents to attend lower river conventions and to advocate channelization to facilitate barge navigation. But during this early period South Dakotans simply participated in the organizations and improvement plans of lower valley inhabitants; they did not assume leadership. In 1910 residents began to hold their own river improvement meetings, making plans to serve their own purposes.[2]

On 30 March 1910 Pierre river boosters hosted a waterways convention. Delegates discussed the possibility of building dams across the Missouri River in South Dakota to facilitate barge navigation, store water for irrigation purposes, and generate electricity.[3] One year later, Doane Robinson, head of the South Dakota State Historical Society in Pierre, contacted the commissioners of Sully, Stanley, and Hughes Counties, located adjacent to the Little Bend of the Missouri (Fig. 8.1). Robinson believed that the Little Bend, an 18.5-mile loop in the river

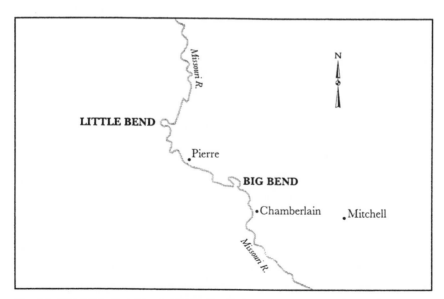

Fig. 8.1. The Little Bend and the Big Bend of the Missouri. Note each bend's location in relation to Pierre, South Dakota.

approximately 30 miles above Pierre, could be profitably developed into a hydroelectric site by building a thirty-foot-high dam across the river and excavating a canal or tunnel across the neck of the bend. The Missouri's water would be diverted from the reservoir through the power canal to a generating plant on the downstream end of the bend. The powerhouse would capture forty-eight feet of head (i.e., potential hydroelectric energy generated from stored water as it descends; a high head generates more electricity than a low head).[4] The three county commissioners responded favorably to Robinson's proposal and hired the engineering firm of Westinghouse, Church, Kerr and Company of Chicago to conduct a study of the site's economic feasibility. Unfortunately for Robinson and the commissioners, the firm did not recommend development of the Little Bend. The amount of earth requiring excavation for the power canal and the Kansas City District's stipulation that the proposed dam possess navigation locks meant the cost of the project would exceed its long-term benefits. According to the private engineers who examined the site, the Corps' insistence that navigation locks be installed ultimately resulted in the project's unfavorable cost-to-benefit ratio.[5]

This incident represented the first time the Corps of Engineers wielded its authority over navigable waterways to kill a South Dakota development proposal. By rejecting the dam, the Corps safeguarded the Missouri River's flow for its lower valley constituency. The engineers kept the river out of the hands of South Dakota interests and ensured its availability for the navigation channel then being built below Kansas City.[6] The Kansas City District also prevented a local governmental entity from making an inroad into an otherwise federal domain.

In 1916, as war between the United States and Germany appeared likely, the Woodrow Wilson administration considered building hydroelectric facilities for munitions production. River boosters from South Dakota, including *Pierre Capital Journal* editor J. M. Hipple and Doane Robinson, hoped to persuade federal officials that South Dakota possessed the best sites for federal hydroelectric plants. Promotional efforts centered on the development of either the Little Bend or the Big Bend of the Missouri. Big Bend is a twenty-six-mile loop in the river approximately sixty-five miles southeast of Pierre and thirty-five miles northwest of Chamberlain. Pierre residents favored federal development of the Little Bend site because its location thirty miles to the north meant that their town would provide the only reasonable market for its hydroelectricity. Individuals from Chamberlain, Mitchell, and Sioux City wanted the Wilson administration to develop the Big Bend site because their towns would most likely receive power from a facility there; at the least they would secure government construction contracts once work commenced on the project.[7]

The engineering firm's rejection of the Little Bend site in 1911 convinced Robinson to support the development of Big Bend. To persuade federal officials, Robinson and two partners formed the Missouri Power Company in 1916 and then went to Washington to discuss Big Bend with officials of the Wilson administration and the War Department.[8] That department had the responsibility of choosing sites for federal hydroelectric development, and Robinson quickly learned that it favored sites outside South Dakota with more favorable cost-to-benefit ratios. Eventually, the War Department decided to build a facility across the Tennessee River at Muscle Shoals, where a greater output of power would be available for the production of nitrates, a compound used in the manufacture of explosives.[9]

Stymied by federal officials twice, South Dakota's river boosters turned to the state government for support. In 1918 the state financed the first comprehensive survey of the Missouri River in South Dakota to determine the most cost-effective locations for building state-financed dams. Governor Peter Norbeck appointed Doane Robinson to supervise the survey.[10] The state government published the results of Robinson's survey in a pamphlet, *Dam Sites on the Missouri River in South Dakota*. Governor Norbeck and Robinson hoped the pamphlet would inform the state's citizens of the great natural resource that flowed through South Dakota, educate them about hydroelectricity's potentialities, and foster public support for a state-financed dam construction program.

In the pamphlet, Robinson proposed seven possible locations for hydroelectric facilities. The report concluded that favorable conditions existed for the construction of either dams or hydroelectric plants at Mulehead (just north of present-day Pickstown), Chamberlain, Big Bend, Reynold's Creek, Medicine Butte (six miles north of Pierre), Little Bend, and Bad Hair (Fig. 8.2). Robinson recommended building dams at all the sites except at Big Bend, where no dam would be necessary for power production because of the site's excessively high natural head. This head could be captured by digging a power canal or tunnel across the bend's neck. The dams proposed for the other locations would be low (approximately forty feet in height), would impound small reservoirs, and

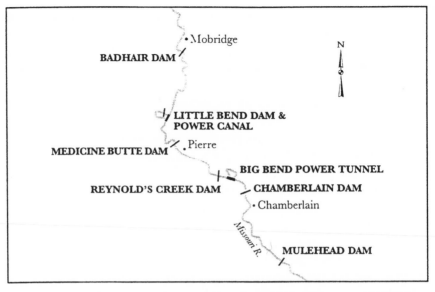

Fig. 8.2. Doane Robinson's dam sites along the Missouri River in South Dakota.

would be used almost exclusively for power production.[11] Any flood-control benefits would be only an incidental consequence of construction. Commercial navigation could never reemerge on the Missouri in South Dakota; locks would not be built into the structures. Robinson concluded that among the seven sites Big Bend possessed the most favorable cost-to-benefit ratio.

To justify the costs of his elaborate hydroelectric system for South Dakota, Robinson argued that the dams and hydroelectric facility at Big Bend would provide cheap electricity for municipalities, farms, railroads, and industries throughout the state and to mining companies located in the Black Hills. Hydroelectricity would even permit the mining of aluminum ore lying beneath the bluffs only a few miles upstream from Big Bend.[12] Robinson admitted that much of the market for this power did not yet exist in 1918, but he alleged, "New uses for current [hydroelectricity] will be developed; the agricultural field is sure to be an extensive one. . . . The farms of South Dakota will afford an outlet for a tremendous amount of current as rapidly as it can be transmitted to them. . . . That the market for the current will develop as rapidly as the power plants can be constructed seems certain."[13]

One year after the publication of *Dam Sites,* the South Dakota legislature created the Hydro-Electric Commission to promote, study, and eventually oversee the construction of hydroelectric facilities on the Missouri River. Robinson was its executive secretary. As its first order of business, the commission financed a thorough engineering survey of dam sites along the Missouri River. Robinson, a historian, did not have the engineering background to determine the cost-effectiveness of dams or power plants, and the state government needed accurate cost estimates before moving forward with any development scheme. In 1919 and 1920 engineers working for the firm of Mead and Seastone of Madison, Wisconsin, roamed up and down the Missouri Valley, making borings, measuring elevations, and examining the mineral composition of the valley wall. The engineers studied the seven sites Robinson had proposed in 1918 and an additional site located four miles north of Mobridge, South Dakota.[14]

Mead and Seastone used five variables to judge each site's cost-to-benefit ratio: length of transmission lines to be constructed from the dam site to existing or potential markets, foundation conditions at the site, power potential of the water stored behind the dam, market value of the lands to be flooded, and proximity of the dam site to available transportation facilities.[15] Mead and Seastone concluded that the proposed Big Bend facility did not have a favorable cost-to-benefit ratio because of the expense of digging the power canal or tunnel across the neck of the bend; too much earth would have to be removed for either the canal or tunnel. The site north of Mobridge had the best cost-to-benefit ratio of the eight locations examined. It had superior foundation conditions, access to a railroad only one mile away, and the existence of a profitable market for its power in the nearby town of Mobridge.[16]

Two years after the submission of the Mead and Seastone report, the citizens of South Dakota held a referendum on whether to issue bonds to finance dam construction on the Missouri River. The dam at Mobridge would be the first structure built. Of course, residents there favored its construction since they would be its main beneficiaries. People living in the counties due west of Mobridge also wanted the dam because a highway would be built on top of it, linking the rural West River country with urban centers in eastern South Dakota.[17]

In early November 1922 state residents voted 106,409 to 55,563 against financing the dam.[18] The vote was sectional, with the southern tier of counties opposed and the northern tier adjacent to Mobridge supporting the dam.[19] The referendum was defeated for several reasons. First, residents in the southern counties did not want to finance the development of the northern counties and the town of Mobridge. Second, rural residents did not want to support a hydroelectric project that would largely benefit urban residents. The high cost of transmission lines to remote areas precluded any possibility that rural residents would receive electricity from the project. Third, the agricultural depression of the early 1920s contracted the money supply. Farmers already strapped for cash did not want to pay higher taxes to finance the project. Fourth, the lobbying efforts of the opposition, especially the South Dakota Taxpayers League and its pamphlet *Hydro Phobia,* persuaded the majority of South Dakota voters that development of the river might cost more money than would ever be returned to the state treasury through electricity sales.[20] Ironically, the defeat of the referendum did not signal public opposition to Missouri River development or to the construction of other dams; rather, the vote indicated opposition to a particular dam that would benefit only a small proportion of the state's total population. Defeat of the referendum also indicated the level of public support needed to implement any future Missouri River development scheme.

Efforts to develop hydroelectric sites on the Missouri River in South Dakota suffered a severe setback with the public rejection of a dam at Mobridge, but this reversal did not stop river boosters from seeking the construction of other hydroelectric projects.[21] In 1924 city leaders from Mitchell advocated the construction of a hydroelectric plant at Big Bend and hoped to persuade South Dakota residents to finance the project. The Mitchell proposal called for diverting a significant portion of the Missouri's flow through a power canal or tunnel constructed across the bend's neck, the same plan put forward earlier by Robinson and rejected by Mead and Seastone. Mitchell's river boosters noted that Big Bend's position in central South Dakota increased its attractiveness; a large number of towns could conceivably receive electricity from a plant there, including Pierre, Winner, Chamberlain, White River, Mitchell, Huron, Redfield, and Murdo. The Mitchell group believed Big Bend's wider potential market would appeal to a larger percentage of South Dakota's electorate than the Mobridge project and thereby would make state financing for it more likely. But state financing for Big Bend never became a reality (Fig. 8.3).

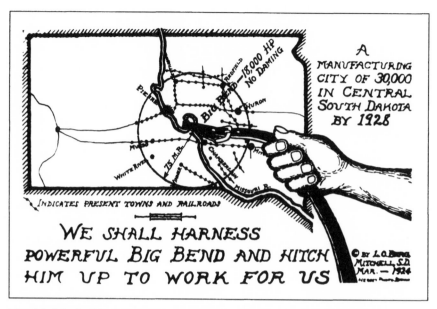

Fig. 8.3. Mitchell hydroelectric enthusiasts published this flyer in 1924 to promote the development of the Big Bend site. (Flyer by L. O. Berg, Mitchell, South Dakota, 1924)

By the early 1930s South Dakota river boosters understood that river development depended solely on federal government support. The inability of South Dakota's residents and interest groups to agree on a suitable location for development, combined with the twin disasters of drought and depression, made it impossible for the state government to generate the revenue necessary for the construction of Missouri River hydroelectric facilities. Only the federal government had the resources at its disposal to build the mammoth river projects.

In order to obtain federal assistance during the 1930s, South Dakotans began earnestly to promote the extension of barge navigation into the Dakotas. Project proposals advocating the construction of a navigation channel through South Dakota were more likely to gain Corps backing than projects designed almost exclusively for hydroelectric generation. A Dakota navigation project could conceivably be coupled to the six-foot channel being built south of Sioux City. South Dakota river boosters also wanted the Missouri developed for irrigation, believing that it would mitigate the negative economic effects of the Great Depression and drought, keep farmers on the land, and foster a general agricultural and industrial recovery throughout the state.

On 18 February 1931 the Pierre Commercial Club sponsored a meeting to discuss the development of the Missouri for hydroelectric generation and navigation. Arthur J. Weaver of the Missouri River Navigation Association, Mayor J. M. Hipple of Pierre, and Doane Robinson were three noteworthy attendees. The Kansas City District sent a representative to Pierre, and Gov. Warren Green of South Dakota wired a statement to the participants expressing support for their efforts to arouse public sentiment in favor of Missouri River development.[22]

During the conference and over the course of the following months, the Pierre Commercial Club formulated a development plan that called for the construction of a series of low dams (approximately forty feet in height) from Gavin's Point, South Dakota (approximately ten miles northwest of Yankton), to the mouth of the Yellowstone River, a distance of approximately 650 river miles. The Commercial Club proposed that seventeen dams be built at intervals of forty miles.[23] Club members believed that these dams, with the addition of locks, would permit slackwater navigation through the Dakotas, which would allow for the use of impounded water to float deep-draft barges. (Open-channel navigation, in contrast, refers to the use of flowing water to carry barge traffic.) The club's recommendation for the Missouri River closely resembled the proposal for a system of locks and dams then being put forth for the Upper Mississippi River. The South Dakotans speculated that slack-water navigation, like open-channel navigation below Sioux City, would create competitive carrier rates between barge lines and railroad companies. This competition would spur economic development by lowering the transportation costs of Dakota and Montana farmers. A further purpose of the seventeen dams would be the generation of hydroelectricity for industrial, mining, and municipal purposes.[24]

Later in 1931 the club received financing from the state government to publish 30,000 pamphlets explaining to the public the purposes of their plan. Doane Robinson authored the pamphlet, pointing out that the series of dams would serve the multiple purposes of navigation, hydroelectricity, irrigation, recreation, flood control, and improved overland transportation between eastern and western South Dakota, with the addition of roadways over the dams.[25] That same year, commercial club members sought a congressional appropriation for a federal engineering survey of their scheme but were unsuccessful.

The commercial club found a supporter for their plan in the Corps' Kansas City District Headquarters, however. District Engineer Theodore Wyman championed the construction of the series of main-stem dams, but he did not convince his superiors at division headquarters in St. Louis of the project's economic or engineering feasibility.[26] The top echelons of the Corps opposed such an extensive program for a number of reasons. The drought of the 1930s lowered the Missouri to unprecedented levels, and Corps officials worried that dams in the Dakotas (especially those built for irrigation purposes) might impinge upon the water supply needed to maintain the already water-deficient six-foot channel south of Sioux City. Furthermore, Corps officials doubted whether the Missouri held enough water during drought periods to fill the seventeen reservoirs. Moreover, the cost of seventeen low dams with accompanying locks would have been exorbitant. Government engineers also understood that the future volume of barge traffic on the river through the Dakotas would probably never reach levels high enough to justify the costs of such an immense undertaking. And Corps officials did not sanction any major dam-building scheme for the Missouri River because proposals for comprehensive, multiple-purpose river-basin development were currently gaining popularity in Congress and the executive branch of the federal government. If a big dam-construction program for the river were to go before Congress, Corps officials feared that their jurisdiction over the Missouri would be challenged by a public corporation based on the soon-to-be-enacted Tennessee Valley Authority legislation.[27]

In spring 1933 South Dakotans renewed their struggle to procure federal aid for the development of the Missouri River to reverse the negative effects of the severe drought and depression that gripped their state. On 4 April a group of individuals held a meeting in the small town of Kennebec, South Dakota, to discuss issues related to the Missouri. Kennebec lawyer Merrill Q. Sharpe, Doane Robinson, and William Robinson (Doane's son) attended.[28] Other river boosters from Murdo, Presho, Chamberlain, and Mitchell participated in the discussions.[29] The attendees resolved to form the Upper Missouri Valley Development Association (UMVDA) and elected William Robinson as president. Like their predecessors in the Pierre Commercial Club, the UMVDA membership sought federal funds for the construction of a series of low dams through the Dakotas.[30] By fall 1933 the UMVDA was lobbying the PWA for a portion of the funds earmarked for Fort Peck Dam.[31] The next year the association's promotional campaign had fizzled out because it did not acquire any funds from the Fort Peck appropriation. The UMVDA's proposal for a series of low dams remained only a dream.

South Dakota's river-development enthusiasts did not accept defeat, however. They persisted throughout the 1930s to seek federal construction of Missouri River dams. In the mid-1930s the Chamberlain Commercial Club advocated the construction of a hydroelectric facility at Big Bend because a dam there would stimulate the economy of the river town. But the club, like all the other organizations before it, failed in its purpose.[32]

Then in May 1937 the Lower Brule Tribal Council and its chairman, Reuben Estes, sought Bureau of Indian Affairs (BIA) and congressional support for tribal development of Big Bend for the production of hydroelectricity.[33] Big Bend sat astride the Lower Brule and Crow Creek Indian Reservations. Estes and the tribe were aware of the activities of the promoters in Chamberlain and Mitchell who had hoped to build a power canal at Big Bend. The tribal council wanted to preempt those efforts and develop a water resource located partially on tribal and individual Indian land.[34] Such a project would bring sorely needed capital into the tribal economy during the midst of the Great Depression.

On 16 May 1937 Chairman Estes wrote South Dakota congressman Francis Case and requested advice on how to proceed with the development of the Big Bend region.[35] Case reacted favorably to Estes's proposal for Indian sponsorship of a construction project at the bend because all previous South Dakota ventures had floundered. Since the State of South Dakota, the Corps of Engineers, and the PWA had been either unwilling or unable to finance any dams or hydroelectric facilities along the river, Case believed the BIA and its parent organization, the Department of the Interior, deserved consideration as possible sources of financing.[36]

Case advised Estes to inform the BIA office in Washington of the Lower Brule Tribe's desire to build a hydroelectric plant at Big Bend. The South Dakota congressman then closed his letter to Estes: "Now this whole idea may be impractical, but it is worthy of investigation. . . . It may be that [the proposed power project] will be too big for us to handle so I do not want you to feel that it must be handled by your organization alone but [the power site] is right there in your reservation and certainly you are entitled to first consideration, if some such program can be worked out."[37]

On 12 June 1937 the Lower Brule Tribal Council followed Case's advice and passed a resolution stating its wish to develop the site at Big Bend for the benefit of the Lower Brule Indians.[38] The tribe reminded BIA officials that its recent acceptance of the provisions of the Indian Reorganization Act made it eligible for federal loan funds. Tribal members then sent the resolution to BIA headquarters in Washington. After its submission, the success of the Lower Brule development proposal depended on the approval of two federal bureaucracies, the Department of the Interior and the Corps of Engineers.[39] The department would actually approve the funding request, but the Corps would determine whether the Indian project possessed a favorable cost-to-benefit ratio. The Corps also would examine the project to ensure that it did not impede navigation on a federal waterway.

Between 1937 and 1940 the Lower Brule tribe labored to gain support from the Department of the Interior and the Corps for their project. To further their cause, the Indians solicited aid from eleven county governments and numerous commercial clubs located in central South Dakota.[40] But by 1940 neither the Interior Department nor the Corps had provided the Indians with a definitive response. Then in early summer 1940, Secretary of the Interior Harold Ickes told Congressman Case that he favored Lower Brule development of Big Bend under the auspices of the BIA.[41] BIA sponsorship of the project would not only contribute to Indian self-sufficiency, but it would also enable the Department of the Interior to expand its influence into a region and a main-stem river system long dominated by its rival bureaucracy, the Corps of Engineers.

But Ickes's endorsement actually carried little weight because the Corps of Engineers had the final decision on the proposal based on its authority over the nation's navigable rivers. In October Corps officials furnished Case and the tribe with a definite response; there would be no development at Big Bend by the Lower Brule or the BIA. According to Corps officials who met with Case, the site had been designated as a lower priority for federal development than the Mobridge and Mulehead locations.[42]

The Corps of Engineers rejected the project for more reasons than its poor cost-to-benefit ratio. Indian development of Big Bend would have allowed the Department of the Interior to control Missouri River water by diverting it through the power canal; such control would have threatened the Corps' authority over the river. Furthermore, water impounded by an Indian dam or diverted through an Indian power canal could have diminished the flow needed to maintain the six-foot channel below Sioux City. In order for the proposed dam and power plant at Big Bend to generate hydroelectricity, a high head of water would have to be stored behind the dam, which would diminish downstream water levels. The Corps would not permit this potential scenario. Too much money had already been invested in the six-foot channel and in Fort Peck Dam by 1940 to allow an Indian dam to threaten the barge channel's future viability. And so another South Dakota development proposal went down to defeat.

At the same time that the Lower Brule Tribe petitioned the Corps of Engineers for approval of their project at Big Bend, a group of businessmen, lawyers, local and state government officials, and other professionals from southeast South Dakota, northeast Nebraska, and northwest Iowa formed the Upper Missouri Valley Association. Thus, its membership was similar to that of the other organizations that had pushed for river improvement since the 1880s. Mayor Ernest A. Crockett of Yankton served as the group's president. The association adopted a broad platform that embraced river development for the sake of soil and water conservation, irrigation, bank stabilization, navigation, flood control, and hydroelectric generation. Federal construction of a dam at Gavin's Point, approximately ten miles from Yankton, was the group's immediate goal. By endorsing multiple-purpose development of the Missouri River, Crockett and the association hoped to gain the cooperation of the Corps of Engineers and lower river interest groups and their congressional representatives. But that hoped-for cooperation never materialized. And to Crockett's utter amazement, he learned that the Omaha District of the Corps of Engineers (which after 1933 supervised work on the river north of Rulo, Nebraska) did not want to build dams along the Missouri River in South Dakota at all.[43]

The failures of the 1930s still did not stop the residents of South Dakota and the upper Missouri Valley from seeking development schemes to alleviate the effects of drought and depression. One week after the bombing of Pearl Harbor and U.S. entry into World War II, businessmen and government representatives from the states of South Dakota, North Dakota, Wyoming, Montana, and Nebraska met with officials from the Bureau of Reclamation and the Corps of Engineers in

Bismarck, North Dakota, to discuss and coordinate their plans for Missouri River development.[44] From this initial conference and from additional gatherings and correspondence in early 1942, upper river interests established the Missouri River States Committee (MRSC) and named Gov. Merrill Q. Sharpe of South Dakota as its head.[45] Sharpe had first become involved with Missouri River issues in 1933 when he joined the UMVDA. He asserted that he and his colleagues "organized the Missouri River States Committee for the express purpose of securing power development, irrigation, flood control, navigation, and related improvements through a valley-wide development of the entire Missouri River system. . . . The general purpose of the committee is to secure unified state action toward accomplishment of this plan of development. It means that the Missouri River states are going to act from a cooperative standpoint instead of going it alone and trying to get individual state projects constructed along the river valley."[46]

The states of the basin thus would work together to secure federal financing for a multiple-purpose project similar to those initiated in the Colorado, Tennessee, and Columbia basins during the New Deal. The MRSC would not push for the adoption of a single project beneficial to only one locale or state. Instead, its membership committed themselves to a broad program that would couple proposed water projects together into a mutually supporting system. This commitment to an overarching, interconnected, basinwide project sharply distinguished the MRSC from previous organizations involved in Missouri River improvement, especially those associations organized in the lower valley for the construction of the barge channel.

In July 1942 the MRSC held its first official meeting in Billings, Montana, and the members agreed to seek the participation of Iowa, Kansas, and Missouri.[47] The inclusion of the three most populous states of the basin would provide a measurable boost to the organization's federal legislative influence. While Sharpe and the MRSC worked to obtain the collaboration of the three remaining states, the Missouri River spilled out of its banks and inundated the lower valley in one of its worst floods in a century. Unlike any previous event, the great flood of 1943 compelled the lower river interests and the Corps of Engineers finally to join with the South Dakotans to seek the construction of dams across the Missouri River.

9 | The Wet Years, 1943–1951

The great flood of 1943 began in late March and early April after a sudden warm-up in temperatures caused the rapid melting of the winter snowpack lying across the northern plains and eastern sections of the Dakotas. Instead of soaking into the soil or evaporating, the meltwater saturated the ground and then drained into the tributaries of the Missouri. Dakota residents prepared for the worst while downstream in Iowa and Nebraska, individuals anxiously watched events in the upper valley, trying to determine whether the river would flood in their vicinity.

By the first week of April, the Missouri began to inundate its valley in North and South Dakota. On Sunday, 4 April 1943, the river level at Pierre measured three and one-half feet above flood stage. Police closed the Highway 14 bridge connecting Pierre with its sister city, Fort Pierre, as water raced over the west approach. In Fort Pierre, numerous homes began to disappear beneath the icy, tawny water. To the dismay of people living near the advancing waters, meteorologists predicted another two-foot rise in the river as the crest passed the two cities.[1]

The flooding intensified farther down the valley, especially between Yankton and Omaha, because two of the Missouri's largest tributaries, the James and the Big Sioux, dumped fantastic amounts of water into the already swollen river. Only a few miles southeast of Yankton, the James River, whose watershed encompasses much of eastern South Dakota, joins the Missouri. It discharged so much water into the Missouri that the big river almost topped its record 1881 flood stage just below Yankton. Along the border between Iowa and South Dakota flows the Big Sioux River; it drains an area comprising far eastern South Dakota, southwest Minnesota, and northwestern Iowa. The Big Sioux gushed into the Missouri a few miles above Sioux City, but the larger river could not take in the additional water. The Big Sioux then backed up and broke through a nine-foot-high dike built to protect Riverside, Iowa. Millions of gallons of water poured into Riverside's residential section, inundating most of the town and driving hundreds of frustrated people from their homes.[2]

As the waters of the James, Missouri, and Big Sioux comingled near Sioux City, the Missouri widened out across its valley and took on the appearance of a vast, wave-tossed sea. Forty square miles of the most productive agricultural land in the world vanished beneath the surging tide. Basements in South Sioux City, Nebraska, filled with infectious refuse from overflowing sewers. Police barred motorists from crossing U.S. Highway 20 between the Iowa border and Jackson, Nebraska, after water began lapping over the pavement. An estimated 250 farm families found themselves surrounded by raging currents, the water moving too fast to risk a passage to safety.[3] Reporter Neil Miller of the *Sioux City Journal* described the scene to the west of Sioux City: "Lakes and the old river shoreline appear to be wiped out as the swollen yellow river spreads over lowlands in all directions."[4]

On 9 April the South Sioux City Police Department deployed thirty flat-bottomed johnboats to evacuate persons in the path of the river, a rescue operation that prevented the loss of life in the area. But people affected by the flood still lost personal property and suffered psychological damage. Charles Brown lived with his dog, Tuffie, in a tiny one-room shack next to the river at Sioux City. Brown reluctantly abandoned his simple home and meager belongings as floodwaters neared his doorstep. Mike Virusa of South Sioux City had just spent sixty-five dollars for seed for a three-acre Victory garden when the river carried the seed and his fledgling garden off and filled his home with muddy water. Looking across a half-mile of former cropland toward his waterlogged house, Virusa said, "I lost everything."[5]

Joe McGinty, who lived with his wife and three children on a 187-acre farm one mile west of South Sioux City, spent from 8 April to 10 April working frantically around the clock to save his home and property. But the river rose too fast and too high, and McGinty watched helplessly as the river swept away his stock animals and feed grain. In a matter of minutes, McGinty lost 5 cows, 4 calves, 6 horses, 2 colts, 150 hens, 1,000 bushels of corn, and 500 bushels of barley, along with his recently planted crops. The stock animals alone were worth $5,000. Trying to keep at least his home, McGinty and his son worked tirelessly to build a makeshift dike around the structure. But the river topped it and filled his living quarters with water. Leaving his flooded farm on Saturday, 10 April, the defeated McGinty went into South Sioux City, where he went berserk. The police arrested him, put him in the city jail, and waited until he calmed down before releasing him to the custody of his family.[6] McGinty's neighbor, Al Austin, watched his own house collapse after water rushed under the foundation. The Missouri River won no friends during the flood of 1943.

Hundreds of valley residents surrounding Sioux City who did not lose their homes or stock animals had to clean putrid mud from their walls, floorboards, and contaminated wells. Removing mud and floodwater from a home was unpleasant at best and sickening at worst. The smell, grime, and potential for disease required that homes be cleansed as soon as possible. After removal of the muck, health officials recommended that chloride of lime be sprinkled on the flooded areas, left for an hour, and then scrubbed clean with a water and chloride solution, time-consuming work. The fetid water in contaminated wells had to be pumped out and a solution of chloride poured in and allowed to sit for twenty-four hours. After waiting the requisite amount of time, the water had to be pumped out again. When this was done, the well water still had to be taken to a health facility for analysis. The cleanup after a flood required patience and fortitude.[7]

The flood crest passed Sioux City late in the night on 10 April. Gauges there read 18.7 feet, still below the flood stage of 19 feet and far below the record stage of 22.5 feet set in 1881. Sioux City did not suffer serious damage because the river north of town had not yet been channelized by the Corps of Engineers. As a result, the Missouri was able to spread across the valley floor before reaching the city and thereby lower the height of its crest.

As the crest moved south along the western Iowa border, its waters covered thousands of acres of farmland but skirted the majority of small towns. When a twelve-foot-high dike gave way in Monona County, Iowa, 1,000 acres of agricultural land disappeared under the deluge and a number of unsuspecting chickens met their deaths.[8] Residents in Onawa, Iowa, grew apprehensive as the river, which normally flowed seven miles west of town, approached within one mile. But the town stood on a small ridgeline, too high to be affected by the flood. Farther south at Blencoe, basements filled with water; at the town of Missouri Valley, the marauding river forced the Iowa State Patrol to close Highway 30.[9]

North of Omaha, Corps pile dikes and revetments funneled the floodwaters downstream toward that city, keeping the river confined and preventing it from naturally reducing its crest. The channelization structures so compressed the river that when the crest reached Omaha it nearly surpassed the record stage of 1881. Omaha sustained heavy damage. Emergency personnel ordered the evacuation of large sections of the downtown area. Government officials redirected civilian and military flights away from the municipal airport when water covered the runway. At the flood's height, the airport sat under seven feet of water.[10] The crest dissipated after it passed south of St. Joseph, where the river had remained low so that it absorbed the floodwaters. By the time the crest reached Kansas City, the river did not top flood stage.[11] Ultimately, in the valley between Bismarck and the vicinity of St. Joseph, the Missouri River inundated 700,000 acres and caused damage estimated at $8 million.[12] Corps officials kept silent about the possible effects of the channelization structures on flood levels, claiming instead that the flood would have been much worse had it not been for the presence of Fort Peck Dam. Colonel Lewis Pick of the Corps of Engineers asserted, "We might have had a new record in this part of the river, if we had not been storing water during that entire time in the Fort Peck reservoir. It has been estimated that if the water from the upper Missouri captured by Fort Peck had been free to come down to join with that from the Yellowstone and the other tributaries, the gauge at Omaha would have read two feet, three inches higher than it did. Not only would Omaha have been inundated but, in my opinion, it probably would have been impossible to keep the floodwaters out of Council Bluffs and Sioux City."[13]

Yet Fort Peck Dam could not halt the continuation of record-setting flooding along the Missouri River during the month of May. Between 6 and 20 May, the channelized river below Kansas City spilled out of its banks after heavy rains fell in the Grand, Gasconade, and Osage watersheds. These three tributaries poured so much water into the Missouri that it capped the level of the 1844 superflood along its lower 140 miles. This second flood submerged an additional 540,000 acres of agricultural land across the central portion of Missouri.

If the second Missouri River flood of 1943 did not push the endurance of valley residents to the limit, the third flood did. This flood resulted from the convergence of two natural events. In June a considerable snowpack above 5,000-feet elevation melted and drained into the Missouri's largest tributary, the undammed Yellowstone River. High water from this stream entered the Missouri below Fort Peck Dam, resulting in the formation of a moderate-sized June rise. At the same time that this June rise passed Omaha, a series of heavy thunderstorms struck Kansas and Missouri. One storm dropped seven inches of rain across the Kaw River basin in a few hours. In a striking similarity to the flood of 1903, a torrent descended the Kaw only to intersect with an already-overflowing Missouri. The resulting ocean covered an estimated 960,000 acres of farmland between St. Joseph and the mouth. During that wet spring and summer, the Missouri inundated a total of 1.8 million acres of agricultural land at least one time. Hundreds of thousands of acres were submerged two or three times. Civil and military authorities estimated that the damages to roads, bridges, farms, and factories equaled $47.3 million.[14]

Besides destroying private property and infrastructure, the floods battered the Corps' piles dikes and revetments. After the waters had receded, engineers from the Kansas City and Omaha district offices traveled up and down the navigation channel, inspecting the status of their work. They discovered a sobering truth; the control structures had failed to contain the river. Officials concluded, "Subsequent high waters have accelerated the destructive erosion of unprotected concave banks, flanked and destroyed many existing installations, and have resulted in complete loss of alignment control in some sites with progressive loss of alignment threatened at additional sites through natural actions of an uncontrolled river reverting to a wild state."[15] The engineers were losing the river.

The floods of 1943 also disrupted rail and river traffic along the Missouri and Mississippi Rivers during the emergency wartime situation. Successive periods of high water prevented the planting of crops in the valley, which in turn lowered agricultural production needed to supply American troops in the field in Europe and Asia. Floodwaters damaged military installations, delayed the training of troops, and required the diversion of supplies and equipment slated for the war front to the flood zone. Eleven people lost their lives to the floods, and untold numbers of hogs, cattle, chickens, and wildlife drowned.[16]

The floods of 1943 had significant consequences for the future of Missouri River development. The repeated freshets convinced the residents of the lower basin states of Iowa, Missouri, and Kansas to join with their frustrated neighbors to the north to push for an extensive dam-building program for the river. During the drought years of the 1930s, lower valley residents and their state and federal representatives had opposed Dakota dams, fearing that the structures would reduce the already depleted flow of the river and deprive the six-foot navigation channel of the water needed to support barge traffic. But after the floods of

1943, lower valley interests realized that the only means of protecting their cities, farms, and $185 million navigation channel from recurring high flows would be through the construction of dams upstream.[17] And the only place where Corps flood-control dams and reservoirs could be built was across the main stem of the Missouri in North and South Dakota.

In order to secure flood protection, the governors of the lower basin states of Iowa, Missouri, and Kansas joined the Missouri River States Committee on 21 May 1943, only days after the second flood had passed through central Missouri.[18] Representatives from these three states joined, however, to advance their own agenda, not to support upper basin development plans.[19] Environmental circumstances forced this reluctant alliance. South Dakota's geographical position along the main stem of the Missouri made it key to any future flood-control program. Cost-effective dams could not be built below Yankton, and reservoirs confined to North Dakota and Montana would not capture enough tributary runoff to significantly lower flood levels at Omaha, St. Joseph, and Kansas City. The failure of Fort Peck Dam to prevent the floods of 1943 clearly demonstrated the danger of building dams too far up the main stem. Dams in South Dakota would capture the runoff from eleven sizable tributaries, the same ones that had caused so much damage in April, May, and June. Hence, local, state, and federal officials from the lower basin states worked to gain the support of the people of South Dakota and their government representatives for their own dam-building program.[20]

Lower valley residents also petitioned Congress to direct the Corps of Engineers to study the feasibility of constructing flood-control dams across the Missouri main stem.[21] In May 1943 Congress ordered the chief of engineers to proceed with such a study.[22] At the time of the 1943 flood, Col. Lewis Pick served as the head of the Missouri River Division (created in 1933 with three subordinate districts at Kansas City, Omaha, and Fort Peck). Pick was charged with the maintenance and management of both Fort Peck Dam and the navigation channel.[23] The chief of engineers commanded Pick to conduct the survey and to provide recommendations on methods to control flooding in the lower valley.

While Pick prepared his survey and recommendations in summer 1943, the MRSC recognized the importance of South Dakota to any future dam-building program by electing its governor, Merrill Q. Sharpe, as the newly reconstituted MRSC's chairman.[24] Under Sharpe's direction, the committee conducted a mammoth promotional campaign throughout the valley to gain public support for dams in the Dakotas, further channelization work, and the construction of a levee system adjacent to the river from Sioux City to the mouth. The MRSC sponsored meetings in cities along the river during 1943, including Bismarck, Pierre, Sioux City, Nebraska City, and St. Joseph (Fig. 9.1).[25]

At these gatherings, army engineers and Bureau of Reclamation field agents explained the technicalities of river development (i.e., how the river would actually be engineered to meet society's demands for water, hydroelectricity, flood control, and navigation). Members of the local chamber of commerce and state political representatives then stepped forward and explained the economic benefits of harnessing the river's

Fig. 9.1. Merrill Q. Sharpe, circa 1942. (Courtesy of the South Dakota State Historical Society, Pierre)

water. At Sioux City's Martin Hotel in August, nearly 200 private citizens and government officials listened to Pick and Sharpe espouse their vision for the Missouri Valley. Pick asserted that the army engineers could build dams that would provide "a source of power to pump water for irrigation, keep the proposed [nine-foot] navigation channel open even in low water seasons and operate industrial and electrical plants." The colonel asked the assembled crowd to lobby Congress for the funds necessary to start the construction of upstream dams following the close of World War II. He continued, "This great project will cost millions of dollars and of course we cannot expect to do very much, if anything, in the way of building until the war is over. But I do not see any reason why this improvement cannot be incorporated in any postwar program which may be inaugurated by the federal government."[26] The colonel recognized that the Corps' control of the Missouri River ultimately rested with the people living in the valley, especially the lower valley. Pick ended his presentation on a cautionary note: "The Missouri River Valley is the last great valley in the United States whose water potentialities have not been developed. . . . If the river is not properly under control the results will be disastrous." Then Sharpe spoke: "Now is the time for action. The prospects for success are excellent. They may never be any better."[27] The timing could not have been better because the floods of 1943 focused congressional, presidential, and national attention on the Missouri. The public-relations strategy of the MRSC resulted in widespread public acceptance of the idea of building dams and reservoirs along the upper river. There was little or no organized opposition within the basin to further damming of the Missouri and using its waters to stabilize and promote the basin's economy.[28]

Congressman Max Schwabe, whose district encompassed several counties along the river in central Missouri, provided members of the MRSC with a clear example of the overwhelming public support that existed in the valley for additional river development, noting that "612 people registered and attended a recent flood conference" in Boonville, Missouri. This group concluded that "flood control is a federal problem and a federal responsibility." With that in mind, the group recommended that "the operation of dams in the Missouri River Valley should be governed in such a manner as to eliminate as far as possible the flooding and damaging of agricultural lands." The river boosters also agreed to "petition our Senators and our Representatives to sponsor and to support all legislation found to be necessary or required to accomplish the purposes set forth in these resolutions." Grassroots organizations once again sought federal cooperation for development of the Missouri.[29]

Any opposition to a basinwide approach to controlling the river arose over the design specifications of the dams, not over the dams themselves. Different economic and political interests wanted certain aspects of the dam-building plan stressed over others.[30] Senator Gerald P. Nye of North Dakota succinctly stated the issue: "In the south end of the valley you have one problem and in the north end we have another. Some want control of these waters, some want access to these waters."[31] Farmers, businesspeople, and politicians from the upper basin (Montana, North Dakota, South Dakota, and Wyoming), represented by the National Reclamation Association, South Dakota Reclamation Association, Montana Stockgrowers Association, and a number of chambers of commerce, wanted dams that met their needs for irrigation and hydroelectric power.[32] Lower basin residents from Kansas, Missouri, Iowa, and Nebraska, led by the Kansas City Chamber of Commerce, the Mississippi Valley Association, and the National Rivers and Harbors Congress, wanted a plan that protected their urban centers from devastating floods, opened their cities to deep-draft barge traffic, and provided them with cheap power.[33] If the upper basin irrigationists received the water they wanted for their crops, commercial interests along the lower river believed they would have to abandon their navigation channel. Both upper and lower basin residents understood that water required to sustain a six-foot or possibly a nine-foot navigation channel for eight months each year would lower the proposed upstream reservoirs and siphon off water required for irrigation. No one in the MRSC had an immediate solution to this conflict of interest.

Pick completed his flood-control survey and recommendations less than three months after being given the assignment and submitted the report to Congress on 10 August 1943.[34] The plan he devised sought to accomplish three interrelated objectives: to provide flood protection to urban centers, infrastructure, and farms in the valley below Yankton; to protect the $185 million navigation channel from eventual destruction by unregulated high flows; and to supply consistent flow volumes to the navigation channel to encourage barge traffic. To achieve these objectives, Pick recommended the construction of four of the world's largest earthen-fill dams along the main stem of the Missouri River in North and South Dakota. They would capture the Missouri's annual spring and summer rise and release the stored water at a uniform rate to maintain a nine-foot navigation channel below Sioux City, a channel that did not exist and had not yet been authorized by Congress.

Under the Pick Plan, the Corps proposed building dams at Garrison in North Dakota and at Oahe (Pierre), Fort Randall (Lake Andes), and Gavin's Point (Yankton) in South Dakota.[35] Dams at these four locations would fulfill lower basin demands for flood control and navigation but provide only incidental irrigation and hydroelectric power benefits.[36] *The Comprehensive Report on Missouri River Development*, a Corps policy paper, stated, "Exclusive power storage would not be provided but power would be generated with water released for navigation and sanitation purposes."[37] The Corps made it clear that upper basin demands for irrigation water and hydroelectricity would be secondary to lower basin demands for navigation. Not surprisingly, lower valley interest groups, such as the Kansas City Chamber of Commerce and the Mississippi Valley Association, fully endorsed the Pick Plan.

The Pick Plan also called for the construction of low, re-regulating dams below the bigger dams, which would eliminate destructive water surges when the big dams released large amounts of water. Re-regulation would be necessary to prevent high water from eroding riverbanks, disrupting downstream navigation, and disturbing municipal water supplies. In its *Comprehensive Report*, the Corps stated that re-regulating dams needed to "be constructed a short distance downstream of each major dam, sufficiently high to create poundage to permit releases from the lower dam at a uniform rate."[38] Under this scheme, re-regulating dams would be built below the dams at Garrison, Oahe, and Fort Randall. The site for the re-regulating dam below Fort Randall had already been chosen at Gavin's Point near Yankton. A dam on the northwest side of the Big Bend of the Missouri would serve as Oahe's re-regulating dam. The Corps had not chosen a definite site for a re-regulating dam below Garrison (Fig. 9.2).

Late in 1943 the Corps submitted the Pick Plan to Congress for authorization. The submission of the Pick Plan to Congress split the Missouri River States Committee along regional lines. Previously, the Corps and its rival bureaucracy within the federal government, the Bureau of Reclamation, had maintained a functional working relationship within the MRSC. The public disclosure of the Pick Plan in February 1944 destroyed that alliance and pitted the bureau and its upper basin constituency against the Corps and its lower basin supporters.

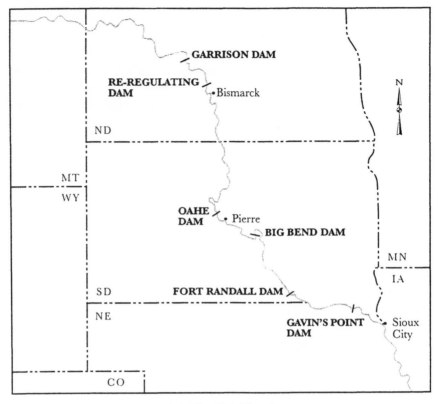

Fig. 9.2. The Pick Plan dams.

MRSC Chairman Merrill Q. Sharpe favored the Pick Plan because it was the first development program ever submitted to Congress that proposed construction of dams in South Dakota.[39] Although it favored navigation interests over irrigation, Sharpe considered it the best plan available. He supported it because he realized that South Dakota would benefit substantially from its implementation. Four of Pick's dams (Oahe, the re-regulation dam at Big Bend, Fort Randall, and Gavin's Point) would be built in his state.

With Sharpe and the South Dakota representatives, including influential newspaper publisher Bob Hipple of Pierre, siding with the lower basin and the Corps of Engineers, lower river interests scored a major political victory in their efforts to develop the river for their particular purposes. South Dakota's defection to the lower basin placed the remaining upper basin states within the MRSC at a distinct disadvantage in the negotiations and discussions concerning the specifications of the proposed dam-building program. But representatives from North Dakota, Montana, and Wyoming, along with officials of the Bureau of Reclamation, could still create federal legislative problems for the proponents of the Pick Plan by delaying or attempting to kill any future river development projects.[40]

Sharpe sought to gain the support of the other upper basin states by convincing them of the Pick Plan's benefits. During congressional hearings held on the plan in February 1944, Sharpe urged cooperation among the various interests. Presenting an insightful analysis of the problems and potentials of river development, the governor noted that the conflict between the irrigation and navigation interests was predicated on a perceived shortage of water. He believed this conflict could be resolved through the construction of dams that had enough reservoir storage capacity for both lower and upper basin needs.[41] Sharpe added, "I think a complete answer for many years to come is found in the single word, storage."[42] He concluded by warning everyone that if agreement on the proper amount of storage did not mend the split in the MRSC and between upper and lower basin state and federal officials, then the entire dam-building scheme would be threatened: "It seems to me that such a result [increasing reservoir water storage capacity] should be reached rather than letting any conflict of interests bring the matter to an impasse which will deprive the Missouri Valley and the nation of the multiple benefits to labor, agriculture, business, postwar adjustment, and other national objectives which require that the project get started now."[43]

Assurances of goodwill by the Corps and Sharpe to build more storage into their Pick Plan reservoirs were not enough to convince the Bureau of Reclamation and upper basin irrigationists that their interests would be satisfied. In May 1944 the bureau responded with its own dam-building plan for the Missouri, which emphasized irrigation and hydroelectric power.[44] The Sloan Plan, named after its author, William G. Sloan, a Bureau of Reclamation field agent stationed in Billings, Montana, called for the construction of dams on the main stem of the Missouri River at Oahe (Pierre), Big Bend (north of Chamberlain), and Fort Randall (Lake Andes) (Fig. 9.3). Like the Corps, the Bureau of Reclamation recognized South Dakota's geographical importance to the construction of main-stem dams. The dams at Oahe and Fort Randall

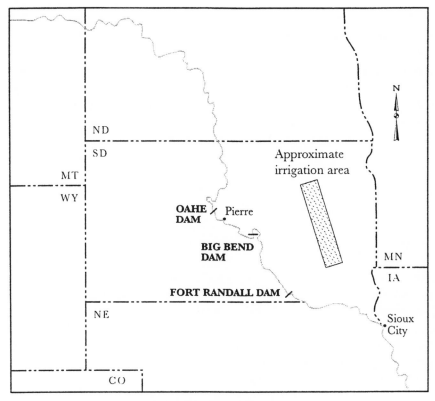

Fig. 9.3. The Sloan Plan dams.

would provide the necessary water storage to irrigate land in both North and South Dakota, and Big Bend would be used almost exclusively for the generation of electricity. The bulk of the land Sloan hoped to irrigate was located in eastern South Dakota in the James River Valley. He proposed that his three dams each produce hydroelectricity to pump water from their reservoirs to the irrigation fields and that any surplus hydroelectricity be sold either to public or private utilities to help offset the costs of the projects.[45] Sloan's plan departed quite significantly from Pick's in that the former did not include Garrison or Gavin's Point Dams in the proposal. Sloan deemed it unnecessary to build Gavin's Point Dam because he did not intend to re-regulate large water discharges for the purpose of downstream navigation. Under Sloan's plan, Missouri River water would be diverted eastward toward the James Valley, not sent downstream to support barge traffic.

The submission of the Sloan Plan led Sharpe on a frantic effort to mend the split between the upper and lower basin states and between the Bureau of Reclamation and the Corps. Sharpe desperately tried to save any plan to build dams in his home state with federal financing. On 5 August 1944 he convened a meeting of the MRSC in Omaha, where the upper and lower basin interests ultimately recognized the folly of attempting to develop the Missouri River without full cooperation. If they went their separate ways, the future dam-building plans would be jeopardized by political and legal infighting. Congress would not authorize the construction of two conflicting programs for the Missouri River. Thus, the previously defiant upper basin states and the Bureau of Reclamation joined South Dakota, the lower basin states, and the Corps to create a revised dam-building plan that supposedly would meet the needs of all interested groups.[46]

At this meeting the MRSC passed a resolution that was crucial to the creation of the Pick-Sloan compromise and then distributed it throughout the federal government's executive and congressional branches. Point five of the resolution declared, "We ask the President and the Congress of the United States to authorize and direct the United States Army Engineers and the United States Bureau of Reclamation to bring before Congress a coordinated plan" (Fig. 9.4).[47]

The success of the compromise was contingent upon the successful site selection and design of multiple-purpose dams. The dams proposed by the bureau in the Sloan Plan and by the Corps in the Pick Plan were designed almost exclusively for their particular constituencies. For the compromise to work and for the interest groups to avoid legal haggling, these original plans had to be altered, new dam sites considered, each previously proposed dam redesigned, and reservoir water-storage capacities increased. Only by making such alterations would it be possible to ensure continued congressional and upper basin support for the damming of the Missouri River.[48]

A number of hurdles had to be overcome before the multiple-purpose dam concept could succeed in the Missouri Valley. Proper sites had to be chosen for the construction of the dams; the dams and reservoirs had to be designed in minute detail to ensure that all interests were met; and the weather had to cooperate by producing enough rainfall to fill the reservoirs. The first two hurdles could be overcome with the proper application of money, science, and technology, but no one controlled the weather, which worried everyone. If the rains did not fall across the

Fig. 9.4. William G. Sloan of the Bureau of Reclamation *(left)* and Maj. Gen. Lewis A. Pick of the Corps of Engineers *(right)*. (Courtesy of the Corps of Engineers)

Great Plains and drain into the Missouri Valley to be stored behind the dams, the political compromise that had created the Pick-Sloan Plan would crumble and the states would fight over the limited water supply. First, though, the Corps, the MRSC, and the Bureau of Reclamation had to agree on the proper sites.[49] Site selection was dependent on geology, cost-effectiveness, demographics, and political considerations.

Geological factors weighed heavily in the selection process. The geological character of the Missouri Valley limited the area of possible sites to the upper basin. From Fort Peck Dam in Montana to Yankton, South Dakota, the valley has a width of from one to five miles. Below Yankton, the valley width varies from five to seventeen miles. A narrow valley is more conducive to dam construction for two simple reasons: cost and safety. Dams in the lower reaches of the river would cost exorbitant amounts of money because of the earth fill required to block the flow of water through the wide valley. Also, long dams would be more likely to fail because subsurface mineral deposits are less stable over long stretches. Thus the engineers and politicians focused their attention on the area in North and South Dakota where the valley was narrower and more stable subsurface minerals existed.[50]

The subsurface mineral deposits in the Dakotas further restricted the available choice of sites. The Missouri Valley in South Dakota is underlain with deposits of Pierre shale and Niobrara chalk, both of which were deemed suitable for the placement of earth-fill dams. The depth of these minerals affected the cost of the dams, however, since the dams had to be attached to the chalk or shale. Therefore, a factor in choosing a dam site was the proximity of these materials to the surface.[51] Another geological consideration was the relation of the sites to tributaries of the Missouri River. The engineers wanted to ensure that the dams captured all or most of the water entering the valley from them. If a major tributary's water was not captured by a dam on the Missouri, its floodwaters could flow downstream and wreak havoc on urban centers and agricultural lands and disrupt navigation.[52]

Engineers also had to consider the location of the sites in relation to available transportation facilities. Large pieces of machinery and equipment would have to be brought in by railroad and highway. If a site was located far from a railhead or highway, the cost of constructing roads to it would lower its suitability.[53] Another consideration was the proximity of the dams to towns, hospitals, housing, and recreational facilities. The construction personnel had to be provided with medical care, food, clothing, shelter, and entertainment. If the Corps had to construct these facilities at the site, the cost of the project would quickly become excessive. Accordingly, sites near cities or towns that had such accommodations were preferable.[54]

Moreover, the engineers had to weigh the difficulty and costs of acquiring the necessary land and of relocating valley residents. Prime lands or expensive urban real estate in the proposed reservoir area would increase the overall cost of the dam; therefore, underutilized or cheap low-quality land was preferable.[55] Moving a large urban population obviously cost far more than moving widely dispersed rural residents. A related consideration was the expense of relocating facilities. Railroad bridges, sewer lines, buildings, and other property would have to be moved out of the reservoir areas. An additional factor in figuring cost-effectiveness was the distance transmission lines had to be built to carry the hydroelectric power from the site to the available market.

The biggest influence on the site-selection process was the relation of the dams and reservoirs to urban centers in the Dakotas. Each dam and its reservoir had to spare the most populous non-Indian towns and cities along the Missouri River while still providing the reservoir storage capacity to meet the water demands of the interest groups. The importance of the population centers to the site-selection process was explicitly stated in the Corps' 1944–1945 *Comprehensive Report*:

In determining the location of the multiple-purpose reservoirs, consideration must be given to the existence of cities which might be wholly or partially inundated by these reservoirs, and the railroads and highways crossing the river in the reservoir areas. Larger cities in this category are Chamberlain, Pierre, and Mobridge in South Dakota, and Bismarck and Williston in North Dakota. Accordingly, the sites described in this report have been selected at such distances downstream from these cities that sufficient storage [in the reservoirs] will be provided without undue flooding of expensive real estate. . . . Thus the height to which Fort Randall Dam can be built is limited by Chamberlain and the railroad and highway crossings in that vicinity.[56]

The report continued, "One of the reasons for selecting the Garrison site was that it is above Bismarck. The storage limit for Garrison reservoir was dictated by damages imposed at and in the vicinity of Williston, near the Montana border."[57]

By late 1944 the Corps, the Bureau of Reclamation, and the MRSC had agreed on the selection of sites. Five dams would be built across the

Missouri main stem. Four—Oahe, Big Bend, Fort Randall, and Gavin's Point—would be located in South Dakota; the fifth would be built at Garrison in North Dakota (Fig. 9.5). The Big Bend Dam slated for construction under the Pick-Sloan Plan would be located at the same site proposed four years earlier by the Lower Brule Tribe but rejected by the Corps of Engineers. The five dam sites were chosen because of their favorable cost-to-benefit ratios and topographical attributes. Most important, the dams and their reservoirs would minimize damage to major urban centers in the Dakotas while still providing the storage capacity to satisfy lower basin demands for navigation and flood control. The storage space would also be used to generate hydroelectricity and to furnish some irrigation water.

The MRSC lacked any Indian representation; only off-reservation interests participated in the hearings, organizational activities, congressional lobbying efforts, and deliberations surrounding site selection. Because of this exclusion from the political process, Indian lands and

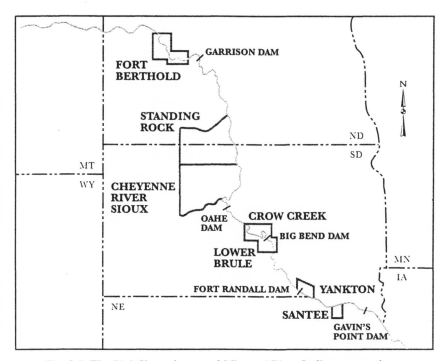

Fig. 9.5. The Pick-Sloan dams and Missouri River Indian reservations.

towns located along the Missouri in the Dakotas did not receive the same degree of consideration as off-reservation cities.[58] The Corps, the Bureau of Reclamation, and the MRSC did not change the sites of any dams or reduce their reservoir storage capacities to spare Indian bottomlands or towns from inundation since doing so would have diminished the benefits received by off-reservation interests. Smaller reservoirs would have spared some Indian land but would have reduced the amount of water available for navigation and irrigation. A reduction in benefits to off-reservation interests might have led to their withdrawal of political support for the Pick-Sloan compromise and prevented the passage of future appropriations bills. Therefore, Indian interests in preserving their lands and communities were ignored in order to make the Pick-Sloan Plan a reality.

After Congress authorized the construction of the five Pick-Sloan Plan dams, Franklin D. Roosevelt signed it into law on 22 December 1944. The power of lower valley interests to direct development became apparent when Congress gave the Corps jurisdiction over the main-stem dams, which would be operated to serve primarily navigation and flood control. In March 1945 Congress, again responding to the political influence of the Mississippi Valley Association, National Rivers and Harbors Congress, Kansas City Chamber of Commerce, and energetic Kansas City mayor John Gage, authorized the construction of a nine-foot-deep navigation channel from the Missouri's mouth to Sioux City. Thus the Pick-Sloan dams would first supply water for the new, deeper channel before irrigating the James River Valley or the parched fields of North Dakota.[59]

Immediately following the end of World War II, the Corps began construction on two of the five dams. In 1946 work commenced on Fort Randall Dam in southeast South Dakota and Garrison Dam in north-central North Dakota.[60] Fort Randall Dam's location far down along the Missouri main stem, along with its tremendous size, made it the key structure of the Pick-Sloan Plan. Situated thirty-five miles above the mouth of the Niobrara River and just a few hundred feet from the site of the old military post bearing its name, Fort Randall Dam would be able to impound water entering the Missouri from nearly all its plains tributaries, including the Milk, Yellowstone, Little Missouri, Knife, Heart, Cannonball, Grand, Moreau, Cheyenne, Bad, and White Rivers. Although Garrison Dam would eventually capture the waters of the Milk, Yellowstone, and Little Missouri, Fort Randall Dam conceivably could have stood alone across the main stem and still provided significant flood control for the lower valley.[61] Engineers claimed that Fort Randall, when closed, would take a minimum of four feet off the crest of any future superflood south of Sioux City. The dam would guarantee substantially lower flood levels along the Missouri Valley in western Iowa but would not stop floods. Uncontrolled tributaries, such as the James and Big Sioux, would still flow into the Missouri below the dam.[62]

Furthermore, Fort Randall Dam was vitally important because it would be the primary supplier of water for the nine-foot navigation channel. Engineers planned to use one-third of the dam's reservoir storage capacity to hold floodwaters. Another one-third or more would generate electricity and maintain flows through the navigation channel. The remaining one-third would serve as a permanent pool. According to the Corps, "The permanent pool provides [the] minimal water level necessary to allow the hydropower plants to operate and provide reserved space for sediment storage."[63] As a further indication of the influence of lower valley residents in directing Missouri River development, none of Fort Randall's water would be made available for use in irrigation.[64]

Because of Fort Randall's import for future flood prevention and navigation, the Corps requested congressional funding for it first. Once Congress allocated the money, the Corps began construction. On 1 August 1946 a crowd of 6,000 restless spectators gathered along the hills overlooking the future site of Fort Randall Dam. People sat in the grass, walked aimlessly along the bluff line, or just stood silently under the bright sun, waiting for the start of the ceremony. On a grandstand in front of the assembled audience stood the puffy-faced Gen. Lewis Pick, Gov. Merrill Sharpe, Gov. Dwight B. Griswold of Nebraska, and Mayor Forrest M. Olson of Sioux City. In the background the American flag flew prominently above the men, snapping as a brisk south wind whipped it back and forth. Sharpe was one of the first to speak. He told his listeners about the many benefits the great dam would provide to residents of the Missouri Valley and beyond. When Pick took the podium, he reiterated the importance of the dam to the stabilization of the area's economy. When the dignitaries had spoken, Pick walked over to an electrical plunger, pushed down the handle, and set off a charge of dynamite that blew away the side of a bluff where the future spillway of the dam would be built. Construction of Fort Randall Dam had begun.[65]

The first order of business for the Corps of Engineers at the dam site was to organize a logistics system to ensure that men, equipment, and supplies could reach the construction area. Engineers built a railroad spur from the Chicago, Milwaukee, St. Paul, and Pacific line that ran through Lake Andes eight miles to the northeast. The railroad was one of the most significant pieces of technology the Corps used to construct the earthen plug at Fort Randall. Over the rails traveled heavy earth-moving equipment, building materials, and eventually the huge turbines to be installed in the dam's powerhouse. A little less than seventy years earlier, the railroad had rendered the Missouri River transportation route obsolete and had contributed to the perception that the river and its valley were wasted natural resources. In the mid-twentieth century, however, the railroad was the main instrument in transforming the river valley to make it useful to a modern, agri-industrial society. The Corps also supervised the construction of a highway from Lake Andes to the bluffs above the dam site.[66] Government engineers erected a new town on a series of bluffs just east of the future dam and named it Pickstown, in honor of the man who tirelessly promoted dams and channelization works along the Missouri River.

By spring 1948 the Corps had completed the necessary logistical base, and work on the dam itself could begin in earnest. The Corps hired thousands of men to drive trucks, operate bulldozers, lay concrete, and perform administrative tasks. A horde of workers and their families descended on the dam site.[67] At the peak of construction activity, over 5,000 men worked on Fort Randall Dam.[68] The number of people temporarily overwhelmed the government housing at Pickstown. Some families actually lived in converted nineteenth-century streetcars that had been purchased in Sioux City and carried to Pickstown to meet the housing emergency. One family even took up residence in a sheep shed, and another hearty individual decided to save on the astronomical cost of rent by living in a filthy coal bin near the railroad tracks.[69] Over the course of the next six years, these men moiled like ants to place a mound of dirt in the path of the Missouri River.

Three of the largest tasks involved in the construction of Fort Randall Dam included raising the embankment, digging the outlet tunnels, and excavating the approach channel from the river to the tunnels. The embankment would stop the flow of the river and impound its waters. The outlet tunnels would allow water to pass around the embankment and downstream. The approach channel would route the river away from its original, natural channel, keep it from abutting against the embankment's upstream side, and direct it to the openings in the outlet tunnels. To accomplish these three tasks, the engineers would adhere to a construction sequence. First, the earthen embankment would be raised on one side of the river to its final height and on the other side of the stream to a height sufficient to avoid being topped by high flows. Second, the outlet tunnels would be completed and the approach channel dug from the river to the tunnel openings. An earth wall would remain in place at the upstream end of the approach channel to prevent the Missouri from flowing through the tunnels prematurely. While this work progressed, the Missouri River would be allowed to flow through a 1,000-foot-wide gap between the two sections of the embankment. Once these three tasks had been accomplished, the Corps would close the gap and route the river through the outlet tunnels. This construction sequence remained essentially the same for all the main-stem dams built under the Pick-Sloan Plan in the 1940s, 1950s, and 1960s.[70]

The earth for the embankment came from the bluffs adjacent to the river valley.[71] Massive Marion 191-M draglines tore 11-cubic-yard strips of dirt from the bluffs and dropped the earth into the back ends of gigantic Mack trucks.[72] Five scoops from the dragline filled each truck with material.[73] The loaded trucks then rumbled down the bluffs to the section of the embankment being raised, where they dumped their loads. Next, a bulldozer spread the earth in an even layer, approximately six inches thick. A sprinkler truck passed over the thin layer and applied just the proper amount of water to moisten it, but not to dissolve it into a muddy mess. Watering the soil ensured a tighter compaction. Finally, a sheepsfoot roller drove over the layer, breaking up any clods, making its texture consistent, and compacting the material. Crews drove trucks back and forth between the borrow pits and the embankment on a round-the-clock basis. At the height of the embankment work, the private contractor installed a lighting system to allow for night work. During this peak period, trucks placed an average of 60,000 cubic yards of earth per day on top of the rising barrier.[74] From November to March the contractor halted work on the embankment; frozen dirt made compaction difficult, and if placed inside the dam, its embedded ice would later melt and weaken the structure (Fig. 9.6).[75]

Building the embankment required more time and effort than any construction task. Embankment work started in 1948. By spring 1952 the completed section on the east bank rose nearly 185 feet above the riverbed, stretched approximately 8,000 feet, and had a base 1,600 feet

Fig. 9.6. Fort Randall Dam, circa 1950. The embankment of the dam rises above the valley floor. (Courtesy of the Corps of Engineers)

wide. Private contractors had dumped over 30 million cubic yards of dirt to form this mound.[76] Yet there still remained closure of the remaining 1,000-foot gap, the raising of that portion of the embankment to the requisite 185-foot height, and completion of the earthwork on the west side of the dam.

While the trucks piled up dirt for the embankment, men and machines dug outlet tunnels. Engineers decided to bore the tunnels through Niobrara chalk located deep within the bluffs on the far east end of the dam site. Chalk formations are less prone than other mineral deposits to shift or crack from excessive water pressure or vibration. Furthermore, chalk is an impervious material. Thus, in the unlikely event that the reinforced concrete lining the tunnel walls fractured, the chalk would prevent or slow a widening of the fissure and thus forestall the failure of the dam.

Tunnel work began in 1949. During construction, instead of using men to drill the tunnels, as had been done at Fort Peck, the private contracting company, Silas Mason, employed a novel tunnel-boring tech-nology, the first of its kind in the world. Engineers mounted a coal saw (similar to a buzz saw) on a notched steel ring that had the same diam-eter as the future tunnel. The saw and ring sat on a contraption known as a jumbo, which rolled along on railroad tracks. During boring opera-tions, the coal saw rotated on the ring while it cut through the chalk. After cutting a two- or three-foot-deep circular outline through the chalk, the jumbo operator backed the machine out of the tunnel, and men armed with jackhammers moved in and reduced the perfectly outlined piece to rubble. By using the saw and jumbo, the engineers removed as much chalk in one and one-half hours as sixteen men had removed in three hours at Fort Peck Dam. The speed and precision of this machine enabled Silas Mason to complete the outlet tunnels by late 1951.[77] The company drilled twelve tunnels, four with diameters of twenty-two feet and eight with diameters of twenty-eight feet, through 875 feet of chalk (Fig. 9.7).[78]

Fig. 9.7. The jumbo and saw used to bore the outlet tunnels at Fort Randall Dam. (Courtesy of the Corps of Engineers)

By early spring 1952 only two major jobs had to be finished before Fort Randall Dam would stem the flow of the Missouri River. The Corps still had to dig the approach channel from the river to the outlet tunnels and fill the last remaining gap in the embankment, where the Missouri continued to pour southward. Closure of the dam would dramatically affect the frequency and height of main-stem floods south of Sioux City. Government engineers planned to close the opening in the embankment sometime during late summer 1952. But just before the engineers attained closure, the Missouri River experienced its greatest flood.

10 | The Mighty Missouri and the Final Quest for Control

December 1951 witnessed the beginning of the wettest, coldest, and deadliest winter on the northern Great Plains since Euro-American agricultural settlement of the area nearly eighty years before. South Dakota received an inordinate share of the harsh weather. Tripp County in south-central South Dakota experienced a blizzard in early December that closed transportation routes and left farmers and ranchers stranded for days. Cold northwest winds blew so persistently after this storm that the county supervisor's office radioed and phoned rural residents to let them know when plows would clear particular sections of highway. After the plow passed their homes, residents jumped in their automobiles, roared down the highway to the nearest town for supplies, and then hurried back before the road closed again from drifting snow.[1] Individuals living in Pierre and the surrounding area endured a series of snowstorms that began on 6 December and lasted for fifteen consecutive days, bringing the central portion of the state to a standstill. By 21 December twenty-six inches of snow stood on the ground at Pierre. High winds and the accompanying drifting snow repeatedly forced the closure of roads into and out of the capital. Such dangerous whiteout conditions prevailed in rural areas that the South Dakota State Highway Office forbade anyone from leaving Pierre during ten days in December.[2]

In January 1952 more blizzards pounded the Dakotas. These additional storms prompted Pres. Harry Truman to extend federal emergency relief to South Dakota so that its highway department could clear state highways and county roads. Relief came in the form of snow-removal machinery dispatched to the area. Yet even with the proper equipment, the wind continued to make snow removal futile; snow often covered roads within hours after the plows had passed over them.

Weather conditions in Montana and along the eastern slope of the Rocky Mountains paralleled circumstances in South Dakota. In January officials working for the Corps of Engineers, clad in snowshoes and heavy coats, hiked into the mountains to conduct a snowpack survey, and discovered a sobering fact. In the areas drained by the Missouri and its tributaries, the mountain snowpack surpassed all recorded levels. To make matters even worse, the deep snow contained a high moisture content. The Missouri River Division Office in Omaha ominously noted that snow amounts across the mountains and northern Great Plains equaled or exceeded the totals present prior to the deluge of 1943, a conclusion that caused severe anxiety among Missouri Valley residents from Montana to the river's mouth.[3]

Meteorologist Ivory P. Rennels of the U.S. Geological Survey Office in Sioux City expressed fear that severe flooding would follow the melting of the heavy snow cover. In early March Rennels confirmed that the northern plains had received 155 percent of the normal amount of precipitation since 1 December 1951. An incredible 460 percent of normal precipitation fell in the area surrounding Pierre during the same period.[4] Rennels understood that the Missouri and its tributaries could not possibly absorb the meltwater from this snowfall without some flooding.[5]

Corps officials and valley residents kept a nervous eye on the sky and the river throughout March. Temperature patterns and precipitation amounts during March often determined whether the Missouri flooded or remained in its banks during the spring. If warm temperatures and heavy rains arrived suddenly across the Great Plains, the consequent snowmelt would quickly saturate the soil and run into the Missouri, causing unprecedented flooding. On the other hand, a slow warming trend accompanied by progressively warmer days and cool or freezing nights would mean a gradual melting of the heavy snows, giving the river time to safely drain away the meltwater streaming off the plains. Everyone's greatest fear was of swiftly rising temperatures and an abrupt melting of the snowpack.

Valley residents also worried about another and more important factor that influenced the extent and duration of any Missouri River flood. If warm temperatures descended on the upper basin before the lower basin, the entire valley from the Dakotas to the mouth might sustain catastrophic flooding because the upper river's high flows would descend the valley first and then combine with the runoff just entering the stream from the lower basin. A simultaneous warming trend in the upper and lower basin would have nearly the same effect; upper river meltwater would be unable to drain off to the south. Ideally, warm temperatures would slowly spread from the lower basin northward, giving the lower river time to carry away the meltwater from Iowa, Nebraska, Kansas, and Missouri before the water from South Dakota, North Dakota, and Montana came down the valley.

Across the northern Great Plains, March 1952 was cold, windy, and exceedingly wet. Heavy snows fell throughout the Dakotas during the second and third week of the month.[6] As April approached and the snow piled up, the possibility of a gradual northward-advancing warming trend grew increasingly dimmer. April carried the real possibility of warm days and warm nights. On 28 March Rennels announced that severe flooding along the main stem of the Missouri River appeared imminent. "The risk of rapid thawing, along with the ice breakup, has increased. The weather the next two weeks to a large extent will determine the intensity of flooding." The meteorologist believed the Missouri River would flood, but just how badly remained to be seen.[7]

Then on 1 April Rennels predicted massive flooding within the Missouri basin. According to the meteorologist, the snows in the region were melting rapidly, the ground remained largely frozen, and a high percentage of the snowmelt went directly into the Missouri's tributaries. During the first days of April, the Big Sioux, James, Niobrara, White, Bad, Cheyenne, Cannonball, Moreau, Knife, Little Missouri, and Milk Rivers became raging torrents, spilling out across their valleys, hurling debris down their channels, and racing toward the main stem of the Missouri (Fig. 10.1).

The Milk River, flowing through northeastern Montana, washed over its banks in a flash flood on 1 April that caught people and animals completely by surprise. Over 3,000 residents hurriedly fled the advancing water. When the Milk River gushed across its valley, stock animals galloped toward high ground to escape death. Numerous animals became disoriented, fell in the rising water, and floated downstream. Many of the animals spared from immediate death took refuge on top of a series of small knolls spread across the valley floor, but the relentless water surrounded the hillocks, moving ever closer to the frightened creatures. Rather than allow their cattle and horses to drown slowly in the frigid water, ranchers rented planes and hired sharpshooters to fly above the stranded animals and kill them with high-powered rifles.[8] Milk Valley farmers and ranchers sustained heavy losses from this flash flood.

At the same time, the Little Missouri River, which flows through western North Dakota's Badlands, reached 23.1 feet at Marmarth, where flood stage stood at 18 feet. Floodwaters inundated approximately 200

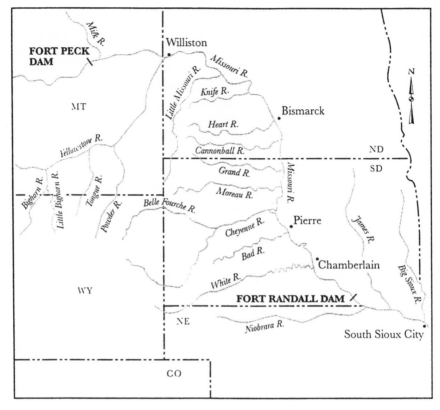

Fig. 10.1. Prairie-plains tributaries of the Missouri River.

homes in the town. Beaver Creek, a tributary of the Missouri located sixty-five miles southeast of Bismarck, overflowed its banks and covered parts of the town of Linton, North Dakota, with three feet of water.[9] As the tributaries pumped their water into the Missouri, its level reached spiraling heights, flooding towns along its banks from North Dakota south to the state of Missouri.

The worst flood in forty-two years hit Bismarck, covering the railroad tracks of the Northern Pacific Railroad and swamping homes near the riverbank. Pierre and Fort Pierre sustained the most extensive flood damage since their founding in the nineteenth century. Fort Pierre, located at the juncture of the Bad and Missouri Rivers, nearly disappeared under the ocean of water. The town's 633 residents evacuated their homes when water lapped over streets, sidewalks, and yards. Portions of Fort Pierre remained submerged for over a week, water reaching to the rooftops of countless buildings.[10] On 9 April the Missouri River stood eight feet above flood stage at Pierre and the water kept going up, expected to reach ten feet over flood stage the next day. The river forced 1,600 people to abandon their homes; thirty blocks of the city sat underwater.

Seventy-five miles southeast of Pierre, the Missouri gobbled up the lower sections of the Indian reservation town of Fort Thompson. Farther south at Chamberlain, the fast river current and huge water volume, combined with gigantic ice chunks, hammered away at the Milwaukee Railroad bridge that spanned the river there. The Missouri undermined a 150-foot-long section of the bridge, causing the span first to slump and then to fall into the river, cutting off a major east-west rail link in South Dakota. Fearing for the remainder of the bridge, railroad officials loaded boxcars with tons of scrap metal and miscellaneous junk and pushed the cars onto the bridge, hoping the added weight would keep it in place. The ploy succeeded and the bridge stood against the fury.[11]

The river streamed south, moving past the Fort Randall Dam site without causing damage to the rising earth structure. At Yankton, the river's enormous water volume was compressed between chalkstone bluffs as it passed through what locals referred to as the Yankton Narrows. Engineers measured the current velocity there at fourteen miles per hour, about six times the average speed.[12] Just below the narrows, the river burst forth into the wide alluvial valley that stretches from Yankton south to the Iowa-Missouri border.

The next sizable towns in the path of the Big Muddy included Sioux City and South Sioux City. The former faced a lesser flood threat than the latter because the majority of its homes and businesses rested on bluffs and a high plateau above the river valley. South Sioux City, on the other hand, lay on top of a slight rise in the valley floor and relied on a levee for protection against the river. In the first days of April South Sioux residents became increasingly concerned about their safety as the Missouri River paraded past the town the evidence of its powerful surge through the Dakotas. The *Sioux City Journal* declared on 8 April, "From the Combination Bridge [linking Sioux City with South Sioux City], evidence of great destruction to the north could be seen in the seething midchannel of the Missouri. Parts of houses, telephone poles, huge uprooted trees and other debris swirled downstream."[13] The river's vivid display of power convinced South Sioux City residents that the dike to the north and west of town required constant surveillance to detect any breaks. It had been designed to withstand a flood stage of 19.4 feet, but meteorologists predicted a flood crest at South Sioux City of 24 feet.[14] Although putting almost no faith in their chances of remaining dry, residents nonetheless made every attempt to maintain the viability of the dike. But vigilance, hope, and willpower could not stop the Missouri. In the early morning hours of 11 April the river breached the South Sioux City levee and ran straight through low-lying neighborhoods.

The worst of the flooding, however, was yet to come. On Easter Sunday, 13 April, Mayor Wilbur Allen of South Sioux City ordered a complete evacuation of the community of 5,557 residents as the river's crest approached and threatened a total inundation (Fig. 10.2). Later that night and early the next morning, the Missouri's crest passed South Sioux City at a height of twenty-five feet. River water almost completely covered the dark, deserted town. On the other side of the Missouri, Sioux City's stockyards, with its hundreds of foul cattle pens, and its riverfront business district slid under the smothering river (Figs. 10.3 and 10.4).[15]

Fig. 10.2. South Sioux City, Nebraska, April 1952. The Missouri inundated most of South Sioux City, including its main thoroughfare, Dakota Avenue, pictured here. (Courtesy of the Sioux City Public Museum)

Fig. 10.3. Sioux City, Iowa, April 1952. The Mighty Missouri flooded the Sioux City stockyards *(top left)* and several blocks near the waterfront. (Courtesy of the Sioux City Public Museum)

Fig. 10.4. An aerial view of Sioux City, Iowa *(left)*, and South Sioux City, Nebraska, at the height of the great flood of 1952. (Courtesy of the Sioux City Public Museum)

During the flood one South Sioux City resident spent five days cling-
ing to rafters in his attic, hoping to be rescued before the water rose any
higher and drowned him. Sixty-nine-year-old Tom Cooper was either
unable or unwilling to leave his property when the river broke through
the levee on 11 April. He hurried to his attic, where he prayed the water
would not rise any higher. Cooper survived for five days on three cans
of cold beans and two quarts of milk. On 16 April his son Harold Cooper and a friend took a motorboat across the river from Sioux City to
the home and pried the white-knuckled, elder Cooper from the rafters.[16]

As the sixty-mile-long crest moved south beyond the Sioux City metropolitan area, small-town residents and farmers in the valley watched
and waited. Corps officials predicted that the river would flood Sergeant
Bluff, Salix, and Sloan, three towns immediately below Sioux City on the
Iowa side of the Missouri. To save their community, residents of Sergeant
Bluff used bulldozers to hastily erect a 9-foot-high, 1,000–foot-long dike,
which not only spared the town but also prevented river water from
overrunning the Sioux City airbase. Corps officials informed Mayor
R. J. Downing of Salix that he could expect from five to seven feet of muddy
water to cover his town.[17] After receiving this news, the Salix town council decided that a dike tall enough to stem such an overflow could not
be built in time; instead, the council focused its energies on ensuring
the orderly evacuation of the town and its surrounding area. Residents
left the community believing that they would return to homes filled with
silt and debris, but miraculously, the river skirted Salix. About one mile
to the west of town, a former river channel had created a four-foot-high
ridge that diverted the water away from Salix. Sloan, six miles below Salix,
was also supposed to receive five feet of water over its streets sometime
during 14 and 15 April. In anticipation of this crest, Sloan residents built
a five-foot-high levee around the town, but the river stayed far from Sloan
and its levee. Residents rejoiced on hearing that an elevated county road
five miles west of the town had blocked the river's floodwaters.[18] The
Missouri flowed so erratically during those first weeks of April that valley residents played a guessing game as to which town would be inundated next. No one really knew where the river would go or how it would
behave. One town might be spared when the river's current suddenly
changed direction, and another town would be unexpectedly flooded.

Amazingly, the river did not inundate the majority of valley towns in
western Iowa. Sergeant Bluff, Salix, Sloan, Whiting, Onawa, and Missouri
Valley stayed dry, and only a portion of Blencoe, Mondamin, and Modale

suffered flood damage.[19] Although the Missouri spared western Iowa towns, it caused extensive damage to farmsteads and agricultural land. The river from Sioux City to the Iowa-Missouri border widened to an average distance of twelve miles and covered roughly 308,000 acres of farmland. Farmers in Monona and Harrison Counties saw more acres inundated than any of the other counties in western Iowa. The overflowing Missouri also forced an estimated 40,000 persons, or 18,496 families (mostly farm families), to leave their homes.[20] Floodwaters utterly destroyed some farmsteads. George Goodwin and his family lived in an area known as Flower's Island in Monona County, Iowa. High water lifted Goodwin's two-story house from its moorings and carried it downstream completely intact, only to drop it into a massive thirty-foot hole formed by an eddy.[21] Goodwin was not alone in his despair; hundreds of other farmers endured similar tragedies.

The total dollar amount of damages in western Iowa alone amounted to $43 million, with the agricultural sector sustaining a $17.6 million loss, mostly from a reduction in potential agricultural earnings and damage to farms and machinery. The flood caused $4,052,000 damage to western Iowa's transportation grid, washing out roads, undermining bridges, and carrying away long sections of railroad. Urban centers sustained approximately $11.5 million in damages. The cost of fighting the flood, in addition to the destruction of communications facilities, utility systems, and levees, equaled $10.1 million.[22]

As the river's crest descended toward Omaha–Council Bluffs, the attention of everyone in the nation, including President Truman, centered on whether the Omaha levee would hold back the approaching tide. At Omaha–Council Bluffs, the twelve-mile-wide river funneled into a 1,200-foot-wide channel confined on both sides by levees protecting the twin cities. The Corps of Engineers built the Omaha levee after the flood of 1943 to protect a business district along the bottoms. The levee possessed an effective height of 26 feet and an actual height of 31.5 feet, effective height meaning that the levee could withstand a crest of 26 feet without being undermined by the tremendous water pressure bearing down on the bottom and side of the levee. The likelihood of a levee failure increased if the water level rose beyond 26 feet. If the river topped 31.5 feet, the levee would suffer a massive failure. The U.S. Geological Survey's Meteorological Bureau predicted a crest of between thirty and thirty-one feet at Omaha, perilously close to the actual elevation of the levee. A crest of this magnitude left little room for confidence; a strong wind could create waves high enough to surmount it. To secure the levee, the Corps deployed National Guard troops to raise its height with sandbags and a wooden fence. Between 14 and 17 April, soldiers elevated the Omaha levee from 31.5 to 34 feet. But even this action provided no guarantee of security. The potential water pressure against the dike created the likelihood of boils forming on the dry side of the structure, an anomaly occurring when the ground becomes so saturated that water actually begins to boil up from under the levee. A boil can get out of control, totally break down the soil, and undermine the levee. Fortunately for Omaha residents, their efforts to strengthen the levee succeeded. On the night of 17 April, a thirty-foot-high crest passed the city, the levee held, and the city did not sustain heavy damage. The Corps calculated that the Omaha and Council Bluffs levee system prevented approximately $62.5 million in damages.[23]

Although the crest moved past Omaha–Council Bluffs without major loss, the state of Missouri shouldered $53.8 million in damages. The total damage estimate throughout the Missouri Valley reached $179 million, with agriculture losing $72.8 million. Astonishingly, the great flood of 1952 took no human lives. Two relatively new forms of mass media, radio and television, allowed disaster services personnel to forewarn Missouri Valley residents of the approaching water. However, an incalculable number of stock animals and wildlife drowned.[24]

The $179 million total damage estimate did not include the losses inflicted on control structures along the navigation channel south of Sioux City. Excessive high flows hastened the deterioration of pile dikes and revetments, eroding the banks behind revetments, undermining the riverbed beneath piles, and outflanking pile dikes. The flood of 1952 came after a decade of high flows and floods wreaked havoc on the navigation channel. In addition to the great flood of 1943, the Missouri had overflowed its banks in 1947, 1949, 1950, and 1951. A Corps official, referring to the dilapidated state of the navigation channel, admitted that "the floods of July 1951 and April 1952 were particularly destructive."[25] Not even considering the devastation wrought during the flood of 1943, the Corps lost a staggering number of pile dikes and revetments between 1944 and 1952 (Figs. 10.5 and 10.6).

On 30 June 1944 the Corps claimed that 90 percent of the six-foot navigation channel from the mouth to Kansas City stood intact; on 30 June 1952 the engineers estimated that 78 percent of that same section of the navigation channel remained in place. During this period, the

Fig. 10.5. Destroyed pile dikes in Monona County, Iowa, circa 1955 *(bottom left)*.
(Top and bottom photos courtesy of the Corps of Engineers)

Fig. 10.6. Flanked control structures at Blackbird Bend, Monona County, Iowa,
circa 1955 *(looking south)*. The Missouri has cut a pile dike into two pieces *(left
center)*, placing one section in the middle of the river channel. Another pile dike
(right center) has been flanked by a side channel.

Missouri rendered ineffective 46.3 river miles of pile dikes and revetments. The destruction along other stretches of the river exceeded the losses below Kansas City. In 1944 the engineers finished 95 percent, or 122.1 miles, of the navigation channel between Kansas City and Rulo, Nebraska. By 1952 only 66 percent, or 84.8 miles, of this portion of the barge channel remained viable. In 1944 the Rulo-to-Omaha reach had been 99 percent complete; in 1952 that reach had degraded to only 67 percent complete. The worst destruction occurred in western Iowa, the reach that the Corps had earlier recognized as being the most unstable. The army engineers finished 78 percent of the six-foot channel between Omaha and Sioux City by 1944; in 1952 a mere 36 percent of this navigation channel continued to serve its design purpose. A total of 54.8 miles of river broke out of its former alignment north of Omaha. These statistics do not include the miles of structures destroyed and then replaced by the Corps during the eight-year period.[26]

The monetary value of the demolished control structures reached shocking figures. The 175.9 miles of navigation channel destroyed and not replaced between 1944 and 1952 equaled $48.3 million in 1944 dollars. Then, during the eight-year period, the Corps spent $75.8 million on maintenance and new work below Sioux City. But this additional investment still did not repair all the damage to the navigation channel. In 1952 the Corps could claim only 511.4 miles of the navigation channel still intact, an amount far below the 687.3 miles of channel completed by 1944. Therefore, of a total investment of $265.7 million in the six-foot, and then nine-foot, channel to 1952, the Missouri destroyed approximately $124.1 million in control structures.[27] President John Forsyth of the Upper Missouri Valley Association, an organization promoting the extension of the navigation channel to Niobrara, Nebraska, confirmed the extent of the devastation. In 1951, even before the flood of 1952, Forsyth said that $30 million in improvements between Kansas City and Sioux City had been lost to the river.[28] He made a conservative estimate, but his figures indicated how much the river cost the Corps and the federal government. To a great extent, the monetary damages to the navigation channel stemmed from the expansion of the project north to Sioux City in the 1930s before the maintenance costs of the control structures had been assessed and before the river's high flows had been curtailed. Between 1930 and 1933 Col. George Spalding of the Upper Mississippi Valley Division had warned his colleagues against taking such action.

After the flood of 1952, referring to the situation north of Omaha, an army engineer confessed, "Loss of alignment and progressive destruction of control works continue in most parts of this section of the river. . . . Much of the river has reverted to its original wild state, and bank erosion is severe at many locations. The rate of the destruction has far exceeded the work accomplished with the limited funds available."[29] The Missouri River had eluded the Corps' harness.

The widespread flooding in spring 1952 led directly to an increase in public, congressional, and presidential support for the completion of two more of the main-stem dams proposed in the Pick-Sloan Plan. The Missouri River had again affected the direction of development. Before the flood, in March 1952, fiscal conservatives in Congress and the Government Accounting Office, seeking to balance the federal budget and redirect resources toward the war in Korea, succeeded in eliminating funding in the annual budget for the start of construction on Gavin's Point Dam; these same interests also substantially reduced the scheduled appropriation for Oahe Dam. The complete denial of funds for Gavin's Point and the reduction for Oahe created the real possibility that the two dams would not receive future appropriations. Congressional representatives found it much easier to eliminate a new project or one barely begun than a project already well under way that represented a large federal investment.[30]

General Lewis Pick, who had been promoted to chief of engineers, and Col. Henry J. Hoeffer of the Omaha District exploited the public outrage after the flood to gain funding for Gavin's Point and Oahe. In April 1952 Pick made the grandiose claim that the completion of the proposed Pick-Sloan dams would forever end the flood threat in the Missouri Valley. The general boasted, "I fought the floods here in 1943. It was from Omaha that the plan for the comprehensive control of the Missouri River was launched and given impetus throughout the valley. It was my privilege at war's end to initiate the projects which will some day soon, I hope, forever end the flood menace in this valley."[31] One month later Pick reiterated, "There would have been no floods on the Missouri last month had the main stem dams, of which Gavin's Point is the last major project to get underway, been completed and operating."[32] In June Hoeffer told a group of individuals concerned with river development, "If our reservoir system had been completed, the river would have been within [its] banks in this whole region and widespread suffering and losses would have been prevented."[33]

Pick and Hoeffer had no trouble selling their idea of additional dams across the Missouri River to anyone that spring. At a meeting between President Truman and the governors of the Missouri Valley states, Pick announced, "All the plans are made. We know what to do and how to do it." He claimed the Corps could end future flooding; the politicians needed only to provide the engineers with the money to do it. President Truman looked at Pick and with an air of frustration remarked, "It's time for action. We've fooled around long enough. . . . Two dams on the upper Missouri have almost been taken out of the budget. I hope that Congress will stick to the budget on flood control."[34]

Congress followed the president's lead. In July 1952 Congress appropriated $3 million for the continuance of work on Oahe Dam and $7.7 million for the start of construction on Gavin's Point Dam. Congressmen from the Missouri basin faced incredible pressure from their constituencies to finance the two projects. Rejecting the construction of more dams across the Missouri after one of the river's largest floods would have been tantamount to political suicide for congressional members during an election year. Thus, the great flood of 1952 enabled the proponents of main-stem dams to defeat a serious challenge to the completion of their development program.[35]

At the same time that the engineers procured funding for Gavin's Point and Oahe dams, they pushed the completion of Fort Randall Dam. By summer 1952 the embankment and tunnel work had progressed to the point where the engineers readied for closure of the dam across the natural channel. Closure, and diversion of the Missouri, began with the digging of the approach channel from the free-flowing river to the opening of the outlet tunnels. To excavate the approach channel, the Corps awarded a contract to the Western Contracting Corporation of Sioux City, which then placed an order with the Tampa, Florida, firm of Erickson Engineering for the world's biggest, most powerful dredge boat. Officials with the Sioux City company named their huge dredge the *Western Chief.* It possessed nine diesel engines that generated 10,950 horsepower, enabling the dredge to suck rocks as large as eighteen inches in diameter from the river's floor and shoot them through hundreds of feet of pipe. The *Western Chief* weighed 1,500 tons, and its nose (the portion sunk into the riverbed) weighed 150 tons alone. The mechanical monster could pump material from forty-eight feet below the river's surface, deeper than any dredge then in operation on the Missouri. The size and velocity of material chewed up by the cutterhead required replacement of its blades every five days. The dredge was too bulky and sat too deep in the water to float up the Missouri, so engineers moved it in twenty-one separate pieces to the dam site and assembled it there. Once in place, the *Western Chief* removed 4.5 million cubic yards of muck to complete the approach channel in spring 1952.[36]

The federal engineers sat poised to close the embankment and divert the river. They scheduled the closure of Fort Randall Dam for July, when river levels dropped after passage of the spring and summer rises. Low water reduced the amount of work necessary to fill the final gap in the embankment; high water and strong currents would wash away the material used to close the gap, costing more money and time. The Corps gave the Western Contracting Company the responsibility to effect closure, and company officials and Corps engineers decided that use of the *Western Chief* offered the safest and cheapest method to achieve it. On 14 July the dredge began pulling up sand, gravel, chalk, rocks, and clay from the riverbed and depositing the slurry across the length of the 1,000-foot gap at the rate of 1,600 cubic yards per minute, much faster than the river could carry it away. Just as the engineers had used the river's silt load below Sioux City to channelize the stream, they now used it to dam the Missouri. The *Sioux City Journal* proclaimed, "The dredge just outsilted the mammoth stream which for many years has carried great amounts of silt down the river."[37] On 20 July, after six days of nonstop dredging, the slurry pile rose above the river's water surface. At 1:10 P.M. the slurry sealed the natural river channel. Within minutes, the Missouri's water backed up, flowed through the approach channel, into the outlet tunnels, and downstream (Fig. 10.7).[38]

During fall 1952 the Corps quickly raised the embankment in the gap section to a height of eighty-five feet. The engineers hurried this work so that the dam could hold back possible high flows in spring and summer 1953, thus avoiding any repeat of the 1952 flood.[39] As the dam rose above the riverbed, the Corps gradually reduced the flow of the Missouri River by lowering giant steel gates over the entrances to the outlet tunnels. Fort Randall Dam tightened its grip on the Missouri River. In November Fort Randall's reservoir began to fill, achieving a depth of thirty-five feet at the dam face by spring 1953 and stretching approximately twenty-three miles upstream. By September, as the entire embankment rose to its maximum height, the reservoir covered 45,000 square acres, and its level climbed at the rate of six inches per day.[40] In Octo-

Fig. 10.7. The world's most powerful dredge, the *Western Chief*, closes the dam at Fort Randall, July 1952. (Courtesy of the Corps of Engineers)

ber and November 1954 the reservoir impounded 2.7 MAF of water and reached beyond Chamberlain, ninety miles upstream.[41]

Closure of Fort Randall Dam and the consequent capture of the river behind its embankment resulted in significant consequences for the navigation channel south of Sioux City. The dam diminished the Missouri's ability to erode and wander through its valley; thus, the danger that unrestricted flows posed to channelization structures decreased in proportion. Recognizing the new environmental situation on the river below Sioux City and responding to the wishes of Missouri Valley residents and their congressmen, Washington began appropriating money for new work on the navigation channel in the mid-1950s. These appropriations came after a fourteen-year hiatus brought on by World War II, the Korean War, and the repeated floods of the 1940s and 1950s. The renewal of funding for the navigation project launched the final push to control the Missouri River.[42]

The methods and technologies employed to narrow and deepen the Missouri in the 1950s and 1960s differed in important ways from those used in the late 1920s and 1930s. New engineering techniques and tools reflected the changing goals of the navigation project and the different environmental circumstances along the river south of Sioux City. During the late 1920s and the depression 1930s, the project's primary objectives included work relief and the establishment of a barge channel. To fulfill these two goals, the Corps employed thousands of men performing labor-intensive tasks. But by the 1950s and 1960s the improved economic situation in the United States and the Missouri Valley eliminated the necessity of using the project to employ thousands of men. Consequently, the Corps used heavy equipment and technology to realign the river. Establishment of barge navigation on the stream did remain a goal; however, bank stabilization and concomitant protection of private property from the river's incursions equaled that objective. Moreover, during this last phase of the navigation project, the Corps displayed an extreme concern for the costs of channelization. The budget-conscious Eisenhower administration forced the army engineers to devise means of decreasing costs while still achieving their goals. Further, by the mid-1950s the upstream dams had reduced the silt load of the Missouri River to a fraction of its predam level.[43] Such a small amount of silt in the water meant the river could no longer redirect its own channel through deposition behind traditional pile dikes. To compensate for the river's smaller silt load, engineers devised new means of realigning the channel, including the use of the toe trench revetment, large quantities of stone, the pile dike revetment, and the pilot canal.[44]

The use of the toe trench revetment indicated how the goals and technologies of the navigation project had changed by the 1950s. Construction of the toe trench revetment began with the placement of a dragline or bulldozer on the surface of a flat barge that carried the machinery to the construction site. Once on location, the dragline or bulldozer dug a seven-foot-deep and fourteen-foot-wide trench along the entire length of the proposed new bank line. After digging the trench, a dragline dumped a blanket of quarried limestone, one or two feet thick, into the bottom of the trench and along its sloping outside edge. With the toe trench completed, engineers then diverted the river's flow into the trench. Over time, the Missouri scoured the earth on the riverward side of the trench, widened itself, and stayed within the imposed confines. The toe trench possessed a number of advantages over the older willow mattress and stone revetment: its construction took less time, cost less money, and required few workers; most important, the structure "healed" itself. Whenever the river undermined a portion of the toe trench revetment, rocks fell into the gaps in the structure, resulting in little or no maintenance costs. Use of the toe trench enabled the Corps to achieve the multiple goals of realigning the river channel, lowering construction costs, securing a stable bank line, and contributing to the establishment of a barge channel along a river with a reduced silt load.[45]

In the 1950s the engineers also began using the simple technique of dropping tons of stone into the river to realign the channel. With this method, the engineers did not engage in any preparatory work grading the bank line, laying a mattress, or driving piles into the clay bed. Instead, a dragline emptied its load of rock into the natural channel to shift the thalweg's direction quickly. Near Sioux City in the mid-1950s a Corps dragline deposited limestone into the river in a series of heaps running perpendicular to the natural bank line. The rock formed wing dams that forced the water away from the natural bank line and into the new channel.[46] The Corps could thus accomplish realignment of the channel in a matter of hours and days instead of years.

The Corps continued to use pile drivers and wooden piles, but in a modified form, to build pile dike revetments. A pile dike revetment consisted of a three-clump, one- or two-row pile dike surrounded by stone along its entire length (Fig. 10.8). The piles and stone reinforced one another, creating an exceptionally strong structure, resistant to powerful currents, high flows, and ice. Most often, the engineers erected pile dike revetments where the full force of the current needed to be deflected downstream, such as across the upstream end of a natural river bend they wanted to cut off or adjacent to the opening in a pilot canal. The Corps of Engineers used pile dike revetments extensively in western Iowa after 1955. Although more expensive than merely dumping stone in the river, pile dike revetments facilitated realignment of the channel and the creation of nearly permanent stone bank lines. The Corps also strengthened old wooden pile dikes with stone, placing rock around the piles with the use of draglines. This technique formed impermeable wing dams that were self-healing, required far less maintenance than the older permeable pile dike, and defied the destructive force of the river.[47]

The engineers relied heavily on the use of pilot canals, which enabled them to cut off long bends deemed impediments to future barge navi-

Fig. 10.8. A pile dike revetment in western Iowa. After 1955 the Corps of Engineers rapidly realigned the Missouri River channel by dumping millions of tons of quarried stone into the river. (Courtesy of the Corps of Engineers)

gation. Pilot canals also allowed the engineers to move the channel quickly. A few of the bends cut off with the use of pilot canals along the western Iowa reach included DeSoto, Decatur, Tieville, and Snyder Bends. The Corps built pilot canals with bulldozers, draglines, dredges, or a combination of all three. They never dug a pilot canal the full width of the proposed navigation channel; instead, men and equipment excavated a canal between 50 and 100 feet wide. Once engineers diverted the river through the canal, the swift-moving, compressed water eroded the canal's banks the remaining 200 or more feet to the edge of a toe trench revetment (Figs. 10.9 and 10.10).[48]

The Decatur Bridge diversion operation represented the height of the Corps' technological prowess along the Missouri River and illustrated how channelization in the 1950s differed from the construction work carried out in the 1920s and 1930s. The engineers used pilot canals, toe trench revetments, pile dike revetments, and even an upstream dam to redirect the Missouri River under the Decatur Bridge. Never before or since has the Corps of Engineers wielded such an awesome array of tools

Fig. 10.9. Pilot canal construction along the Missouri River. In the photograph, a pilot canal's upstream plug is removed with a dredge while a pile driver hammers piles into the riverbed in preparation for closing the old channel area from the future navigation channel. Notice the toe trench revetment on the right side of the pilot canal; the river will eventually occupy the area up to it. (Courtesy of the Corps of Engineers)

to manipulate the Missouri River. The Corps reached the pinnacle of its power along the Missouri in summer 1955.

The story of the Decatur Bridge diversion operation began in fall 1946 when the Burt County Bridge Commission petitioned the Omaha District of the Corps of Engineers for the right to build a bridge across the Missouri River, linking Decatur, Nebraska, with Onawa, Iowa. The Corps, ever protective of its prerogatives along the Missouri, examined the proposed bridge's design specifications to ensure that it would not hinder the future construction of the barge channel. With this in mind, Corps officials approved construction of the bridge, stipulating that it span the future course of the navigation channel, which sat 500 feet west of the actual unchannelized river. Following the Corps' instructions, the county commission built the bridge over a bone-dry expanse of valley bottomland covered with sand, thistle, small willows, and cottonwood trees. In 1951 the county commission finished the bridge and

Fig. 10.10. The natural channel area of the Missouri River is sealed from the navigation channel. The Corps has dropped quarried stone into the river along a row of piles, forming a pile dike revetment. The new navigation channel is widening itself to the bottom of the toe trench revetment. (Courtesy of the Corps of Engineers)

asked the Corps to furnish them with a river, but the Corps did not have any money to divert the Missouri under the span. Consequently, from 1951 to 1955 the Decatur Bridge sat idle, a bridge without a river. Only after persistent lobbying by members of the Burt County Bridge Commission and congressional representatives from western Iowa and eastern Nebraska, including Ben Jensen of Iowa, did Congress eventually appropriate the $11 million to move the river under the $2 million bridge.[49]

One and one-half miles north-northeast of the Decatur Bridge, the Missouri River made a wide loop, approximately 3,000 feet wide, only a few feet deep, and covered with sandbars and islands, before traveling south past the east end of the span. In order to move the river under the bridge, the Corps needed to construct a stable bank line to guide the river away from the loop and to the bridge.[50] The engineers planned to divert the river under the bridge in four stages.

The Corps, working with private contractors, completed the first stage in early spring 1955. The engineers built a stone revetment on the Nebraska side of the river one mile above the bridge, which ensured that the river did not outflank the control structures built farther downstream and which kept the river directed toward the future navigation channel. Next, the Corps supervised the construction of a one-and-one-half-mile-long pile dike revetment to deflect the river's flow from the wide, shallow loop. But the river still did not flow under the bridge; instead, the Corps kept a 200-foot-long opening in the south end of the pile dike revetment to allow the river to continue to run east of the bridge (Fig. 10.11).[51]

The third stage of the diversion project involved the use of dredges, which dug a pilot canal from south of the bridge, under the span, north to the point where the Missouri River flowed through the gap in the

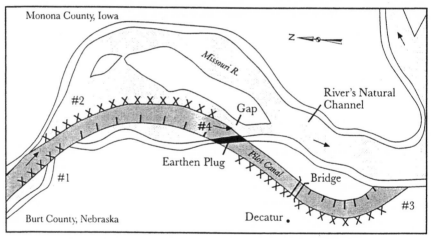

Fig. 10.11. The Decatur Bridge diversion operation, summer 1955. The first step in the diversion of the Missouri River under the Decatur Bridge involved the construction of a stone revetment one mile north of the bridge on the Nebraska shore. The second stage entailed construction of a one-and-one-half-mile-long pile dike revetment to block the flow of the river through its natural channel. The engineers left a 200-foot-long opening in this revetment to allow the river to escape south. During stage three, the Corps dredged a pilot canal from the natural river channel north under the bridge to the edge of the 200-foot-long gap. In the final stage, the Corps, with the assistance of Fort Randall Dam, closed the 200-foot gap, removed the coffer dam at the upper end of the pilot canal, and forced the river under the bridge.

pile dike revetment. At the upper end of the pilot canal, the Corps maintained a coffer dam to keep the river out of the pilot canal until they finished dredging. The final stage of the scheme involved the most sophisticated application of technology. The engineers stationed at the Decatur site coordinated the diversion of the Missouri under the Decatur Bridge with the closure of Gavin's Point Dam at Yankton, South Dakota. On Friday, 29 July 1955, Fort Randall Dam pinched down the flow of the Missouri River to a mere trickle, 3,000 cfs, far beneath the normal flow volume of 28,000 cubic feet per second.[52] The Missouri had never been lower, probably not even since the glacial formation of the stream 30,000 years earlier. This low flow allowed the engineers to close Gavin's Point Dam on Sunday, 31 July, without having to battle a strong current. As the low water level lazily drifted downstream, the *Sioux City Journal* reported, "The lack of water proved that man had at last controlled the impetuous river."[53] At Sioux City, the low water exposed the river bottom to view, and from the depths appeared rusty old cars, discarded home appliances, and miscellaneous junk, testament to years of neglect.

The engineers at Decatur began the actual diversion when the low flow reached the construction site. Over the weekend of 30 and 31 July crews began dumping rock along the 200-foot-wide aperture in the pile dike revetment northeast of the bridge. By Monday morning, 1 August, only a few feet remained to be sealed in the dike before the river would be forced toward the pilot canal. To achieve total diversion, the engineers had to remove the coffer dam at the head of the pilot canal. The Corps initially planned on removing the plug with a simple dredge; however, representatives from the media wanted something more dramatic to mark the end of what had become known nationally as the Decatur Dry Land Bridge. The Corps acquiesced in this request and placed a pickup truck load of dynamite on the coffer dam. Crews detonated the dynamite, but the resulting explosion blew only a small hole in the earthen plug, and very little water flowed into the pilot canal and under the bridge. In an anticlimactic conclusion to the entire diversion sequence, a dredge moved into position and excavated the remainder of the coffer dam. Cheers went up from the crowd as the Missouri's channel began to stream through the pilot canal and under the bridge. The Decatur Dry Land Bridge was no more (Fig. 10.12).[54] A few days later, the engineers opened the gates at Fort Randall Dam to allow a higher water volume to flow downstream. It quickly scoured the origi-

Fig. 10.12. Looking north toward the Decatur Bridge, circa 1980. During the Decatur Bridge diversion operation, the *Sioux City Journal* claimed that humanity "had at last controlled the impetuous river." (Courtesy of the Corps of Engineers)

nal 80-foot-wide pilot canal into an approximately 450-foot-wide channel, capable of holding the full volume of the Missouri.

The Corps continued to use many of the channelization methods and technologies employed during the Decatur Bridge diversion operation into the late 1950s and 1960s. These techniques, in combination with further congressional assistance, enabled the engineers to press forward with completion of the navigation channel. For all intents and purposes, the Corps finished the channel from Sioux City to the mouth in 1970, although the engineers kept fine-tuning the river to deepen it (Fig. 10.13).[55] Meanwhile, the Corps wrapped up construction on the series of dams and reservoirs authorized in the Pick-Sloan Plan. Besides Fort Randall, Garrison, and Gavin's Point, closed in 1952, 1953, and 1955, the engineers closed Oahe Dam in 1958 and Big Bend Dam in 1963.

Big Bend was unique among the five Pick-Sloan main-stem dams. By the early 1950s the army engineers displayed ambivalence toward, if not a downright lack of interest in, its construction. They wanted the other four structures but appeared willing to forgo Big Bend. The

Fig. 10.13. The completed navigation channel, western Iowa, circa 1965. The symmetry of the navigation channel and its control structures contrasts sharply with the irregular outline of the natural channel area. (Courtesy of the Corps of Engineers)

Corps recognized that a dam at Big Bend would no longer be necessary for re-regulation of Oahe's releases, their earlier justification for it. Re-regulation alone would not repay the expense of building the structure. Moreover, the infrequent water surges bursting forth from Oahe's powerhouse would be captured and dissipated by the reservoir behind Fort Randall Dam. Big Bend Dam would not contribute to flood control or the navigation channel below Sioux City. Garrison, Oahe, and Fort Randall reservoirs had enough storage space for both of those purposes, and Gavin's Point Dam would discharge steady water volumes for downstream navigation. Nor did the Corps want to build the dam to furnish irrigation water to fields in South Dakota; irrigation meant water depletion and Bureau of Reclamation influence on the Missouri main stem, and the Corps would not tolerate either possibility. Further, the engineers did not want to build a dam for the exclusive purpose of hydroelectric generation. They wanted multiple-purpose and mutually supporting dams along the main stem. A multiple-purpose dam delivered numerous benefits to society, including hydroelectricity, flood control, and aid to navigation. A mutually supporting dam provided benefits to other dams within the hydraulic system. Garrison, Oahe, Fort Randall, and Gavin's Point extended each other's longevity by capturing a portion of the Missouri's silt load. The four dams also increased the others' operational efficiency by holding the high tributary inflows of spring for regulated release during the dry summer and fall. Without Garrison and Oahe, for example, the release rates at Fort Randall and Gavin's Point would have oscillated so dramatically each year that their usefulness to the navigation channel would have been negligible. The small size of Big Bend Dam's proposed reservoir and its location above Fort Randall and below Oahe meant it would be neither multiple-purpose nor mutually supporting.

The Corps did not seek funding for Big Bend until South Dakota interests pressured them, and even then the engineers wavered in their commitment. Two South Dakota senators did more to obtain federal financing for the dam than the Corps itself. Only after South Dakota threatened to build the dam on its own, thereby challenging Corps control over its Missouri River hydraulic system, did the engineers finally acquiesce.

The history of Big Bend Dam is significant for several reasons. The dam illustrates how a local initiative compelled the Corps to further develop the Missouri River, not to advance its interests but to protect them. The controversies surrounding the construction of Big Bend Dam also signaled the beginning of South Dakota's discontent with the Pick-Sloan Plan. The dissatisfaction grew from the perception held by many South Dakotans and their political leaders that their state had sacrificed more valley bottomland to Pick-Sloan than any other state and therefore deserved more in return from the development plan. Disenchantment with the Pick-Sloan Plan temporarily subsided after the Corps built Big Bend Dam, but dissatisfaction resurfaced again in the 1970s, 1980s, and 1990s over the issues of irrigation, water diversion, and reservoir fisheries. Moreover, Big Bend's history provides insight into the details of the Pick-Sloan site-selection process and its repercussions for the Indian population living adjacent to the Missouri River.

In 1944 Congress authorized the construction of a dam at the northwest side of Big Bend and a power canal across the bend's neck. For ten years the Corps did no work on the dam; the army engineers did not even request funds for planning it. Then in 1954, after prodding by *Pierre Capital Journal* editor Robert Hipple and U.S. senator Francis Case of

South Dakota, the Corps conducted a preliminary site survey of the Big Bend area as a prelude to the design and eventual construction of the dam. Before carrying out the survey, Corps officials admitted that Big Bend Dam's sole purpose would be to generate electricity.[56]

The Corps studied three sites in the Big Bend region (Fig. 10.14). The engineers wanted a dam site that would maximize power output and be the most cost-effective, "based on foundation, topography, materials, and access." Corps officials referred to the three sites under consideration as the Bend site, the Lower Bend site, and the Fort Thompson site. Officials immediately disqualified the Bend site because they believed it showed an unfavorable cost-to-benefit ratio. The army engineers concluded, "The major disadvantage of this location is that cuts through Pierre shale would be from 250 to 300 feet deep. . . . This site is considered the least feasible of the three sites studied."[57] The rejection of the Bend site reversed the 1944 decision made by Congress, the Corps, and the Missouri River States Committee to build a dam there.[58] Officials ruled against the Lower Bend site, on the southeast side of the bend

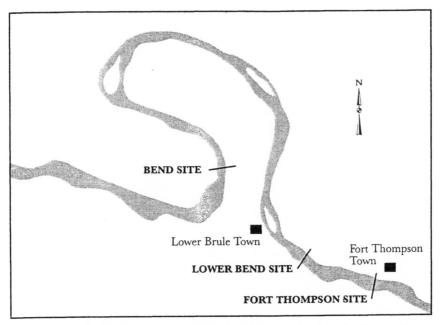

Fig. 10.14. The three sites in the Big Bend region examined by the Corps of Engineers in their 1954 site-selection survey.

just below the Indian community of Lower Brule, because of poor foundation conditions. The engineers favored the Fort Thompson site, adjacent to the Indian community of Fort Thompson and thirty miles southeast of the Bend site, because there the valley walls stood closer together and impermeable chalk rested near the surface, and a dam there would store more water than the other two sites, consequently generating more electricity. The submission of this preliminary site study dramatically altered the proposed location of Big Bend Dam.[59]

Although the Corps found the Bend site unsatisfactory and seriously contemplated building the dam at Fort Thompson, the engineers did not inform the Indians on the Lower Brule and Crow Creek Reservations of this possible change in plans. A dam at the new site would force the relocation of hundreds of Indians on the two reservations, inundate the Indian town of Lower Brule, and flood the remaining bottomlands of the Crow Creek and Lower Brule Tribes, but the Corps kept quiet. It was not until October 1955, when the *Sioux Falls Argus Leader* printed an article addressing the results of the preliminary site survey, that anyone living on the reservations learned that the dam might be moved downstream.[60]

The Lower Brule Tribal Council decided to do all within its power to protest the revised location of the dam. On 4 January 1956 the council unanimously passed a resolution: "This Tribal Council . . . hereby register and publish on behalf of said tribe their opposition to changing the said site of said Big Bend Dam and project and allege that such change would result in heavy loss and extreme hardship." They sent the resolution to South Dakota state and federal representatives, including Sen. Karl E. Mundt, who sat on the influential Senate Appropriations Committee.[61]

Ironically, at the very time the Lower Brule sent their resolution to his office, Mundt was seeking the first congressional appropriations for Big Bend Dam. Mundt used the cost-effectiveness of the planned dam as his most persuasive argument in the Senate chambers to procure funding for further site studies, a prerequisite for actual construction. Because Big Bend would be a single-purpose dam, its cost-effectiveness depended entirely on how much electricity it could produce. And high electrical output depended on locating the dam at Fort Thompson, inundating the upstream lands of the Crow Creek and Lower Brule Indians.

In spring 1956 Mundt received letters from the Mississippi Valley Association, the National Rural Electric Cooperative Association, the South Dakota Farmer's Union, the city of Chamberlain, and the Chamberlain Community Club urging him to obtain an appropriation for Big Bend Dam so that the Corps could conduct the final site-selection study. Mundt responded to these requests for action with vigor and determination. He understood how the dam would benefit his off-reservation constituents in South Dakota, and he worked hard for their interests.[62]

Mundt told the army engineers to place a request for funds before his Senate committee; then he fought to include that request in the annual budget. With this maneuver, Mundt, not the Corps, became the key player in pushing the construction of Big Bend Dam. But Mundt's fight to include the dam in the budget met with resistance from colleagues. The dam competed for limited funds with other public works projects throughout the United States. However, on 21 June 1956 Mundt secured an appropriation of $150,000 for the final site-selection study. After his victory the senator expressed great pride in having kept Big Bend Dam away from the budget ax. In a letter to John F. Lindley of Chamberlain, Mundt gloated, "You are dead right that it took a little 'doing' in the subterranean recesses of our Subcommittee room to have Big Bend included and hold the line when it came to the Conference Committee. All's well that ends well, however, and we are getting every dime *the Army Engineers requested* for their planning and study of *their* proposed project at Big Bend."[63]

The final site-selection studies moved forward. In 1957 federal engineers examined six sites in the bend region. After months of intense analysis, the engineers chose Site D1/D2, which sat very close to the Fort Thompson site first examined in 1954. Impermeable chalk lay closer to the surface here than anywhere else, men and materials could easily access Site D1/D2 from Highway 34–47, and Chamberlain, with its schools, restaurants, churches, medical facilities, and entertainment possibilities, was only twenty-seven miles south along the highway. Most important, the engineers claimed that at Site D1/D2, "Reservoir storage and power production would be a maximum among the sites investigated." After finishing the final site studies in late summer 1957, work could have begun on the dam, but the Corps encountered unexpected opposition from South Dakota's other senator, Francis Case.[64]

Case, who sat on the Senate Public Works Committee, believed passionately in the Pick-Sloan Plan. But he had one major qualm with its Preference clause, which stipulated that public utilities, rural electric cooperatives, and federal facilities have first preference for power generated at hydroelectric dams built across the Missouri River. The clause meant that South Dakota, a state of private utilities, would receive only a small fraction of the power from any future Big Bend Dam.

The Preference clause disturbed Case. He believed South Dakota should receive its fair share of the hydroelectricity from the dam because its residents had already given up so much land to provide water-storage space for Pick-Sloan's reservoirs. Since at least 1949 Case had been working for the repeal of the Preference clause, but to no avail. By the mid-1950s the power from Gavin's Point Dam and Fort Randall Dam had already been allocated to out-of-state preference customers by the Federal Power Commission. The power from the Oahe Dam would soon be allocated to out-of-state public utilities. Since Big Bend would be the last main-stem dam built under the Pick-Sloan Plan, the last hope for Case, and for South Dakota, for receiving hydroelectricity rested on securing power from Big Bend. Case was aware of this fact. He was so intent on receiving power from Big Bend that he told his South Dakota constituents in 1955 that "personally, I shall not press for appropriations to start Big Bend Dam until we get some plan officially approved or legislation passed that will make Big Bend power available to South Dakota consumers before it is exported outside the State."

Case's opposition to Big Bend Dam represented a major obstacle to its completion. The senator possessed the institutional and political power either to halt or to slow its construction. In fall 1955 Case objected to the Corps' recommendation that Big Bend Dam be moved from the Bend site to the Fort Thompson site. The senator opposed the latter site because a dam there would inundate yet more of South Dakota's precious Missouri Valley bottomlands.[65]

As the final site studies neared completion in summer 1957, Case made a bold move to gain power for South Dakota's off-reservation population. On 20 August he proposed that South Dakota finance the construction of Big Bend Dam through the issuance of a bond. Desperate to gain hydroelectricity for his state, Case introduced S.R. 2822, which would grant federal permission to South Dakota to build Big Bend Dam.

Case's action stunned Corps officials. The passage of S.R. 2822 and the construction of Big Bend Dam by the state would threaten the efficient operation of the entire Missouri River main-stem system of dams and reservoirs. Since Big Bend Dam would stand squarely in the middle of the other Pick-Sloan dams, South Dakota's control of its reservoir waters would imperil the Corps' control over the river and possibly disrupt the flows needed to maintain the navigation channel south of Sioux City. Case's proposal presented the same threat posed by the previous South Dakota dam projects that had been vetoed by the Corps of Engineers.

The bill troubled Corps officials. On 11 September 1957 Chief of Engineers Maj. Gen. E. C. Itschner wrote Case,

The construction and operation of Big Bend by non-Federal interests would present some unusual and complicated problems. . . . If all interested parties will work together in a spirit of cooperation, it is believed that these problems can be overcome. Accordingly, we are willing to work with the interested parties to arrive at a mutually acceptable arrangement. . . . Big Bend project is not a separate entity, and cannot be operated independently of the other main-stem projects without loss of effectiveness of both Big Bend and the remaining system.[66]

Case had made a dramatic move, and the Corps took notice. Congress also took notice. New York had recently received congressional and Federal Power Commission approval for a state-financed power project on the Niagara River. Thus, the precedent for Case's proposal of state-financed dams on national waterways had already been set. Congressmen realized they would have difficulty denying South Dakota the authority they had granted New York.

The lower Missouri Valley states of Iowa, Nebraska, Kansas, and Missouri feared that if South Dakota built Big Bend Dam on its own, the state could deny Missouri River water to them. Moreover, Congress and lower valley government officials understood that federal construction of Big Bend Dam could not go forward without the cooperation of South Dakota's federal and state government representatives, including Mundt, Cong. George McGovern, and Gov. Joseph Foss, who backed Case in his attempts to gain hydroelectricity for their state. The lower valley states and the Corps faced a great dilemma. If the federal government failed to finance the construction of Big Bend Dam, South Dakota could possibly build the structure in the near future and endanger their interests.

On the other hand, if the Corps and lower valley representatives continued to insist on the application of the Preference clause, the dam probably would not be built, for lack of South Dakota's support. Either way, the Corps and the lower valley states had a lot to lose. The only way out of the dilemma Case had created was to compromise. Such a compromise was forthcoming.

During spring 1958 Case, the Corps, and lower valley congressional representatives and state officials hammered out an agreement. In March Congress reversed the Preference clause and granted South Dakota 50 percent of the power from the future Big Bend Dam. Two months later, Mundt's appropriations committee granted $600,000 to begin its construction. Lower Missouri Valley congressmen voted for this allotment and ensuing allocations to forestall the construction of a Big Bend Dam by South Dakota.[67]

Guaranteed 50 percent of the dam's future electrical output instead of a specified number of kilowatts, Case wanted the planned dam to produce as much energy as possible. Therefore in fall 1958 he changed his mind about the location and dimensions of Big Bend Dam and gave Site D1/D2 (near Fort Thompson) his full endorsement. He also approved a Corps proposal to raise the planned height of the reservoir by an additional 8 feet, to 1,422 feet above sea level. The Corps estimated that the extra 8 feet of water storage would more than double the dam's electrical output, from approximately 220,000 kW to 480,000 kW.[68]

In fall 1958 the Corps publicly announced its intention to build the dam at Site D1/D2 with a reservoir level of 1,422 feet above sea level. Colonel David Hammond of the Omaha District admitted that the army engineers made this decision only after consultation with South Dakota's government representatives. In other words, Case, Mundt, and Foss assented to the dam's final location and dimensions.[69]

After hearing the definitive news on Big Bend Dam's height and location, members of the Lower Brule Tribe expressed dismay. Twenty years earlier, Francis Case had aided the tribe in its attempt to build a hydroelectric facility at the Big Bend, only to fail because of Corps opposition. In the 1930s Case believed the Indians deserved first claim to any power project at the Big Bend; in the late 1950s, however, Case wanted to flood their lands to advance his own political fortunes and to enrich his off-reservation constituency. In more ways than one, Case wanted power. On 16 February 1959 Lower Brule Tribal Chairman J. W. (Jiggs) Thompson notified Case of his tribe's opposition to Big Bend Dam:

We are opposed to increasing the elevation of Big Bend Dam to 1,422. In fact, we are opposed to the construction of Big Bend Dam. It is the wish of our people that no more land be taken from us. With us, the point is simple. When our land is gone, our way of life is gone, our tribes are destroyed. The bottom lands the Corps of Engineers want to take are the very best on the reservations. They are our heart lands. They can never be replaced. No similar lands are for sale. We depend on land for our livelihood, it furnishes us our income. To take our land is to take our homes and income, and a part of our history and heritage.[70]

Case heard Thompson's plea and ignored it.

By mid-1959 the Corps of Engineers completed the site selection and design phase of Big Bend Dam. At the insistence of Francis Case, the Corps lowered the dam's planned reservoir water level to 1,420 feet above sea level, a decrease of 2 feet. The senator wanted to spare Fort Pierre and the state park at Farm Island from any water damage, not to preserve any Indian land. The Corps signed the first construction contracts, using the money Mundt had obtained, and began work on the dam's access roads in 1959 and on the dam itself in 1960. In July 1963 the engineers impounded the Missouri River behind Big Bend Dam. By spring 1964 the reservoir submerged the Indian town site of Lower Brule and the remaining Missouri Valley bottomlands on the Lower Brule and Crow Creek reservations. In September 1966 Secretary of State Dean Rusk dedicated Big Bend Dam (Figs. 10.15 and 10.16).[71] The dedication ceremony marked a triumph for South Dakota's off-reservation residents. They had successfully pressured the Corps and its lower valley benefactors into building Big Bend Dam to supply South Dakota with hydroelectricity. This victory for one group of South Dakotans spelled defeat for another group, however, the Indians on the Crow Creek and Lower Brule Reservations, who forfeited the land for the reservoir.

The filling of the reservoir, along with the other four Pick-Sloan reservoirs, resulted in the inundation of 650 of the 780 miles of river valley between Yankton, South Dakota, and the mouth of the Yellowstone River.[72] With the Dakota dams in place and work on the channelization project winding down, the Corps publicly claimed to have tamed the Missouri and made it work for humanity. But the river eluded complete mastery. The dams, reservoirs, and channelization structures could not halt the occurrence of floods along the valley south of Sioux City, prevent the onset of a phenomenon known as stream-bed degradation, stop tributary stream-cutting, or lessen the effects of drought and high flows on the navigation channel. From the 1960s into the 1990s, a host of nega-

Fig. 10.15. Big Bend Dam and powerhouse under construction, April 1962. (Courtesy of the Corps of Engineers)

Fig. 10.16. The relocated Indian community of Lower Brule, January 1964. Lake Sharpe inundated the original town of Lower Brule *(background)* in spring 1964. (Courtesy of the Corps of Engineers)

tive environmental repercussions cropped up as a consequence of the development projects of the preceding decades. These problems, in conjunction with a rising public awareness about issues related to environmental quality, led to the first significant criticisms of the navigation project and its supporting system of dams and reservoirs. A period of public disillusionment with Missouri River development began in the 1970s, intensified in the early 1980s over the issue of water diversion, grew stronger during the severe drought of the late 1980s and early 1990s, and reached a fever pitch in the wake of the flood of 1993.

11 | The Untamable Missouri

Although the Corps of Engineers had been channelizing the Missouri since the 1890s, the river and valley maintained a semblance of their presettlement environmental character into the 1950s because channelization structures and Fort Peck Dam failed to keep the stream from meandering and eroding a new course. In 1952, for example, 83 of the 130.5 river miles between Sioux City and Omaha remained unchannelized and unencumbered by pile dikes or revetments. The free-flowing Missouri hindered the advance of agriculture, industry, roads, and urban sprawl into the river corridor.[1]

The river corridor extended from one to four miles across the valley and consisted of four distinct subregions[2]—the water area, the channel area, the active erosion zone, and the meander belt (Fig. 11.1).[3] The water area embraced the Missouri River itself, its thalweg, side channels, sloughs, and connected oxbow lakes, anywhere that water flowed. The Iowa Geological Survey estimated that the water area of the Missouri River in western Iowa before channelization covered approximately 24,637 surface acres.[4] The channel area stretched from the waterline on the left bank to the waterline on the right bank and comprised the water area as well as sandbars and islands. Along the Iowa border, this area embodied roughly 42,682 acres, or 66.6 square miles, before channelization.[5] The active erosion zone lay adjacent to the channel area on either side of the river and could be inundated, scoured, or eroded each year. Its physical features included sand flats on the water's edge, willow groves along the bank, and timber tracts that stretched to the bluff line. A government estimate placed this area from Sioux City to the mouth at 364,000 acres, or 564 square miles.[6] In western Iowa there existed approximately 44,915 acres, or 70.1 square miles, inside the active erosion zone.[7] The meander belt sat the farthest from moving water. The swerving Missouri usually bypassed this area, only infrequently submerging it or tearing up its vegetation. It possessed timber tracts, marshland, pasture, native grasses, and cropland and totaled 31,864 acres, or 49.7 square miles in Iowa. In sum, the river corridor through western Iowa

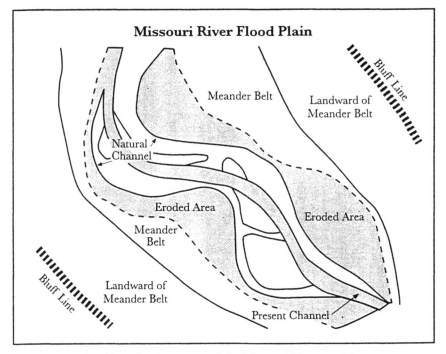

Fig. 11.1. The four areas of the Missouri River corridor.

comprised 186.4 square miles of various types of habitat for fish and wildlife (Fig. 11.2).[8]

The unchannelized and undammed Missouri River perpetually washed away sandbars and islands, undermined trees and brush along the shoreline, and overtopped its banks during the spring and summer months. The river thus prevented any one area in the corridor and its accompanying habitat from gaining supremacy within its ecosystem. Nothing in the river or the adjoining valley remained standing against the power of moving water for very long. Yet even as it destroyed one habitat, it created another. As the sandbars that served as nesting sites for shorebirds disappeared beneath the rising river, fish habitat increased proportionally; or when the river quit inundating a sand flat, willows and cottonwoods took root and provided cover and forage for birds and mammals. Through an endless process of formation and disintegration, the Missouri nurtured biological diversity. Additionally, the unregulated

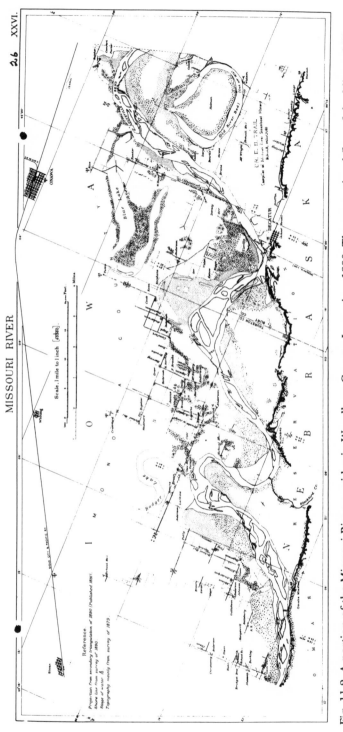

Fig. 11.2. A portion of the Missouri River corridor in Woodbury County, Iowa, circa 1890. The unrestricted flow of the Missouri River fostered biodiversity by constantly creating and destroying species habitat. No single habitat and its concomitant life forms could achieve dominance within the ecosystem as long as the river remained free to erode, meander, and flood. Closure of several Dakota dams in the 1950s and the resultant regulation of flow volumes, in concert with channelization work south of Sioux City, dealt a severe blow to the corridor's biodiversity. (Courtesy of the Western Historical Manuscript Collection)

Missouri and undeveloped valley floor served the purpose of biological dispersal. Plant, fish, bird, and animal species moved up and down the Missouri River or Valley, venturing into new territories, establishing fledgling colonies, and affecting the species composition, and thereby biological diversity, of a particular habitat type. The Missouri River and Valley represented a biological thoroughfare.

Moreover, the unrestricted flow of water contributed to the health of all life forms in the river and valley. When high water eroded a timber tract and sunk its trees to the bottom of the river, the deer, turkeys, coyotes, beavers, and skunks that had lived in the drowned forest moved to another grove. These displaced creatures competed for food and mates with wildlife already occupying the remaining woodlands, competition that strengthened the species.

Everything imaginable lived in this disparate, unsettled habitat. Abundant numbers of blue, channel, and flathead catfish swam in the Missouri's warm, muddy, nutrient-rich water and its moderate-to-fast channel chutes. Among valley residents, the blue catfish gained notoriety because they grew to such large sizes. According to officials of the Missouri Department of Conservation, "[In the Missouri River] legendary blue catfish were caught frequently. Reports include one of 315 pounds, another of 242 pounds."[9] The number and size of blue catfish decreased in the early and mid-twentieth century because of commercial fishing and the elimination of habitat. But even in the 1950s, stories still circulated of huge blue catfish being caught by surprised anglers.[10]

Paddlefish cruised the dark waters of the Missouri main stem, feeding on plankton and using their long snouts as sensory devices to find their way. Because of their feeding practices, paddlefish preferred to lie in the deeper sections of the river, in nine feet or more of water, leaving the depths only to migrate upstream to ancient spawning grounds and there, as the grayish blue backs of the females protruded above the water surface, to lay eggs over hundreds of feet of shallow gravel and sand riffles. Dispersal of the eggs guaranteed against destruction of the entire nesting population.[11] Paddlefish also reached admirable sizes. Fishers in the 1950s, using stout poles and large-diameter treble hooks, frequently snagged paddlefish ranging from 50 to 100 pounds. Legions of other fish lived in the shallow, calm side channels and connected oxbow lakes, where a teeming mass of plankton, insects, larvae, crustaceans, and reptiles appeased the appetites of largemouth bass, small-mouth bass, white bass, black crappie, white crappie, blue sucker, gold-eye, walleye, northern pike, shovelnose sturgeon, bigmouth buffalo, smallmouth buffalo, white sucker, pallid sturgeon, bluegill, and the ever-present and versatile carp.[12]

The channel area and its sandbars, gravel bars, islands, and marshy sloughs afforded habitat to reptiles, shorebirds, geese, and ducks. Turtles, frogs, and snakes swam in the shallow water of sloughs or sunned them-selves on the beaches and bars that blanketed the river. Birds, such as the piping plover and least tern, with their long, thin legs, danced along the edge of bars, eating aquatic insects, snails, seeds, berries, and the occasional, unalert fish. Canada geese, lesser snow geese, blue geese, and ducks of various sorts, including the mallard, ring-necked duck, and ruddy duck, migrated and nested along the river corridor. Canada geese depended heavily on the Missouri River flyway during their annual jour-neys north and south. The bars in the river furnished crucial resting sites for migrating birds needing protection from predators. Bars also sup-plied waterfowl with nesting areas, providing a safe haven for the eggs and brood from weasels, badgers, raccoons, and skunks patrolling the banks.[13]

Sand flats, sand dunes, willow groves, stands of cottonwood, tracts of elm, ash, and bur oaks, tangled masses of poison ivy, wild grapevines, chokecherry bushes, and saw grass stretched across the active erosion zone. Wood ducks, woodpeckers, and eagles nested in tall, dead trees that towered above the river. Coyotes, red foxes, gray squirrels, fox squir-rels, cottontail rabbits, raccoons, opossums, beavers, weasels, muskrats, skunks, badgers, bobcats, and mink scurried along the ground, either trying to avoid their neighbors or attempting to eat one of them. Bob-white quail, Hungarian partridge, ring-necked pheasants, and mourn-ing doves fed on kernels of corn left in nearby fields in fall, cowered in the brush during the snows of winter, and made a noisy racket as they sought mates during spring.[14]

The meander belt maintained the most stable land forms and flora within the river corridor. Relative stability in habitat meant the presence of long-established oxbow lakes, mature forest tracts of bur oak, elm, and ash, pastureland occupied by cattle and hogs, and agricultural crop-land. Many of the creatures that lived within the active erosion zone ventured into the meander belt for food and cover.

Beyond the meander belt lived the valley's human inhabitants. For over 100 years the residents of the valley from Montana to Missouri had for the most part kept their distance from the river for a simple reason: to avoid having their homes, crops, livestock, towns, and cities swept downstream. In western Iowa, along the margins of the valley or on top of low ridgelines that ran along the bottomlands, sat towns, including Sergeant Bluff, Salix, Sloan, Holly Springs, Luton, Whiting, Turin, and Onawa. In Monona County, settlers platted their towns from four to ten miles away from the river or directly under the shadow of the Loess Hills. Railroads and highways, including Highway 75 and the Chicago and Northwestern Railroad, ran beside the bluff line or far from the river on top of inclines. Valley residents positioned grain elevators, warehouses, industrial sites, and farmhouses away from the river. Common sense dictated that structures and people stay clear of the river corridor and not get close to it.[15]

Closure of the Dakota dams and resumption of work on the navigation channel in the 1950s set off a series of physical and ecological changes in the river corridor, which occurred both simultaneously and over a short period of time. The closing of Fort Randall Dam in 1952, Garrison Dam in 1953, and Gavin's Point Dam in 1955 put an end to the Missouri's spring and summer rise south of Yankton. Furthermore, the regulated Missouri maintained a fairly even discharge rate during eight months of the year, about 25,000 to 30,000 cfs at Sioux City. Uniform flow volumes markedly decreased the river's ability to erode, meander, and flood (Fig. 11.3).

The dams and reservoirs in the Dakotas considerably reduced the amount of silt, minerals, and organic matter in the river downstream from Yankton. The Corps of Engineers estimated that before the 1950s, the Missouri carried 142 million tons of silt past Sioux City each year; after closure of the dams, the river hauled a scant 4 million tons past the same location.[16] A private study concluded that 138 million tons of silt rolled by Yankton every year, an amount that decreased to 1.9 million tons.[17] Noting the decline in the river's silt content, Gerald Jauron, Missouri River coordinator for the Iowa Conservation Commission, remarked, "They closed the dam [Gavin's Point] last summer. For a couple of days the Mo practically stopped running, and you could almost spit across the river when they shut off the flowage. Then it began to flow over the spillway and the river began to rise again. When it did, I'd never

Fig. 11.3. Fort Randall Dam, circa 1965. (Courtesy of the Corps of Engineers)

seen the Missouri cleaner."[18] Accordingly, residents in the valley boasted that the Missouri had become one of the clearest rivers in the Midwest, and its nickname, Big Muddy, was no longer applicable.[19]

The narrowing of the channel area's width below Sioux City from an average of 2,363 feet to a mere 739 feet, combined with the straightening of the river (the Corps shortened the Missouri by seventy miles from Sioux City to the mouth), resulted in a threefold increase in the river's current velocity.[20] Before the navigation project, the river flowed between one and two miles per hour; after channelization, it rocketed downstream at six mph (Fig. 11.4).[21]

Cleaner water, a straighter channel, a faster current, and confinement of the water area within stone-lined banks caused streambed degradation, or the lowering of the riverbed through erosion. The army engineers called the clear water exiting the dams "hungry water," which seeks sedimental material in order to slow its momentum; it did so by eating away the riverbed of sand, gravel, and clay. Degradation occurred

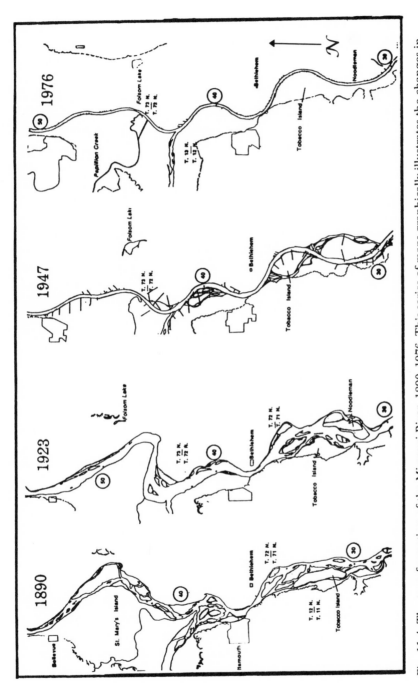

Fig. 11.4. The transformation of the Missouri River, 1890–1976. This series of maps graphically illustrates the changes in the Missouri River that resulted from construction of the navigation project and Dakota dams. (Courtesy of the Iowa Geological Survey)

from Yankton to the Platte River confluence. Below the Platte, a number of factors mitigated against degradation, including the presence of bedrock near the surface. By 1980 the river had dug down 8.5 feet at Sioux City, and approximately 5.5 feet at Decatur (Fig. 11.5).[22] No one knew how much lower the river would dig into its bed; some officials speculated that it would degrade another 15 feet at Sioux City.[23] The government engineers predicted the river would lower itself only a few more feet because the hungry water flowed over increasingly coarser bed materials, consisting of large stones and even boulders that resisted erosion.

Regulation of flows, channelization, and degradation produced a noticeable reduction in the size of the river's water and channel areas. By 1980 the water area along the Iowa border dropped from 24,637 acres to 7,637 acres, a net loss of 26.5 square miles. The channel area fell from 42,682 acres to 7,682 acres. Essentially, the engineers succeeded in joining the water area with the channel area and in the process eliminated the river's islands and sandbars. Of the roughly 18,000 acres, or 28 square miles, of bars and islands that existed in western Iowa before the navigation project, less than 60 acres remained by the early 1970s.[24] The Iowa Geological Survey figured that the channel area of the Missouri River from Sioux City to the mouth "had been decreased by more than 132,000 acres—over 206 square miles—about a 40% reduction from 1879. Even

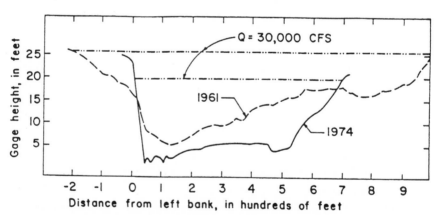

Fig. 11.5. Streambed degradation at Sioux City, Iowa. Degradation of the Missouri's bed began immediately after the closure of Fort Randall and Gavin's Point Dams in the 1950s. (Courtesy of the Iowa Geological Survey)

more striking is that over 103,000 acres—161 square miles—of water area have been lost, over 57% of the 1879 water area."[25]

The decrease in the size of the water and channel areas meant a corresponding increase in accreted land. The former islands, sandbars, side channels, and shallow sloughs became firmly attached to the new bank line. Accreted land represented a boon to valley farmers, who quickly laid claim to the new terrain. With the river restricted inside rock-lined pile dikes, or wing dams, and revetments, the Dakota dams holding back high flows, and the channel digging itself ever deeper into bedrock north of the Platte River confluence, valley farmers, for the first time in history, planted crops to the water's edge.

Before crops could be sown within the river corridor, the vegetation growing along the accreted acres needed to be cut down. Valley farmers often waited until the winter months to clear the land. By December or January, plant growth had ceased for the year, and the cold, brittle trees and shrubs could be easily snapped in half or knocked down. Farmers used a number of technologies to denude the land, including chain saws, bulldozers, triangular bulldozer blades, and a recent invention, the Crossville Clearing Blade.

Farmers operated chain saws to fell large-diameter trees, and bulldozers uprooted the smaller willows and cottonwoods. Then Russell E. Long of Gray Ridge, Maine, invented the Crossville Clearing Blade and patented the device in September 1953. Within months, farmers employed this tool in the Missouri Valley. The Crossville Clearing Blade was V-shaped and razor sharp, and it had a staggered edge. A bulldozer pushed the blade along only an inch above the surface of the ground, where it sliced through trees up to thirty-six inches in diameter. D. M. Babbitt, who lived in the valley just south of Council Bluffs, owned 600 acres of bottomland that had once been an island before channelization work fixed it to the bank line. Using the Crossville Clearing Blade, Babbitt and his sons removed an average of ten acres of trees and shrubs per day from the former island. In a month of irregular work, the men toppled ninety acres of timber and brush and intended to destroy the rest as soon as possible.[26] In western Iowa, owners of bulldozers hired themselves out to farmers to defoliate land in the river corridor. In winter 1954 a crew of three men, working west of Sloan, laid bare 200 acres of accreted land in just a couple of months. Another bulldozer operator cleared 500 acres for several farmers near Onawa during winter 1955–1956. Once the land had been stripped of foliage, farmers planted crops. Charles Scebold, who lived north of Council Bluffs, plowed his furrows within feet of the Missouri. Farmers along the river from Sioux City to the mouth repeated the actions of men like Scebold and Babbitt.

Studies on clearing operations in Nebraska along the Missouri River between 1955 and 1971 concluded that 50 percent of the forest cover present in 1955 did not exist sixteen years later.[27] This figure contrasted to a rate of destruction of only 5 percent on lands adjacent to unchannelized streams or rivers, where most of the timber had been removed by the stream itself. More forestland may have been cleared in Nebraska because state law permitted valley farmers to acquire the land accreted through channelization. In Iowa, accreted land within the former highwater line of the river belonged to the state. Thus, the state government held forestland in preserves that did not exist on the other side of the Missouri. Nonetheless, the amount of privately owned forestland cut down in Iowa probably equaled the volume removed by farmers in Nebraska. The rate of clearing accelerated after 1971, spurred on by a jump in land values and a rise in commodity prices as the Soviets purchased vast stores of American grain.[28] Approximately 80 percent of privately owned forestland in western Iowa had been destroyed by the 1980s.[29] Neil Heiser of the Woodbury County Conservation Board admitted that he "did not know of a single 40-acre or more patch of native bottom timber left on private land anywhere along the Iowa side of the Missouri between Sioux City and Omaha."[30] The forests of bur oak, ash, elm, and cottonwood located in the erosion zone and meander belt had fallen in only thirty years.

Industry moved into the river corridor after 1955. Factories, coal-burning power plants, docks, and grain elevators sprang up along the Missouri from Sioux City south. The army engineers encouraged this industrial expansion. In January 1955 Gen. William Potter, head of the Missouri River Division, proclaimed to the *Omaha World Herald* that the dams and channelization structures made industrial development possible in the bottomlands. The general believed the relatively sediment-free river could supply the water to cool machine tools used in the manufacturing process. The navigation channel could provide a low-cost route for shipment of raw materials and finished products to and from the new industrial sites.[31]

Later in 1955 Potter told a group of Omaha business representatives that the federal projects in the Missouri Valley had laid the groundwork for industrial expansion along the river's banks, but valley residents had to take the initiative themselves to exploit these opportunities.[32] Business interests in Sioux City, Omaha, Council Bluffs, and Kansas City did not need much encouragement to build in the river corridor. The valley floor held comparatively inexpensive land, free water could be readily accessed, industrial sites on flat land needed little preparation for the placement of buildings, and roads could be cheaply and easily graded from any facility to the closest highway.

In the mid-1950s Sioux City businessmen established the Industrial Development Expansion Association. As its first order of business, the association acquired sixty-five acres of bottomland on the west side of Sioux City, just below the Loess Hills and slightly east of the mouth of the Big Sioux River. In 1958 the association employed bulldozers to remove trees and brush from the area, leveled the land, and filled ponds and marshland with sand and gravel dredged from the Missouri. By the late 1970s and early 1980s this former channel area contained a Zenith Electronics plant, a Holiday Inn, and numerous factories, retail stores, and restaurants. Sioux City developers named the complex the TriView Industrial Park (Fig. 11.6).

In late 1959 Sioux City, with the backing of the business community, annexed a 4.4-square-mile section of river bottomland south of town. Within twenty years this area housed gas stations, trucking firms, the Big Soo Barge Terminal, an extensive blue jeans manufacturing plant, and a Swift Packing Company hog-processing plant. The same year the Iowa Public Service Company announced that it would build a $25 million coal-burning power plant on the river west of Salix, a facility that expanded over the years and became known as the Port Neal Industrial Area. In 1980 the Port Neal complex operated four electrical generating plants, a massive Archer Daniel Midlands grain elevator, and the largest nitrate plant in Iowa, owned by Terra Chemical Incorporated.[33] All the way down the valley, the story repeated itself. Industries pushed into the river corridor.[34]

Industrial growth in the corridor occurred concurrently with and was facilitated by the construction of roads, especially Interstate 29 and a network of county highways. President Dwight D. Eisenhower's Interstate Highway Program authorized the construction of Interstate 29 from Kansas City north to the U.S.–Canadian border, skirting the Missouri River as far as Sioux City. Work on the section in Iowa began in 1958 and progressed steadily until final completion in 1973. Interstate 29 did

Fig. 11.6. The site of the TriView Industrial Park at Sioux City, Iowa. The top photograph shows the valley floor in 1939 just east of the mouth of the Big Sioux River. The bottom photograph shows the same location over fifty years later. (Top photograph by Robert Joseph Schneiders; bottom photograph by author)

not wind through the Loess Hills or along the foothills as had roads constructed in the late nineteenth and early twentieth centuries. Instead, it stretched along the lowlands, in close proximity to the Missouri. In several spots the interstate approaches the river to within one-half mile, and just south of Sioux City it comes within fifty feet of the waterline. Before construction of Fort Randall Dam and the channelization project, constructing roads this close to the river would have been inconceivable.

Before the 1950s the few roads that led to the Missouri required the frequent expenditure of funds for maintenance because the river periodically inundated the routes. If the river did not actually wash out a road, the high water table, poor drainage, and heavy spring and summer rains turned the lanes into muddy bogs. The engineering projects allowed county governments to construct hard-surface highways and gravel roads to the stream's banks.[35] The ever-expanding road network stimulated the construction of boat ramps up and down the Missouri. In the Sioux City area, government agencies constructed four boat ramps. The roads and ramps afforded unprecedented access to the river corridor to residents of the valley and beyond. Recreational boaters became a common sight on the river during the summer months.

As the river became narrower and deeper, V-bottom sport boats with powerful inboard motors replaced the traditional Missouri River flat-bottom johnboats and their small outboard motors. The number of private sport boats on the Missouri increased spectacularly in the 1950s, 1960s, and 1970s. In 1954, for example, the Sioux City Boat Club had eight members and eight boats. Three years later, the club claimed eighty-six members with 100 boats. And the numbers kept going up. By the late 1970s hundreds upon hundreds of boats raced up and down the river in the vicinity of Sioux City. Some of these craft were colossal cruisers with 500-horsepower engines. Along with the boats emerged a supporting system of harbors, gas stations, convenience stores, and restaurants.[36]

Agricultural and industrial growth transformed the former active erosion zone and meander belt areas. During the early twentieth century the active erosion zone held 44,915 acres (70.1 square miles) from Sioux City to the Iowa-Missouri border. In 1980 the Corps of Engineers estimated that 90 percent of this area had been converted from fish and wildlife habitat to crops, industries, roads, and residences. Only 4,491 acres (7.1 square miles) of the zone remained undeveloped.[37] Changes in the meander belt mirrored events in the active erosion zone. By 1980 nearly 100 percent of the meander-belt land area had been remade to serve human purposes. In western Iowa this sector decreased by 31,864 acres (49.7 square miles).

Federal officials concluded that since the navigation project's inception in the late nineteenth century, nearly 500,000 acres of the water area, channel area, and active erosion zone from Sioux City south had been cleared, cropped, paved, or covered with buildings. An additional 242,000 acres in the meander belt had been eliminated as habitat.[38] The amount of land affected by the navigation project reached astronomical proportions. As a result of the project and its consequences, 1,150 square miles of the river valley had been altered.

Replacement of the richest continuous stretch of species habitat in the Midwest with an urban-industrial-agricultural complex benefited numerous valley residents. Secure roads, a more extensive highway network, accreted farm land, the decreased threat of floods, low-cost land for industrial sites, water for cooling power plants and machine tools, and the presence of a barge channel profited farmers and businessmen. Yet the same environmental changes that profited some caused harm to others, including the fish and wildlife species that had lived in the corridor.

By the 1980s the only regions in the river corridor where fish and wildlife could find nesting and feeding sites existed in the shrunken water area and along narrow strips of accreted former channel not yet cleared of vegetation for agricultural production or industrial use. According to data provided by the Corps of Engineers, the U.S. Fish and Wildlife Service, and the Iowa Geological Survey, a mere thirty-seven square miles of the former corridor remained available as habitat in western Iowa. This amount represented a decrease of 150 square miles since 1950.[39] Even more significant, the last thirty-seven square miles of habitat did not remotely resemble what had existed there before the navigation project and dams.

The channelized water area of the Missouri River no longer possessed the diversity of depths and current velocities of the previous water area. The U.S. Fish and Wildlife Service claimed, "In place of a wide range of aquatic niches, there now exists a swift-flowing channelized river containing hostile conditions for most organisms. . . . This study indicated that no fish species prefers, or is even commonly found, in the main channel."[40] The water flowed inordinately fast, and fish expended too much energy fighting the current. The new aquatic environment made life tough, if not impossible, for most of the river's original fish species.

The loss of shallow, slow-moving water, connected oxbow lakes, marshes, and sand and gravel bars eliminated the spawning sites used by the majority of fish. The only areas conducive to spawning existed behind the stone wing dams, where the water slowed enough for fish to lay their eggs. But even there, few species could survive, let alone spawn. In place of the dissimilar species that once thrived in the Missouri, three species reigned supreme in the river by 1980: the carp, the buffalo fish, and the channel catfish. The remainder of the fish population consisted of declining numbers of shovelnose sturgeon, gar, pike, flathead catfish, paddlefish, blue catfish, and the occasional freak exotic. Big blue catfish and paddlefish became relics of the past. An almost complete absence of snags meant blue catfish could not find nests and feeding lies.[41] Paddlefish numbers declined precipitously because of the elimination of sand and gravel bars and the closure of the dams, which blocked the fish from visiting their prehistoric spawning grounds. Gavin's Point Dam and reservoir sharply curtailed the annual run to the spawning beds at the mouth of the Niobrara River. State fisheries biologists maintained the paddlefish population through artificial propagation at hatcheries.[42] As the river changed, exotic fishes entered the new environment. People reported catching brown trout, rainbow trout, chinook salmon, and even piranhas in the Missouri near Sioux City. These species could not have survived a single day in the former silt-laden stream. Officials with the Missouri Department of Conservation confirmed, "These changes [in the fish population] have paralleled the physical changes in the river and, while proof of a cause and effect relationship is lacking, the circumstantial evidence of a direct relationship between decreased diversity in the habitat and decreased diversity in the fish population is very strong."[43]

Reptiles such as snakes, frogs, and turtles suffered. Elimination of beaches, sandbars, and marshy bogs expelled these creatures from the corridor. The variety of birds and their numbers dipped. Obliteration of sandbars kept geese and ducks from resting along the river during their migrations. A dispersed flyway consisting of artificial impoundments and managed refuges replaced the primordial Missouri River flyway. Migratory waterfowl flew in fragmentary patterns across the Great Plains and over the states of North Dakota, South Dakota, Nebraska, and Iowa. Geese and ducks became wholly dependent on the system of refuges established in the upper Midwest by the U.S. Fish and Wild-life Service and by state conservation departments. These refuges concentrated the birds, made the populations more susceptible to the spread of disease, and presented hunters and natural predators with easy targets.[44]

Birds, such as the piping plover and least tern, lost habitat as regulated water releases curtailed the scouring of bars and sand flats and allowed for plant growth that eliminated potential nesting locations. To add to the birds' hardships, the Corps of Engineers let large amounts of water out of the dams at the same time the birds usually nested in the spring, drowning eggs and chicks. Increased human activity along the river disturbed least tern and piping plover nests; people fished and sunbathed on the same beaches and bars the birds needed to survive.[45]

The near-total removal of timber, brush, and native grasses from the active erosion zone and meander belt precipitated a sharp decrease in a wide array of terrestrial species. Raccoon, weasel, deer, rabbit, skunk, beaver, squirrel, fox, coyote, mink, and bobcat populations plummeted. Fox squirrel numbers declined with the destruction of the timber tracts. A few species actually benefited from the changes. As corn and soybeans replaced the native cover, the quantity of mourning doves, common fieldmice, and Norway rats increased.[46]

The Corps' projects disrupted the plant-succession process. The river no longer formed new plant communities or overturned older, stable communities, a process indispensable for biodiversity. By 1980 all terrestrial habitat in the corridor approached the climax forest stage; mature forests favored only the few species adapted to it.[47] Thus, even the land not converted to human purposes rendered limited assistance to fish and wildlife.

Any remaining habitat, however marginal in quality, faced extensive human interference. High-powered motorboats tore through the navigation channel, their operators oblivious of the effects of the churning waves, leaking oil, gas fumes, and noise on fish, birds, and animals. Power plants pumped water from the river and put it back much warmer and more deadly to creatures. Farmers, in huge tractors, plowed and planted to within feet of the Missouri, regularly spraying gallons of chemicals on the land to boost crop yields. Herbicides, pesticides, and fungicides found their way into the river since little or no vegetation grew on the river's edge to halt the flow of pollutants. People in cars came close to habitats and upset mating, nesting, or feeding species. The human advance into the river corridor after 1955 presented species with so many challenges that the majority of them quickly perished in the face of the onslaught.

The loss of fish and wildlife species in turn affected people, especially commercial fishers, sport fishers, and hunters. Commenting on the effect of the barge channel on the annual commercial harvest of fish from the river in Missouri, John L. Funk and John W. Robinson of the Missouri Department of Conservation acknowledged, "Since 1945 the trend of the annual commercial catch has been generally downward from 1,724,000 lb in 1947 to 342,000 lb in 1963, a decline of 80%. These are extremes, but they mark the trend of the catch. Many factors may affect the commercial catch in a body of water, but the one steady, consistent change in the Missouri River has been the reduction and deterioration of fish habitat resulting from the navigation and stabilization project."[48] The two officials also said that the number of commercial fishers decreased from 771 in 1945 to 404 in 1970.[49]

Only small numbers of sport fishers used the channelized Missouri, and those who did often caught rough fish such as buffalo and carp. Steve Jauron of the Iowa Department of Natural Resources remarked, "There's very few people fishing the Missouri River. It's not a very good fishery. It's just a canal. . . . The channel is for navigation. It's not for fish. It's not for ducks."[50] As early as 1954 the hunters along the Missouri in western Iowa noticed declines in the number of ducks and geese using the flyway. In 1955 Gerald Jauron (Steve's father) noted, "The hunting on the Missouri River from Sioux City to Omaha has been the worst in years. And it'll get worse. . . . There's not a reserve in this stretch; not a point where birds can congregate in breaking their flight. So what happens? The birds move straight through."[51] And the birds never returned. In the 1970s scientists noted that an estimated 400,000 ducks and geese used the unchannelized river reach between Ponca, Nebraska, and Yankton as a food source or resting site, but none used the channelized river below Sioux City.[52] The navigation project ended the river's role as a hunting ground for ducks and geese and reduced its value as a commercial and sport fishery.

Since the nineteenth century, the oxbow lakes scattered across the river valley had served urban and rural residents as places of recreation. People went to the lakes to fish, swim, sunbathe, hunt, and boat.[53] The most popular lakes in southeast South Dakota, eastern Nebraska, and western Iowa included McCook in Union County, South Dakota (ten miles northwest of Sioux City), Crystal (situated near the city limits of South Sioux City), Brown's (just ten miles south of Sioux City), Blue (due west of Onawa), and Manawa (a couple of miles south of Council Bluffs). The popularity of these lakes resulted from their proximity to urban centers, which afforded city dwellers the chance to visit their waters easily. Lesser known and more remote oxbow lakes in western Iowa included Round, Badger, Modale Flats, Horseshoe, Folsom, Noble's, New, and Forney's.[54] Beginning in 1954 and 1955 water levels dropped in these oxbow lakes; the dip in lake levels generated a great deal of public attention. Sportsmen's clubs, conservation groups, lakeside property owners, and state game and parks departments wanted to prevent the loss of this natural resource.[55] But no one knew the reason for the low water; hence, no one had a viable means of saving the oxbows. Erv Krogh of the Nebraska Izaak Walton League assumed the lakes suffered from excessive evaporation rates. Residents of the resort community of McCook Lake speculated that the great flood of 1952 had filled their lake with silt and clogged the underground springs that maintained water levels. Others believed that below-average precipitation since 1953 had affected the lakes.[56]

On 22 September 1955 more than 500 people packed the small Izaak Walton League clubhouse at Brown's Lake to discuss the situation. Representatives from the Iowa Conservation Commission, the Corps of Engineers, the Iowa legislature, and the U.S. Congress attended the meeting. A. B. Kidd, representing the army engineers, hinted that the upstream dams on the Missouri might be the cause for the drop in lake levels. He said that before the dams, the Missouri had flooded the valley on a regular basis, and these floods poured water into the lakes, raising their levels. Since floods had become a thing of the past, the lakes did not receive the water needed to sustain their levels.[57] Later in 1955 staff writer George Mills of the *Des Moines Register* proposed another cause for the deterioration of the oxbows. He pointed out that "stabilizing the channel . . . is likely to speed up the flow of water. That means the river bed will be lowered over the years by water action. As a result, instead of water seeping from the river into these lakes, the reverse will be true. The combination of no floods and loss through seepage is likely to shorten the lives of these lakes."[58] Mills correctly identified the cause as degradation.

To prevent the total loss of the oxbows, valley residents devised ingenious and expensive methods to raise their levels.[59] At McCook Lake, the South Dakota Game, Fish, and Parks Department and the Corps of Engineers dredged the oxbow at a cost of $300,000.[60] But this operation did not guarantee against future reductions in water volume. The Izaak Walton League spent $6,800 to dig a well and build a pump to supply water to Crystal Lake.[61] When the pump failed to save the dying lake, the league proposed to the Corps that it finance a $1 million restoration project. The Corps turned down this request.[62] The Iowa Conservation Commission devised an innovative method to restore Lake Manawa by allocating $270,000 to divert the water of nearby Mosquito Creek into the lake.[63]

In the 1950s and 1960s no one had the means or the money to restore water to Brown's and Blue Lakes. But in the 1970s officials sent cooling water from the Iowa Public Service power plant at Port Neal into Brown's Lake and pumped water into Blue Lake from a series of wells. Those oxbow lakes not receiving water through artificial means shrank or completely dried up as degradation progressed in the 1980s.[64] The dams and channelization structures forced valley residents to relinquish an important recreational resource. Nevertheless, the formation of new oxbow lakes along the channelized river gave them hope that they could replace this loss.

While the Corps built the navigation channel, it created channelized oxbow lakes. These formed in much the same manner as the natural oxbow lakes, except that the engineers, not the river, created the cutoff. Members of state conservation commissions, state and local governments, county conservation boards, sporting clubs, and the Corps of Engineers believed these channelized oxbows would become playgrounds for residents of the Missouri Valley and the nation. Cartoonist Ding Darling and conservationist Gerald Jauron believed the channelized oxbows could be developed either into a national park or into one of the most valuable recreational assets in the Midwest. The two men reasoned that the series of new lakes would make up for a major deficiency in parks and outdoor recreation facilities between the Appalachians and the Rocky Mountains.[65]

Jauron proposed the construction of boat ramps, picnic areas, and beaches at twenty-one channelized oxbows in western Iowa, including Snyder Bend, Winnebago Bend, Tieville Bend, Middle Decatur Bend, Wilson Island, Nottleman Island, and State Line Island. Jauron predicted that Snyder Bend and Winnebago Bend, fifteen miles south of Sioux City, would achieve the status of true recreational meccas, drawing visitors from throughout the United States. Both oxbows offered white sand beaches, high sand dune formations, deep blue water, and tall groves of trees.[66] But Darling and Jauron's vision for the channelized oxbows was never fulfilled: degradation drained the water from the lakes. By the mid-1980s, weeds and trees grew where water once had gleamed.[67]

Degradation contributed to other problems. Lowering of the streambed threatened the structural integrity of bridges that crossed the river at Yankton, Sioux City, Decatur, and Blair as the river tore away the bed material that had provided support to the spans.[68] Degradation also caused the Missouri's tributaries to experience "stream cutting," a tributary stream's erosive action to lower its elevation to meet the Missouri River. Streamcutting began at the mouth of rivers and creeks and progressed backward, or upstream. As the tributaries cut into their beds to join the Missouri, their slope increased. A steeper slope led to higher current velocities and more erosion along the tributaries. The highly erodible alluvium present in the Missouri Valley worsened the effects of stream cutting, particularly in the Loess Hills, which extend along the entire western Iowa border and consist of windborne silt, extending seventy feet down in some places. Accordingly, creeks running through the hills toward the Missouri gouged deep ravines before hitting bedrock. Farmers and government agencies further exacerbated the effects of stream cutting by straightening the Missouri's feeder streams to increase their tillable acreage.

The effects of stream cutting appeared everywhere in western Iowa. In Pottawattamie County, the banks of several Missouri tributaries descended only a few feet to the water's edge in the 1950s; by 1980 these same streams had eroded thirty-five- to forty-foot-deep chasms. In other western Iowa counties, creek banks that fell six feet in the 1950s dropped twenty-five feet or more by the early 1980s. The Boyer River, which drains into the Missouri near Loveland, Iowa, possessed a ten-foot-deep, thirty-eight-foot-wide channel area in 1947; in 1982 the tributary flowed through a twenty-two-foot-deep canyon with a 100- to 150-foot width.[69]

A government study concluded that stream cutting damaged or imperiled 931 bridges in thirteen western Iowa counties. Residents of Woodbury County faced the most acute threat; one-third of its 597 bridges had been damaged by excessive erosion. The problem went beyond western Iowa. Residents in southeast South Dakota and eastern Nebraska faced similar troubles with their infrastructure. The navigation project clearly resulted in unforeseen financial and environmental repercussions for people living in the Missouri Valley.[70]

Moreover, degradation led to a lowering of the water table. Wildlife biologist Robert Dolan of the Iowa Department of Natural Resources said that for every foot the Missouri lowered itself, the adjacent water table fell a foot.[71] Degradation thus forced hundreds of farmers to deepen their wells. And the lower water table weakened buildings erected along the valley floor. A high water table saturated the soil, sands, and gravels that upheld these structures; once water drained from these subsurface deposits, buildings slumped and shifted. In Elk Point, South Dakota, fissures ripped through the high school and the Catholic church as the buildings settled.[72] Degradation also compelled the operators of power plants and industrial facilities repeatedly to extend their inlet pipes to the receding water line (Fig. 11.7).

The flooding along the Missouri River main stem did not end after completion of the five Pick-Sloan Plan dams, although Gen. Lewis Pick had asserted in the 1950s that his engineers would end it in the valley

Fig. 11.7. The effects of degradation in Monona County, Iowa. Degradation required the repeated extension of boat ramps to the receding river and its adjacent oxbow lakes. (Photograph by author, 1996)

forever. High flows south of Sioux City and especially below Kansas City persisted for a number of reasons, including destruction of wetlands, possible changes in climate attributable to global warming, and the extension of paved areas within the Missouri River watershed. A reduction in the Missouri's carrying capacity and the existence of uncontrolled tributaries contributed more than anything else to the continuance of flooding along the main stem. Ironically, the navigation project's effect on the river's carrying capacity negated some of the flood protection provided by the Dakota dams. Confinement of the Missouri between pile dikes and revetments lowered the stream's ability to transport high flows; consequently, it took less water for the Missouri to overtop its banks. In the 1920s, before channelization work at Waverly, Missouri, the river carried 150,000 cfs without flooding. But after completion of the navigation project through central Missouri, the river flooded at Waverly in 1931, 1935, 1941, 1942, 1943, 1944, 1945, 1947, 1948, 1949, 1950, 1951, and 1952 at 150,000 cfs.[73] Charles B. Belt Jr. of the Department of Earth and Atmospheric Sciences concluded, "This [navigation] project . . . has greatly reduced the channel area and given the river less space to spread out in times of high flow. . . . A water volume of 618,000 cubic feet per second raised the river at Hermann [Missouri] to a gauge height of 33.3 feet in July 1951 at the peak of flooding there. . . . a volume of only about 500,000 cubic feet per second produced a higher gauge reading of 33.7 feet in an April 1973 flood."[74]

Tributary streams contributed to the perpetuation of flooding along the main stem. Some of the larger undammed tributaries included the James, Big Sioux, Little Sioux, Boyer, Nishnabotna, Platte (in Missouri), Grand, and Gasconade. Deep snows and heavy rains in their watersheds pushed the Missouri out of its banks repeatedly after the completion of the Dakota dams. To add to the problems, once the channelized Missouri overtopped its banks, the accelerated current took a heavy toll on the increased number of roads and buildings in the valley. Floods occurred along the main stem in 1960, 1971, 1973, 1984, 1993, and 1995.[75]

By the 1980s everyone in the valley, including the Corps of Engineers, admitted that the 8,300 training structures (rock-lined pile dikes and revetments) and the six earthen dams had failed to achieve their primary purpose, the establishment of barge traffic. Barges stayed away from the river. From 1935, the first year of navigation below Kansas City, to 1951 over 90 percent of the traffic hauled on the Missouri consisted of sand, gravel, clay, stone, and building materials for the navigation channel itself.[76] In 1951 the Corps, providing tonnage estimates to Congress once again to justify the cost-effectiveness of the navigation project, predicted that the Missouri would carry an average annual commercial tonnage of 5 million tons by 1980. In 1960 operators hauled 1.4 million tons of cargo. In 1970 barge companies shipped 2.4 million tons. In 1979 the Missouri River carried a record 3.2 million tons of material, but this still fell short of the projected 5 million tons. In comparison, by the late 1970s and early 1980s, the Mississippi annually transported 300 million tons of cargo. The Missouri hauled less than 1 percent of the barge traffic moving in the United States. Even more astonishing, the river reach between Omaha and Sioux City conveyed only 15 percent of this minuscule amount. A study completed by the Mid-America Regional Council concluded that 90 percent of the cargo to and from Kansas City and its surrounding region went over the rails; most of the remaining 10 percent went by semitrailer truck.[77] Even this small amount of barge traffic declined as a result of floods and drought in the 1980s. By 1985 only twelve people worked in Kansas City, Missouri, in positions directly related to Missouri River navigation.[78] The era of prosperity that was to follow the commencement of barge service on the river, and promised by river boosters since the 1880s, never arrived in Kansas City or the upper Midwest.

The costs of development for residents of the Dakotas were also high. Over .5 million acres of the most fertile land in North and South Dakota were inundated to provide storage space for the reservoirs, a loss that negated the gains in agricultural land south of Sioux City. Furthermore, South Dakota residents were able to irrigate only 1 percent of the land area originally planned for irrigation as part of the Pick-Sloan Plan. The Missouri River did not have enough water to maintain a navigation channel and to supply water to parched regions.

Only a few years after finishing the navigation channel, the Corps of Engineers, the U.S. Fish and Wildlife Service, and several county conservation boards and state natural resources departments tried to reverse some of the negative environmental effects of the channelization project. More specifically, these institutions worked to restore aquatic and terrestrial habitat in the modified river corridor.

In the early 1980s army engineers and government biologists believed notched dikes would foster a healthier, more diverse fish population in the channelized river. The notch dike had an added advantage: its construction would not require any dismantling of the navigation channel. Barges would still be able to use the river. The needs of fish would in no way impinge upon the demands of society. For many people, the notch dike represented an excellent compromise of interests. Fish and wildlife could coexist with people in a reengineered environment. To form a notched dike, the engineers punched a hole in the center of a rock-lined pile dike. A portion of the river's flow moved through the opening and carried away the sand that previously had accumulated on the downstream side of the structure, eventually scouring a calm-water area hospitable to fish. The dikes achieved only marginal success. A number of factors limited their effectiveness, including high flows that over-topped the dikes, low flows that altogether bypassed the openings, and the absence of any alternative habitat for fish to retreat to when hostile conditions prevailed behind the structures. The engineers could have torn a larger breach in each dike to increase its chances for success, but they chose not to. The Corps feared that large notches would lead to excessive downstream bank erosion and cause a detrimental realignment of the barge channel. By the 1990s the army engineers discontinued use of the notched dike.

In the early 1990s Larry Hesse, a biologist for the Nebraska Game and Parks Commission, proposed that the Corps allow communities along the Missouri to dump their residential yard waste into the stream. Grass clippings, brush, and tree branches would add desperately needed organic matter to the river, which in turn would increase the variety and distribution of insects eaten by fish. Hesse wanted to restore the food chain disrupted by the upstream dams and channelization structures, but this plan encountered immediate opposition. Several biologists feared that the yard waste contained too many chemicals. The discarded foliage might harm the fish population rather than help it. Some of the stiffest resistance came from the operators of coal-burning power plants who complained that the added debris would clog their water-intake pipes. Instead of removing flotsam from the pipes once a year, managers worried that they might have to clear the pipes two or three times a year or every month. Members of boat clubs grumbled that the floating vegetation would make the river less user-friendly. Drifting tree branches or shrubbery might keep boaters off the water, inflict damage to boats and motors, or injure skiers. Hesse's proposal was scuttled.

When farmers, businesspersons, and homeowners bulldozed the river corridor's timber and underbrush, they exposed all kinds of wildlife to the vagaries of the weather. During December, January, and February creatures in the valley, largely left out in the open after the harvest of the corn and soybean crop, had to contend with deadly northwest winds, subzero temperatures, and blowing snow. Lacking food or cover, birds and animals froze to death. County conservation boards wanted to lower winter mortality by furnishing wildlife with shelter and feed. Toward that end, county governments in western Iowa planted trees and brush on small parcels of public land, which formed life-saving windbreaks, aiding deer, rabbits, ring-necked pheasants, coyotes, and songbirds. The windbreak refuges presented problems, however. Because the small preserves existed on isolated acres surrounded by cultivated land, any creatures inhabiting the areas faced higher incidences of predation, disease, and human interference.

In the 1990s, but especially after the flood of 1993, biologists and environmentalists, including members of the Audubon Society, Sierra Club, and American Rivers, began to push for the restoration of former channel areas within the river corridor since allowing water to flow through the natural channel would benefit both people and wildlife. Most important, these projects would not impair the barge channel. Allowing the river to spread itself out would lower the crest of any future flood, a major concern among valley residents below the mouth of the Platte River. The new habitat would be a boon to hunters and fishers and to the state governments that sold them licenses. Fish would be able to swim in calm and fast water and occupy a diversity of depths, factors necessary to maintain a disparate fish population. Terrestrial species would have new nesting and feeding sites. In order to restore a former channel area, the army engineers first knocked down a pile dike revetment and then redirected a portion of the river's flow into the natural channel. In western Iowa and eastern Nebraska, they restored the channel areas at Hamburg Bend, Louisville Bend, and the Boyer Chute and planned to restore the channel at Blackbird Bend, Tieville Bend, Upper Decatur Bend, Middle Decatur Bend, Tobacco Island, Kansas Bend, Langdon Bend, and Rush Bottom Bend. The effectiveness of this method has yet to be proven, but the results are likely to be positive.

But channel restoration did not offer the catchall solution to habitat loss and reductions in species diversity. Above the mouth of the Platte River, the engineers and biologists had to address the problem of degradation. Since the navigation channel flowed from five to eight-and-one-half feet below the natural channel, water would not always move through the restored channels. For extended periods of time each year, fish, ducks, geese, and furbearers would be without water. The only method for alleviating this situation involved pumping water from the barge channel into the restored channels—an expensive process. Moreover, regulated, uniform flows down the navigation channel and into the restored side channels did not provide the variability in discharge rates necessary for habitat and species diversity. Vegetation in the channel area would progress toward the mature forest stage unless floodwaters frequently washed over the lowlands, and restored channels would be discontinuous, providing only detached pockets of habitat. Therefore, the channel areas and their inhabitants would confront the same challenges experienced by their neighbors in the windbreak refuges. Commenting on the difficulties of restoration in the river corridor, Thomas Bruegger of the Monona County Conservation Board lamented, "Just because we're getting mitigation [funds] doesn't mean we're going to solve our problems. . . . It's going to be a long time before we repair the damage."[79]

Ironically, probably the most successful restoration efforts along the Missouri occurred in 1993, without human intervention. The great flood of 1993 tore apart Corps pile dikes and revetments at forty-five locations, enabling the river to flow into former channel areas, dig new holes, drop trees into the thalweg, and rearrange habitats. Of course, regulation of flows by the Dakota dams limited the effects of this upheaval. And the army engineers wanted to hurriedly spend $20 to $30 million to fix the damage to the barge channel. Nonetheless, conservation officers in the state of Missouri noted that the river had increased habitat for a multitude of fish species, including the long-abdicated king of the Missouri— the blue catfish.

While efforts at restoration moved forward under a cloud of uncertainty, the Corps of Engineers had to contend with additional problems of a political nature. By the 1980s and early 1990s individuals and interests began to question the Corps' day-to-day management of the river. At times, private citizens bombarded the engineers at the Missouri River Division's Reservoir Control Center with demands to alter the release rates of the Dakota dams in order to meet particular, immediate contingencies. Barge company executives, for example, asked the engineers to increase discharge rates to float their barges. Marina operators sought higher releases for boaters during summer holidays. Homeowners who built next to the river wanted the engineers to hold back water to protect their property. Or when thunderstorms dumped inches of rain over central Missouri, farmers there requested that the engineers cut the river's volume to allow their fields to drain. The engineers tried their best to accommodate these requests, turning the reservoir plumbing on and off and yo-yoing water levels up and down. But on a river as long as the Missouri, the engineers found it difficult, if not impossible, to meet all the demands placed upon them and the river. When certain vocal interests failed to have their demands met, they accused the Corps of mismanaging the Missouri.

Discontent of another sort surfaced in the upper valley in the 1980s. In 1981 Gov. Bill Janklow of South Dakota signed an agreement with Energy Transportation Systems Incorporated (ETSI) to sell 54,300 acre-feet of Missouri River water for a coal-slurry pipeline. The water for the slurry would be pumped out of Lake Oahe to Wyoming, where it would be mixed with coal. From there, the slurry would be sent to power plants in Oklahoma and Arkansas. South Dakota would make approximately $1.4 billion over the fifty-year life of the project. Even though the South Dakotans and ETSI wanted to divert only 1/1070 of the Missouri's annual flow, downstream interests vehemently opposed the project. Iowa, Nebraska, Kansas, and Missouri representatives objected to ETSI (the name given the entire project) because its implementation would supposedly set a dangerous precedent: South Dakota would gain access to the Missouri River's water. ETSI did not immediately threaten downstream flows, but future, larger diversion projects might compromise the navigation channel, deplete drinking-water supplies, and harm fish and wildlife habitat.

To strengthen their position in the dispute, the Dakotans aligned themselves with the Bureau of Reclamation and the controversial Secretary of the Interior James Watt. In 1982 Watt granted a permit to South Dakota to take the water from Oahe to sell to ETSI. The lower basin states, led by Missouri, then sued to block the sale. After years of litigation and an eventual hearing before the Supreme Court, the lower basin succeeded in killing South Dakota's development plan. The Supreme Court ruled that jurisdiction over the Missouri River reservoirs rested with the Corps of Engineers and indirectly with their lower valley supporters. The lower valley again laid claim to the Missouri River, as it had done since the first decade of the twentieth century. After being stymied by lower basin interests, Bill Janklow expressed the sentiments of most

South Dakotans: "For the first time in my life, I honestly don't understand the selfishness and greed that comes from all sorts of people." He later added, "We're [the lower valley's] water tower, and that's all we are. When they're short of water, they want to drain us. And when they have too much water, they want to hold it back and fill up the tower."[80]

With ETSI dead, lower valley government representatives, including Missouri Attorney General John Ashcroft and Sen. Jack Danforth, believed they had finally, irreversibly, put the South Dakotans in their proper place. Then in 1986 a drought began across the northern Great Plains, and conditions worsened in 1987 and 1988. The Dakota reservoirs dropped to levels not seen since the engineers first built the dams in the 1950s and 1960s. The drought devastated the fisheries program on the five Dakota reservoirs. Walleye and northern pike (the two most popular sport fish) no longer found the habitat necessary for survival. To protect their fishery and the $67 million tourist industry that depended on it each year, the South Dakotans, led by Sen. Tom Daschle, and their neighbors to the north pressured the Corps of Engineers to revise its master manual, which determined the annual discharge sequence at the reservoirs. South Dakota wanted more water in the reservoirs to protect the fish spawn. In 1989 the Missouri River Division agreed to revise the master manual, but the lower basin, again led by Missouri's representatives, opposed revision. Danforth and his cohorts wanted the army engineers to drain the reservoirs, as they had always done, to support a barge industry that added a meager $14 million a year to the lower valley's economy. Despite lower valley opposition, the Corps rewrote the master manual.

In 1994 the army engineers publicly disclosed the contents of the revised manual, which tried to meet the demands of all interests. The Corps proposed releasing significant volumes of water in the spring months. These regulated high flows would imitate the former spring and summer rises, aid the fish spawn in the lower river, and fill the Missouri with needed nutrients. This change represented a concession to environmental interests. The engineers would then decrease release rates in summer and fall, keeping the Dakota reservoirs high for recreational users. The plan meant more water in the Dakota reservoirs and less in the navigation channel. The engineers wanted to shorten the navigation season by one to two months each year, an aspect of the proposal that pleased the South Dakotans.

The revised master manual drew immediate and concentrated fire from residents living in the lower valley. Valley farmers worried about the high releases each spring. A heavy thunderstorm over the lower valley, in concert with the Corps' proposed spring rise, might send the Missouri out of its banks and onto their fields. Moreover, the struggling barge industry would be hurt by the shorter navigation season. Fierce resistance to the new master manual forced the Corps to ditch the plan in 1995 and to return to the drawing board. At this point the South Dakotans wondered whether their demands for water would ever be met.[81]

By 1995 the Missouri River flowed through a land of discontent. Few people expressed satisfaction with the engineered river and its government overseers. This general discord and uneasiness stemmed from one simple, irrefutable truth; the Missouri compelled people to look at themselves and to question their faith in technology, their commitment to progress, and their motives. The river had rendered some of the most sacred American ideals irrelevant. At one time or another, science, technology, expectations for a brighter future, and enlightened self-interest had been pulverized and carried away by the Mighty Mo. The Missouri River confounded people. Yet few individuals entertained any thoughts of simply letting the river go, of taking down the dams and training structures and abandoning the traditional paradigm, even though that seemingly radical alternative possessed many obvious, tangible advantages.

12 | Conclusion

In the early and mid-nineteenth century, the Missouri River and Valley provided an environment conducive to the success of European-American agricultural settlement. American explorers, adventurers, fur traders, miners, military personnel, and agricultural settlers depended on the river and valley for nearly all the necessities of life, including drinking water, food, fuel, building materials, and furs. The Missouri River made its greatest contribution to American settlement as a transportation route, however. Between 1803 and 1880 keelboats and later steamboats carried passengers and manufactured products to the frontier regions and hauled agricultural commodities downstream to eastern U.S. markets.

Steamboat traffic on the Missouri River diminished with the arrival of the railroad in the valley. Railroad tracks reached St. Joseph in 1859, Council Bluffs in 1867, Sioux City in 1868, and Yankton in 1873. Steamboats, with their incessant delays, small cargo-carrying capacities, high insurance rates, and uncomfortable passenger accommodations, could not compete against the faster, more efficient, reliable, and comfortable railroads. As a result, by the early 1880s steamboat operations on the Missouri River came to an end.

The steamboat's demise and the establishment of a railroad monopoly over transportation into and out of the Missouri Valley contributed to a shift in perception among valley residents. Instead of considering the river and its valley as adding to their economic success, valley residents began to view the Missouri as a wasted natural resource, a threat to civilization, and a stream in need of improvement for navigational purposes.

Beginning in the late 1870s and early 1880s, individuals from a number of river towns began to lobby Congress for funds to channelize the river. Steamboat company executives, lawyers, businessmen, and other professionals sought to create competitive carrier rates through the establishment of deep-draft barge traffic on the Missouri, but they confronted a reluctant Congress. Federal officials did not automatically approve of Missouri River channelization. Therefore, local organizations, led by the members of the Kansas City Commercial Club, had to convince federal authorities repeatedly that the river deserved federal dollars and engineering expertise.

In 1890 Congress appropriated money for the first time for the channelization of the Missouri from the mouth to Kansas City and ordered the Corps of Engineers and the Missouri River Commission to supervise construction of the barge channel. The engineers possessed only twelve years of continuous daily stream-flow data for the river. Consequently, they were unsure of how deep or wide to design the navigation channel. Yet the Corps pushed ahead with construction, hoping to learn the proper channel dimensions as work progressed. Engineers employed a system of permeable pile dikes and willow mattresses and stone revetments to concentrate the flow of water, realign the channel's direction, deepen the thalweg, and make the river navigable. After six years the Corps and the commission had improved a mere forty-five miles of river. Congress, disappointed with these results, the rising cost of the channelization structures, the complete lack of any barge traffic on the stream, and the absence of valleywide support for channelization, slashed funding. By 1896 appropriations did not even cover the cost of maintaining the existing pile dikes and revetments. Then in 1902 Congress disbanded the Missouri River Commission. Valley residents and the federal government in effect abandoned the Missouri River.

During the first decade of the twentieth century the Midwest and northern Great Plains experienced a series of wet years, which caused the Missouri repeatedly to flood, refocusing local and federal attention on the river. Thus did the Missouri itself contribute to the formulation and implementation of development plans. Valley residents, however, sought federal assistance to lessen the threat of floods, not to improve the river for navigation. The public favored channelization as a means of hastening the movement of floodwaters through the state of Missouri. The federal government balked at funding flood-control projects, and the local lobbyists failed to garner Washington's cooperation.

Also during the first decade of the twentieth century, the progressive conservationists pushed for the development and sustained use of natural resources, including the nation's rivers. Missouri Valley residents, particularly the Kansas Citians, effectively tied their own goals for the Missouri into the larger progressive conservation movement. As a result of these efforts, Congress authorized the construction of a six-foot navigation channel from Kansas City to the mouth in 1912.

After 1916 work on the navigation channel slowed down, mainly because of erratic and inadequate appropriations from Congress. Then in 1925 a group of Kansas Citians formed the Missouri River Navigation Association, which gained federal cooperation for the renewal of large-scale construction on the channel. The association also convinced Congress to authorize the extension of the barge channel to Sioux City, even though the channel below Kansas City had not yet been opened to traffic. Although Congress concurred with the expansion of the project, the War Department and the Calvin Coolidge and Herbert Hoover administrations did not support the construction of the Upper River Project. These federal authorities wanted to determine whether barge traffic would emerge along the Kansas City–to–mouth reach before channelizing the stream to Sioux City.

Two events in the 1930s had a major effect on the development of the Missouri. In 1929 a dry precipitation cycle began across the plains states. The drought dropped the Missouri to unprecedented levels and convinced Corps officials that the six-foot channel was already obsolete. Again the Missouri River influenced the formulation of development plans. In order to protect the federal investment in the completed pile dikes and revetments, and to ensure the future viability of the navigation channel, the Corps' Kansas City District Office advocated the construction of Fort Peck Dam. President Franklin D. Roosevelt concurred, and Fort Peck's construction began in 1933.

The Great Depression, followed by Roosevelt's efforts to restore the national economy, led to the reversal of federal policy toward the Upper River Project. Beginning in summer 1933 the Roosevelt administration, through the Public Works Administration, directed large appropriations toward the construction of the six-foot channel from Kansas City to Sioux City. The techniques and technologies the Corps of Engineers used reflected the government's desire to employ men.

While the Corps built the navigation channel below Sioux City, South Dakotans organized to promote the construction of dams and hydroelectric facilities along the Missouri River. They failed in their efforts because the army engineers refused to cooperate with them in order to protect the navigation channel and the Corps' lower valley constituency. The Corps itself did not wield arbitrary power over the South Dakotans; rather, its actions reflected the wishes and political power of lower valley residents.

By the early 1940s the six-foot channel from the mouth to Sioux City neared completion, and Fort Peck Dam provided partial regulation of the river's flow volume. In 1940 the first barge arrived at Sioux City, docking at that city's small port facility. River boosters proclaimed the beginning of a new era in water transportation for the region. But the advent of World War II interfered with the completion of the barge channel. The federal government cut funding to all programs not deemed essential to the war effort, including the Missouri River navigation project.

In 1943 a series of floods struck the Missouri Valley and convinced lower valley residents that storage reservoirs in the upper valley, particularly in South Dakota, offered the only means of protecting the navigation channel, their urban centers, and their agricultural lands from high flows. Thus the lower basin states for the first time cooperated with the South Dakotans to push for a federal dam-building plan. In 1944 Congress and the president authorized the Pick-Sloan Plan for Missouri River Development, calling for the construction of five dams along the main stem of the Missouri.

In 1946 construction began on two of the main-stem dams, Fort Randall in southeast South Dakota and Garrison in north-central North Dakota. The Corps did not plan on closing these dams until the early 1950s. In the meantime, the lower valley and the Corps' channelization structures remained vulnerable to the destructive power of high flows. In the late 1940s and early 1950s a series of floods descended the valley. The water carried away an estimated $124 million-worth of channelization structures and made it apparent to everyone that the Corps had moved forward with construction of the navigation channel without a thorough knowledge of the river and its variable flow rates. By mid 1952 Corps officials admitted that the Missouri had reverted to a wild, uncontrolled river over much of the reach south of Sioux City.

The closure of Fort Randall Dam in summer 1952, Garrison Dam in 1953, and Gavin's Point Dam in 1955 noticeably altered the river environment. Specifically, the curtailment of high flows meant the construction of the navigation channel could proceed without the threat of immediate destruction. In the 1950s and 1960s Corps construction techniques differed radically from those employed during the depression years, as the engineers applied technologically intensive methods instead of labor-intensive procedures. The Decatur Bridge diversion operation signaled the height of the Corps' technological prowess during the construction of the barge channel. Dredge boats, pile drivers, bulldozers, and even an upstream dam were used in the diversion operation. With so many tools at its disposal, the Corps completed the navigation channel to Sioux City in the 1970s. Effective regulation of the Missouri still eluded the federal engineers, however.

A number of environmental changes occurred in the Missouri River corridor after 1955, producing mixed results for the people living in the valley. Channelization, in concert with the Dakota dams, allowed farmers to clear land to the river's edge but also contributed to degradation, tributary stream erosion, and a lower water table. Declines in habitat produced a corresponding decrease in the number of fish and wildlife species. Thus, the Corps' projects diminished the value of the Missouri River as a recreational resource for valley residents. Beginning in the 1970s the Corps of Engineers and several other agencies tried to restore fish and wildlife habitat in the Missouri River corridor, projects that did provide habitat for a variety of species. But streambed degradation, predation, human interference, and the relatively small scale of such isolated projects limited their effectiveness. In the 1980s and 1990s South Dakotans made further attempts to develop and manage the Missouri River to their advantage. Yet the lower basin interests, adhering to past precedent, prevented South Dakota from achieving its goals.

The history of Missouri River development provides a number of lessons. First, the success of the Kansas Citians in achieving their objectives over all apparent odds illustrates what local grassroots organizations can accomplish within the institutional system that operates in the United States. A well-organized and highly motivated group of individuals did more than any other organization to develop the Missouri River. Admittedly, the Kansas City Commercial Club cooperated with the Corps of Engineers and other federal officials to channelize and dam the Missouri, but it also organized the people of the valley, publicized the cause of development, and effectively lobbied Congress and the various presidential administrations. The system of dams, reservoirs, and channelization structures that line the river today is largely the result of the Kansas City Commercial Club.

Second, a water elite did not, and does not, exist in the Missouri Valley. The Corps of Engineers and the federal government never arbitrarily directed Missouri River development. Furthermore, the Corps is not the sole entity responsible for the environmental transformation of the lower valley. Granted, the engineers built the pile dikes, revetments, and dams; but the majority of farmers and businessmen living in the lower valley wanted the federal government to build those structures. And after the completion of the navigation channel and upstream dams, countless individuals and organizations cleared land in the river corridor for crop production, roads, industry, boat ramps, harbors, and homes. Thus, the Corps of Engineers and their public supporters were responsible for the environmental transformation of the Missouri River and the problems resulting from it.

Third, the costs of Missouri River development in monetary and environmental terms may have been greater than its benefits. Reservoirs in Montana and the Dakotas offer limited flood protection to the lower valley while requiring the permanent inundation of the upper valley. Channelization structures provided lower valley farmers with more land but contributed to a host of other problems, including degradation, habitat loss, and a channel that flows too fast for upstream barge traffic. Valley residents and the general public might have been better off if the Missouri River had been left alone.

Fourth, self-interested individuals labored for over 100 years to channelize and dam the Missouri River, believing that such projects would directly or indirectly profit them and the public. Self-interest, as represented in the Kansas City Commercial Club, Congress, and the Corps of Engineers, facilitated the radical transformation of the Missouri River environment. Many people did benefit from that transformation, but many others did not. The Indians of the Dakotas forfeited most of the land for the Pick-Sloan reservoirs; lower valley hunters, bird watchers, commercial fishers, and sport fishers lost a vast recreational resource; and city and county governments in the lower valley had to contend with an infrastructure damaged by degradation and continuing floods. Self-interest led to bitter political conflicts between the lower basin and South Dakota, crippled attempts at habitat restoration, and forced the Corps of Engineers to micromanage a huge hydraulic system. By the mid-1990s people began seriously to doubt the efficacy of institutionalized self-interest, but no one had an alternative to it as a means of relating to the Missouri River. No one has spoken of or proposed dismantling the dams and channelization structures and restoring the Missouri's hydrologic processes in a renunciation of self-interest. Yet applying the principles of ecosystem management to the Missouri would result in numerous positive changes, including the emergence of .5 million acres of inundated land in North and South Dakota, the rebirth of a biodiverse ecosystem along 1,500 miles of river, the cessation of streambed degradation, the fertilization of the valley's soil through deposition of silt, the growth of timber tracts, the establishment of numerous recreational opportunities, and an end to the vicious water wars that have been waged over the Missouri River.

No one will ever know enough about the Missouri River to regulate its flows effectively: it possesses too many characteristics; it is influenced by innumerable external factors; and its waters behave in an unpredictable fashion. An agricultural-urban-industrial society demands uniform flow volumes for the generation of firm hydropower, the irrigation of fields on schedule, and the shipment of cargo over standard depths. But the Missouri never delivered uniform flows and never will. No amount of damming or channelizing will keep the river in check. The drought of the 1930s, the floods of the 1940s and 1950s, the drought of the late 1980s and early 1990s, and the great flood of 1993 proved that the Missouri River cannot be regulated for barge traffic, flood control, or irrigation. One might conclude that to continue to try to regulate the river to produce these supposed benefits is a waste of effort and money. As Claude Strauser of the Corps of Engineers admitted, "In the long run the Missouri will have its way."

Notes

1. Introduction

1. Elliot Coues, ed., *The History of the Lewis and Clark Expedition by Meriwether Lewis and William Clark*, 3 vols. (1893; reprint, New York: Dover Publications, n.d.); Gary E. Moulton, ed., *The Journals of the Lewis and Clark Expedition*, 6 vols. to date (Lincoln: University of Nebraska Press, 1983–), vol. 1.

2. Henry M. Brackenridge, *Views of Louisiana; Together with a Journal of a Voyage up the Missouri River, in 1811* (1814; reprint, Ann Arbor: University Microfilms, March of America Facsimile Series, no. 60, 1966), 200.

3. John Bradbury, *Travels in the Interior of America, in the Years 1809, 1810, and 1811; Including a Description of Upper Louisiana, Together with the States of Ohio, Kentucky, Indiana, and Tennessee, with the Illinois and Western Territories, and Containing Remarks and Observations Useful to Persons Emigrating to Those Countries* (1817; reprint, Ann Arbor: University Microfilms, March of America Facsimile Series, no. 59, 1966).

4. Edwin James, ed., *Account of an Expedition from Pittsburgh to the Rocky Mountains, Performed in the Years 1819 and '20, by Order of the Hon. J. C. Calhoun, Sec'y of War: Under the Command of Major Stephen H. Long, from the Notes of Major Long, Mr. T. Say, and Other Gentlemen of the Exploring Party* (1823; reprint, Ann Arbor: University Microfilms, March of America Facsimile Series, no. 65, 1966).

5. Thaddeus A. Culbertson, *Journal of an Expedition to the Mauvaises Terres and the Upper Missouri in 1850*, ed., John Francis McDermott, Smithsonian Institution, Bureau of American Ethnology, Bulletin 147 (1952; reprint, Lincoln: J and L Print Company, Reprints in Anthropology, 22, 1981).

6. Hiram Martin Chittenden, *History of Early Steamboat Navigation on the Missouri River: Life and Adventures of Joseph La Barge, Pioneer Navigator and Indian Trader for Fifty Years Identified with the Commerce of the Missouri Valley*, 2 vols. (New York: Francis P. Harper, 1903).

7. John G. Neihardt, *The River and I* (1910; reprint, Lincoln: University of Nebraska Press, 1938, 1968).

8. Melvin R. Gilmore, *Uses of Plants by the Indians of the Missouri River Region* (Lincoln: University of Nebraska Press, 1977).

9. Michael L. Lawson, *Dammed Indians: The Pick-Sloan Plan and the Missouri River Sioux, 1944–1980* (Norman: University of Oklahoma Press, 1982).

10. John E. Thorson, *River of Promise, River of Peril: The Politics of Managing the Missouri River* (Lawrence: University Press of Kansas, 1994).

11. John R. Ferrell, *Big Dam Era: A Legislative and Institutional History of the Pick-Sloan Missouri Basin Program* (Omaha: Missouri River Division, U.S. Army Corps of Engineers, 1993).

12. Donald Worster, *Rivers of Empire: Water, Aridity, and the Growth of the American West* (New York: Oxford University Press, 1992).

13. John Opie, *Ogallala: Water for a Dry Land, a Historical Study in the Possibilities for American Sustainable Agriculture* (Lincoln: University of Nebraska Press, 1993).

14. Norris Hundley Jr., *The Great Thirst: Californians and Water, 1770s–1990s* (Berkeley: University of California Press, 1992).

15. James Sherow, *Watering the Valley: Development Along the High Plains Arkansas River, 1870–1950* (Lawrence: University Press of Kansas, 1990).

2. The Modern Missouri

1. Waterscape refers to the natural and human-made features present in a river system.

2. Missouri Basin Inter-Agency Committee and the Missouri River States Committee, *The Missouri River Basin Development Program* (Washington, DC: GPO, 1952), 3–5.

3. *Montana, Official Highway Map 1995–1996* (Helena: Montana Promotion Division, 1995).

4. Henry Hart, *The Dark Missouri* (Madison: University of Wisconsin Press, 1957), 155. One acre-foot equals one acre of land covered by one foot of water.

5. Ibid., 158.

6. Coues, ed., *Lewis and Clark Expedition,* 1:426, 427.

7. Ibid., 2:385.

8. Josyln Art Museum and University of Nebraska Press, *Karl Bodmer's America* (Omaha: Josyln Art Museum, 1984), 229.

9. Ibid., 232.

10. U.S. Army Corps of Engineers, Missouri River Division, *Missouri River Master Water Control Manual: Review and Update Study, Draft Environmental Impact Statement* (Omaha: U.S. Army Corps of Engineers, Missouri River Division, 1994), 3–5, 3–7.

11. Ibid., 3–17, 3–18.

12. Ibid., 3–5.

13. *Sioux City Journal,* "Indians Lose in Taming of Missouri," 7 September 1991.

14. U.S. Army Corps of Engineers, Missouri River Division, *Missouri River Master Water Control Manual,* 3–5.

15. The word "headwaters" refers to the upstream end of a reservoir, the section where flowing water slows as it enters the reservoir proper.

16. U.S. Army Corps of Engineers, Missouri River Division, *Missouri River Master Water Control Manual,* 3–18.

17. *American News,* "Reservoirs Termed More Treacherous Than Ocean," 10 June 1966.

18. *Sioux Falls Argus Leader,* "Big Bend Popular Spot," 17 May 1964.

19. *Rapid City Journal,* "Big Bend Dam Nominated for Engineering Award," 4 January 1967.

20. U.S. Army Corps of Engineers, Missouri River Division, *Missouri River Master Water Control Manual,* 3–16.

21. U.S. Army Corps of Engineers, *The Federal Engineer, Damsites to Missile Sites: A History of the Omaha District, U.S. Army Corps of Engineers* (Washington, DC: GPO, 1985), 107.

22. *Sioux Falls Argus Leader,* series titled "Down by the River: Life Along the Missouri," 21–25 July 1991.

23. U.S. Army Corps of Engineers, *Federal Engineer,* 168.

24. Ibid., 147.

25. *Sioux Falls Argus Leader,* "Down By The River," and "Crowd Control, State Officials Consider Plans for Lewis and Clark Lake," 24 July 1991.

26. U.S. Army Corps of Engineers, Missouri River Division, *Missouri River Master Water Control Manual,* 3–37.

27. *Omaha World Herald,* "New Center Here Achieves World's Best Water Control," 24 May 1956.

28. *Sioux City Journal,* "Corps Stuck in Middle of River Muddle," 18 September 1991.

29. *Des Moines Register,* "Clobbered by Raging River," 25 October 1993.

30. U.S. Army Corps of Engineers, North Central Division, *The Great Flood of 1993, Post-Flood Report, Upper Mississippi River and Lower Missouri River Basins, Main Report* (Chicago: U.S. Army Corps of Engineers, North Central Division, 1994), 60.

31. *Des Moines Register,* "River Resists Path Charted for It by Man," 24 October 1993.

3. The Missouri River Yesterday

1. Lewis R. Freeman, "Trailing History Down the Big Muddy," *National Geographic,* July 1928, 73; Frederick Simpich, "Taming the Outlaw Missouri River," *National Geographic,* November 1945, 569; *Time Magazine,* "Land of the Big Muddy," 1 September 1952.

2. George R. Hallberg, Jayne M. Harbaugh, and Patricia M. Witinok, *Changes in the Channel Area of the Missouri River in Iowa, 1879–1976* (Iowa City: Iowa Geological Survey, 1979), 17, Appendix (river maps); Moulton, ed., *Journals of Lewis and Clark Expedition,* 1:14, Clark-Maximillian Sheet 3, route about August 3–8, 1804, 15; Sheet 4, route about August 8–13, 1804, 16; Sheet 5, route about August 13–21, 1804; Chittenden, *Early Steamboat Navigation,* 1; 154, 155, and map, "Changes of the Channel of the Missouri River Through Monona County, Iowa," drawn by Paul Burgoldl, comp. Mitchell Vincent, Onawa, Iowa; B. Shimek, "Geology of Harrison and Monona Counties" *Iowa Geological Survey Annual Report,* 20, (Des Moines: Emory H. English, 1910), 293.

3. U.S. Army Corps of Engineers, Missouri River Division, *Comprehensive Report on Missouri River Development, Appendix 8, Plan of Improvement, Section A: Introduction* (1944?), 11.

4. Shimek, "Geology of Harrison and Monona Counties," 287.

5. Coues, ed., *Lewis and Clark Expedition*, 62, 63.

6. Ibid., 73; Moulton, ed., *Journals of Lewis and Clark Expedition*, 1:15, Clark-Maximillian Sheet 4, route about August 8–13, 1804.

7. Maria R. Audubon, *The Missouri River Journals, 1843,* in *Audubon and His Journals,* ed. Elliot Coues, 2 vols. (1897; reprint, New York: Dover; 1960), 1:483.

8. Hallberg, Harbaugh, and Witinok, *Changes in the Channel Area of the Missouri River,* 17.

9. Chittenden, *Early Steamboat Navigation,* 154, 155.

10. *Sioux City Journal,* "Stabilizing Missouri River Will Affect Brown's Lake," 30 September 1954.

11. Willard Robbins, *Recollections of Monona County Pioneers* (Published by author: n.d.), listed under "The Story of a Pioneer," 2.

12. U.S. Army Corps of Engineers, *Federal Engineer,* 45; Hallberg, Harbaugh, and Witinok, *Changes in the Channel Area of the Missouri River,* 7.

13. *Sioux City Journal,* "Sea of Water Extends from South Sioux City to Jackson," 10 April 1943.

14. Chittenden, *Early Steamboat Navigation,* 83.

15. Audubon, *Missouri River Journals,* 2:53.

16. Brackenridge, *Views of Louisiana,* 232.

17. B. Shimek, "Geology of Harrison and Monona Counties," 287; *Kansas City Star,* 7 May 1911.

18. U.S. Army Corps of Engineers, *Annual Report of the Chief of Engineers, 1939,* pt. 1, vol. 2 (Washington, DC: GPO, 1939), 1273, 1308 (hereafter *ARCE*).

19. *Yankton Herald, The Great Flood* (Yankton: Herald Press, 1881), 3.

20. A. H. Lathrop, *Life in Vermillion Before the 1881 Flood and Shortly After* (Vermillion, SD: Clay County Historical Society, 1970), 38.

21. *Sioux City Journal,* "Damaging Missouri River Flood of 1881 Recalled on 60th Anniversary of Outstanding Event in the History of This Area," 30 March 1941.

22. Ibid., "Enraged Missouri River Carries Vermillion Away: It's April 6, 1881," 5 July 1953.

23. Lathrop, *Life in Vermillion,* 37.

24. U.S. Army Corps of Engineers, *ARCE, 1891,* graph, "Mean Daily Gauge Height and Discharge in Cubic Feet Per Second for a Period of Twelve Years. 1879–90. Missouri River, Sioux City. To accompany annual report for 1891 of A. H. Blaisdell, Asst. Eng'r."

25. U.S. Army Corps of Engineers, *Federal Engineer,* 7; William E. Lass, *A History of Steamboating on the Upper Missouri River* (Lincoln: University of Nebraska Press, 1962), 110.

26. "Account of a Steamboat Voyage on the Missouri River, May–August, 1859, by Elias J. Marsh, M.D.," in *South Dakota Historical Review* 1, no. 2 (January 1936): 110.

27. Coues, ed., *Lewis and Clark Expedition,* 8.

28. Brackenridge, *Views of Louisiana,* 215.

29. Coues, ed., *Lewis and Clark Expedition,* 127; William L. Heckman, *Heckman's Hand Book of Information About the Missouri River* (Hermann, MO: published by author, 1933), 8, 9.

30. Culbertson, *Journal of an Expedition to the Mauvaises Terres and the Upper Missouri in 1850,* 17.

31. Chittenden, *Early Steamboat Navigation,* 83.

32. Coues, ed., *Lewis and Clark Expedition,* 62, 63.

33. Audubon, *Missouri River Journals,* 1:525.

34. Coues, ed., *Lewis and Clark Expedition,* 103, 113; Audubon, *Missouri River Journals,* 1:508.

35. Coues, ed., *Lewis and Clark Expedition,* 103, 104.

36. B. Shimek, "Geology of Harrison and Monona Counties," 411, 412.

37. Culbertson, *Journal of an Expedition to the Mauvaises Terres and the Upper Missouri in 1850,* 36.

38. Joslyn Art Museum, *Karl Bodmer's America,* 150, painting listed as 152, *Snags on the Missouri,* watercolor and pencil on paper, 8 3/8 × 10 ¾.

39. Annie Heloise Abel, ed., *Tabeau's Narrative of Loisel's Expedition to the Upper Missouri,* trans. Rose Abel Wright (Norman: University of Oklahoma Press, 1939), 61.

40. Chittenden, *Early Steamboat Navigation,* 122.

41. Lathrop, *Life in Vermillion,* 13, 14.

42. Coues, ed., *Lewis and Clark Expedition,* 75.

43. Ibid., 63.

44. Brackenridge, *Views of Louisiana,* 204.

45. Bradbury, *Travels in the Interior of America,* 15.

4. The Missouri Valley and American Settlement, 1803–1880

1. Coues, ed., *Lewis and Clark Expedition,* 7, 8, 9.

2. Ibid., 1211, 1212.

3. Brackenridge, *Views of Louisiana,* 211.

4. Herbert S. Schell, *History of South Dakota* (Lincoln: University of Nebraska Press, 1961): 71, 72, 73; James Sterling Pope, "A History of Steamboating on the Lower Missouri: 1838–1849, St. Louis to Council Bluffs, Iowa Territory" (Ph.D. diss., St. Louis University, 1984): 97; James R. Shortridge, "The Expansion of the Settlement Frontier in Missouri," *Missouri Historical Review,* 75 (October 1980): 68, 73, 77; Raymond D. Thomas, "Missouri Valley Settlement—St. Louis to Independence," *Missouri Historical Review* 21 (October 1926): 24–40; Sam T. Bratton, "Inefficiency of Water Transportation in Missouri—A Geographical Factor in the Development of Railroads," *Missouri Historical Review* 14 (October 1919): 82–88; Edward J. White, "A Century of Transportation in Missouri," *Missouri Historical Review* 15 (October 1920): 126–62; Jonas Viles, "Old Franklin: A Frontier Town of the Twenties," *Mississippi Valley Historical Review* 9, no. 4 (March 1923): 270; Hattie M. Anderson, "Missouri, 1804–1828: Peopling a Frontier State," *Missouri Historical Review* 31 (January 1937): 150–80; Stuart F. Voss, "Town Growth in Central Missouri, Part 3," *Missouri Historical Review* 64 (April 1970): 322–50; Stuart F. Voss, "Town Growth in Central Missouri, 1815–1880, An Urban Chaparral, Part 1," *Missouri Historical Review* 64 (October 1969): 64–80; Culbertson, *Journal of an Expedition to the Mauvaises Terres and the Upper Missouri,* 21–25.

5. Audubon, *Missouri River Journals*, 2:14; Joyce Estes, interview by author, tape recording, Lower Brule, South Dakota, 12 March 1992; Coues, ed., *Lewis and Clark Expedition*, 82, 83.

6. Brackenridge, *Views of Louisiana*, 203.

7. "Account of a Steamboat Trip," 86, 95; Audubon, *Missouri River Journals*, 1:502.

8. Ibid., 2:15; Chittenden, *Early Steamboat Navigation*, 117, 118.

9. John Perlin, *A Forest Journey: The Role of Wood in the Development of Civilization* (Cambridge: Harvard University Press, 1991).

10. *Sioux City Journal*, 4 January 1941.

11. Robbins, "Story of a Pioneer," 3.

12. Chittenden, *Early Steamboat Navigation*, 125, 126.

13. Audubon, *Missouri River Journals*, 2:21.

14. James J. Dinsmore, *A Country So Full of Game: The Story of Wildlife in Iowa* (Iowa City: University of Iowa Press, 1994), 116; Robbins, *Recollections of Monona County Pioneers*, story, "Wild Life in 1855," Brackenridge, *Views of Louisiana*, 214; Culbertson, *Journal of an Expedition to the Mauvaises Terres*, 31; *Sioux City Journal*, "Thanksgiving Dinner in Sioux City was an Enjoyable Occasion Although Prepared and Eaten as Hostile Indians Looked On," 15 January 1938; and "Sioux City's Earliest Settler Tells of Her Arrival at Frontier Settlement," 16 December 1923.

15. Coues, ed., *Lewis and Clark Expedition*, 76.

16. Audubon, *Missouri River Journals*, 2:56.

17. Patrick Gass, *A Journal of the Voyages and Travels of a Corps of Discovery, Under the Command of Capt. Lewis and Capt. Clarke of the Army of the United States, from the Mouth of the River Missouri through the Interior Parts of North America to the Pacific Ocean, During the Years, 1804, 1805, and 1806* (Minneapolis: Ross and Haines, 1958), 35.

18. Robbins, *Recollections of Monona County Pioneers*, "Early Day Farming Methods," 1; Bradbury, *Travels in the Interior of America*, 14.

19. *Sioux City Journal*, "Tame Fertile Bottom Land," 25 July 1954.

20. Robbins, *Recollections of Monona County Pioneers*, "The Prairies," 2; Marie George Windell, ed., "The Road West in 1818, the Diary of Henry Vest Bingham, Part 2," *Missouri Historical Review* 40 (January 1946): 188; *Sioux City Journal*, 4 January 1941.

21. Windell, ed., "The Road West in 1818," 188.

22. Moulton, ed., *Journals of Lewis and Clark Expedition*, vol. 1, *Atlas of the Lewis and Clark Expedition*, 3.

23. Depth of hold refers to the depth of the keelboat's hull.

24. Stephen Ambrose, *Undaunted Courage, Meriwether Lewis, Thomas Jefferson, and the Opening of the American West* (New York: Simon and Schuster, 1996), 107, 128; Coues, ed., *Lewis and Clark Expedition*, 4; Blair Chicoine, interview by author, Sioux City, Iowa, 14 June 1996; Chittenden, *Early Steamboat Navigation*, 102.

25. Coues, ed., *Lewis and Clark Expedition*, 73.

26. Chittenden, *Early Steamboat Navigation*, 105.

27. Coues, ed., *Lewis and Clark Expedition*, 6, 80; Brackenridge, *Views of Louisiana*, 200, 231; Bradbury, *Travels in the Interior of America*, 12, 69.

28. Viles, "Old Franklin," 274, 275.

29. Pope, "History of Steamboating on the Lower Missouri," 92.

30. *Omaha World Herald*, "Steamboats' Banner Year Was 1859," 9 May 1954.

31. Lass, *History of Steamboating on the Upper Missouri*, 42; Chittenden, *Early Steamboat Navigation*, 217.

32. William E. Lass, "Missouri River Steamboating," *North Dakota History, Journal of the Northern Plains* 56, no. 3 (summer 1989): 13.

33. Lass, *History of Steamboating on the Upper Missouri*, 15, 16, 17, 18.

34. Chittenden, *Early Steamboat Navigation*, 80, 81.

35. Hiram M. Chittenden, "Report on Steamboat Wrecks on Missouri River," *Nebraska History Magazine* 8, no. 1 (January–March 1925): 21, 22.

36. Ralph E. Nichol, "Steamboat Navigation on the Missouri River with Special Reference to Yankton and Vicinity" (Master's thesis, University of South Dakota, 1936), 13.

37. Ibid.

38. Coues, ed., *Lewis and Clark Expedition*, 6, 80; Brackenridge, *Views of Louisiana*, 200, 231; Bradbury, *Travels in the Interior of America*, 12, 69.

39. Chittenden, *Early Steamboat Navigation*, 417, 421.

40. *ARCE, 1902*, 203.

41. Robert L. Branyan, *Taming the Mighty Missouri: A History of the Kansas City District, Corps of Engineers, 1907–1971* (Kansas City, MO: U.S. Army Corps of Engineers, Kansas City District, 1974), 4.

42. *ARCE, 1884*, 1532; *ARCE, 1885*, 1635; *ARCE, 1886*, 1394; *ARCE, 1891*, 3726.

43. Chittenden, "Report on Steamboat Wrecks on Missouri River," 24.

44. *Omaha World Herald*, "Steamboat's Banner Year Was 1859," 9 May 1954.

45. Chittenden, "Report on Steamboat Wrecks on Missouri River," 20, 21, 22, 24; Transportation Commission of the State of Iowa, *Transportation Map, Iowa.*

46. Chittenden, "Report on Steamboat Wrecks on Missouri River," map, 20–21.

47. Chittenden, *Early Steamboat Navigation*, 81; Annalies Corbin, "Shifting Sand and Muddy Water: Cartography and River Migration as Factors in Locating Steamboat Wrecks on the Far Upper Missouri River," *Historical Archaeology* 32(4), in press; Annalies Corbin and Kenneth W. Karsmizki, "Steamboats in Montana: Wrecks of the Far Upper Missouri–Yellowstone River Drainage Area, Phase 1—The Search for Historical Evidence," *Underwater Archaeology*, 1997, 64.

48. Lass, "Missouri River Steamboating," 13.

49. *Account of a Steamboat Trip on the Missouri River*, 85, 89.

50. Chittenden, *Early Steamboat Navigation*, 417, 418, 419; Herbert S. Schell, "The Dakota Southern: A Frontier Railway Venture of Dakota Territory," *South Dakota Historical Review* 2, no. 3 (1937): 99; Lass, *History of Steamboating on the Upper Missouri*, 137.

51. Chittenden, *Early Steamboat Navigation*, 417.

5. The River Abandoned

1. Lass, *History of Steamboating on the Upper Missouri River*, 141, 142.

2. *Congressional Record*, 15 December 1875, 228, 229.

3. *ARCE, 1885*, 2990.

4. *Congressional Record*, 8 January 1877, 488.

5. U.S. Congress, House, *Appointment of a Missouri River Commission, Report to Accompany H.R. 6330*, 18 May 1884, 2.

6. Ibid., 3; Missouri River Improvement Convention, Official Report of the Proceedings of the Missouri River Convention, Held in Kansas City, Mo., December 29 and 30, 1885 (Kansas City: Lawton and Havens, 1885), 6; *ARCE, 1890–91,* 3821, 3822, 3831.

7. *Sioux City Journal,* "Mill Tail of Hell," 8 June 1940, "Speaking of Floods," 23 May 1942, and "Enraged Missouri River Carries Vermillion Away: It's April 6, 1881," 5 July 1953; Lathrop, *Life in Vermillion,* 33–39; *Yankton Herald, Great Flood.*

8. Missouri River Improvement Convention, Official Proceedings, 1885, 4, 5.

9. Ibid.

10. *ARCE, 1885,* 2991.

11. Ibid., 2990.

12. Ibid., 2990, 2991.

13. U.S. Army Corps of Engineers, *Federal Engineer,* 7.

14. *ARCE, 1885,* 2989, 2990; U.S. Congress, House, *Appointment of Missouri River Commission,* 1.

15. U.S. Congress, House, *Appointment of Missouri River Commission,* 2.

16. *ARCE, 1885,* 2992.

17. *ARCE, 1886,* 2167.

18. Lass, *History of Steamboating on the Upper Missouri River,* 124, 149; *Missouri River Convention,* Official Proceedings, 7.

19. Lass, *History of Steamboating on the Upper Missouri River,* 130.

20. *Missouri River Convention,* Official Proceedings, 16–18.

21. Ibid., 13.

22. Ibid., 20.

23. Ibid., 28.

24. Ibid., 62, 63.

25. *ARCE, 1890–91,* 3730, 3732.

26. Ibid., 3723, 3726.

27. Ibid., 3726.

28. U.S. Army Corps of Engineers, *Federal Engineer,* 7.

29. U.S. Army Corps of Engineers, *Missouri River,* 73d Cong., 2d sess., H. Doc. 238 (Washington, DC: GPO, 1935), 272.

30. Simpich, "Taming the Outlaw Missouri River," 589.

31. *ARCE, 1894,* 3134, 3148.

32. Ibid., Plate 2, *Missouri River Commission, Osage Division, First Reach. Method of bracing dikes adopted for works constructed during fiscal year 1894,* 3134; Chittenden, *Early Steamboat Navigation,* illustration, *Improving the Missouri River,* 424; *ARCE, 1891,* illustration, *Missouri River Commission, Omaha Division, Sketch and Cross-Section Showing Waling and Willow Curtains Constructed May and June 1891 on Dykes at Sioux City, IA,* insert, page 3833.

33. *ARCE, 1894,* 3076, 3077; John Ferrell, *Soundings: One Hundred Years of the Navigation Project* (Washington, DC: GPO, 1996), 13, 14, 15; Chittenden, *Early Steamboat Navigation,* 424.

34. U.S. Army Corps of Engineers, Committee on Channel Stabilization, C. P. Lindner, "Channel Improvement and Stabilization Measures," in *State of Knowledge of Channel Stabilization in Major Alluvial Rivers,* ed. G. B. Fenwick, Technical Report no. 7 (Vicksburg, MS: U.S. Army Corps of Engineers, 1969), 8:7.

35. *Sioux City Journal,* "Harnessed: Revetment Job Near Salix Illustrates How Uncle Sam Is Preparing Missouri River for Opening of Navigation," 3 March 1940; U.S. Army Corps of Engineers, *Federal Engineer,* 9.

36. U.S. Army Corps of Engineers, *Federal Engineer,* 8, 9; Thomas Bruegger, personal photograph collection, Missouri River willow mattress construction in the 1930s in western Iowa.

37. *ARCE, 1894,* 3142, 3143, illustration, *Missouri River Commission, Osage Division, First Reach. Osage Chute Dam, Plate 4.*

38. Missouri River Improvement Association, Proceedings of the Missouri River Improvement Convention, Held at Kansas City, Mo., December 15 and 16, 1891. (Kansas City: Missouri River Improvement Association, 1891), 23.

39. *ARCE, 1894,* 3077.

40. Missouri River Improvement Association, Proceedings, 1891, 6.

41. Ibid., 32.

42. Ibid., 79–85.

43. Ibid., 36.

44. Ibid., 42.

45. Ibid.

46. Ibid., 41.

47. Ibid., 35–43.

48. Ibid., 151.

49. Ibid., 155, 156.

50. Ibid., 155.

51. *ARCE, 1902,* 176, 177.

52. Ibid., 186.

53. *ARCE, 1902,* 184–88; L. E. Bradley, "Government Ice Harbors on the Upper Missouri," *North Dakota History* 60, No. 3 (summer 1993): 28–37; Nichol, "Steamboat Navigation on the Missouri River with Special Reference to Yankton and Vicinity," 14.

54. *ARCE, 1913,* 930.

6. *The River Rediscovered*

1. A 100-year flood is a measurement of water discharge and is considered the highest water level possible during a 100-year period; the odds for that are 1 in a 100 each year.

2. U.S. Army Corps of Engineers, *Missouri River,* 73d Congress, 2d sess., H. Doc. 238 (Washington, DC: GPO, 1935), 80.

3. Ibid., 751.

4. Branyan, *Taming the Mighty Missouri,* 43.

5. U.S. Army Corps of Engineers, *Missouri River,* 91; *ARCE, 1891,* 3826.

6. U.S. Army Corps of Engineers, *Missouri River,* 80, 386.

7. *Sioux City Journal,* "Ignore Navigation," 11 June 1903.

8. *Kansas City Star*(?), "The River Congress Opens," 9 October 1903; *Kansas City Times,* "Appeals to Congress," 9 October 1903.

9. *Kansas City Star,* 24 June 1932.

10. Branyan, *Taming the Mighty Missouri,* iii.

11. *Kansas City Journal,* "To Use the River, Business Men Hold Meeting to Further the Movement," July 1906; *Kansas City Star,* 24 June 1932.

12. *Kansas City Star*(?), July 1906, and 24 June 1932.

13. Missouri Valley River Improvement Association, "The Way to Navigate Is to Navigate: The Missouri, a Deep Waterway, a 12-Foot Channel Would Save Its Cost Every Year," Work of Missouri Valley River Improvement Association for the Development of River Navigation (Kansas City, MO: Missouri Valley River Improvement Association, 1907), 7; *Kansas City Star,* 24 June 1932.

14. *Kansas City Star,* 24 June 1932.

15. Roderick Nash, *Wilderness and the American Mind,* 3d ed. (New Haven: Yale University Press, 1982), 162, 163; John F. Reiger, *American Sportsmen and the Origins of Conservation* (Norman: University of Oklahoma Press, 1986), 148–51; Theodore Roosevelt, "Publicizing Conservation at the White House," in *American Environmentalism: Readings in Conservation History,* ed. Roderick Nash, 3d ed. (New York: McGraw-Hill, 1990), 84–89; George R. Call, *The Missouri River Improvement Program As I Have Known It,* 1967, manuscript, Sioux City Public Library, 2, 3.

16. *Kansas City Post,* 3 November 1907; Roosevelt, "Publicizing Conservation," 84–89; J. Leonard Bates, "Conservation as Democracy," in Nash, ed., *American Environmentalism,* 98–101; Samuel P. Hays, "Conservation as Efficiency," in Nash, ed., *American Environmentalism,* 102–4.

17. *Kansas City Post,* 3 November 1907.

18. Missouri Valley River Improvement Association, "The Way to Navigate Is to Navigate," 7.

19. Ibid., 5–31.

20. Missouri River Navigation Congress, Proceedings of the First Annual Convention of the Missouri River Navigation Congress, Sioux City, Iowa, Wednesday and Thursday, Jan. 22–23, 1908 (Sioux City[?]: Missouri River Navigation Congress, 1908), 25.

21. Ibid., 27, 28.

22. Missouri Valley River Improvement Association, "The Way to Navigate Is to Navigate," 14.

23. *ARCE, 1913,* 936; Missouri Valley River Improvement Association, "The Way to Navigate Is to Navigate," 5, 8; *Kansas City Times,* "Kansas City Must Be Its Own Seaport," 10 April 1909.

24. *Kansas City Star,* 5 July 1908.

25. Ibid., and "How a Canal Would Reduce the Height of the Missouri at Kansas City," 13 June 1908.

26. Edgar C. Ellis to Louis Benecke, 23 July 1908, Louis Benecke Family Papers, no. 3825, Box 50, Folder 2044, Western Historical Manuscript Collection, Columbia, Missouri.

27. Louis Benecke to Edgar C. Ellis, 8 September 1908, and Resolution to form a local office of the Missouri River Navigation Congress, Benecke Family Papers.

28. Resolution to form a local office of the Missouri River Navigation Congress, and Edgar C. Ellis to Louis Benecke, 9 September and 18 September 1908, both in no. 3825, Box 50, Folder, 2045, Benecke Family Papers.

29. *Kansas City Times*, "Missouri River Work Insured," 3 January 1909.

30. *Kansas City Star*, "Build the Boats—Burton, Rivers and Harbors Chairman Says He's Watching the Situation," 29 September 1909, no. 3825, Box 50, Folder 2048, Benecke Family Papers; Robert Pearson and Brad Pearson, *The J. C. Nichols Chronicle* (Lawrence: University Press of Kansas, for Robert Pearson and Brad Pearson, 1994), 83.

31. *Kansas City Star*, 5 February 1910; *Kansas City Times*, 9 December 1910, and 24 December 1910.

32. Ferrell, *Soundings*, 35.

33. *ARCE, 1885*, 2992; Lindner, "Channel Improvement and Stabilization Measures," 8:6.

34. *ARCE, 1913*, 933.

35. *Kansas City Times*, 27 April 1914.

36. Ibid., 6 August 1915; Ferrell, *Soundings*, 27.

37. The Board of Engineers consisted of seven high-ranking army engineers. A project receiving board approval went to the House Rivers and Harbors Committee for further review and legislative action. If the committee accepted the board's endorsement, it recommended inclusion of the project in the Annual Rivers and Harbors bill.

38. *Kansas City Times*, 6 August 1915; *Kansas City Star*, 9 August 1915; *Kansas City Times*, 10 August 1915, and 16 October 1915; *Kansas City Star*, 11 November 1915.

39. *Kansas City Times*, 10 August 1915.

40. Ibid., 6 August 1915.

41. Ibid., 10 August 1915.

42. Ibid., 21 October 1915.

43. *Kansas City Star*, 7 April 1916; Ferrell, *Soundings*, 46.

44. *Kansas City Times*, 10 March 1916.

45. Ibid.

46. Ibid., "The Frear Attack," 11 January 1916.

47. Ibid.

48. Ibid.

49. Ferrell, *Soundings*, 51.

50. *Kansas City Star*, "What of New River Plan? Navigation Company Officials Asked How to Proceed," 15 November 1923.

51. *Kansas City Star*, 1 September 1918; *Kansas City Times*, 16 July 1919.

52. *Kansas City Star*, "What of New River Plan?"

53. Call, *Missouri River As I Have Known It*, chap. 2, 6.

54. *Kansas City Star*(?), "Arrival of 'Mark Twain,' 'Gen. Ashburn,' and Towboats Marks Opening of River for Barge Lines," 26 June 1932; Missouri River Navigation Association, *What the Missouri River Navigation Association Has Accomplished* (Kansas City, MO: Missouri River Navigation Association, 1927), 3.

55. Missouri River Navigation Association, "What the Association Has Accomplished," 3; *Kansas City Star*(?), "Missouri River Project," 16 October 1925.

56. Hoover, "The Need of Inland Waterway Transportation," 9.

57. Ibid., 6.

58. Ibid., 7.

59. Ibid., 11.

60. Pearson and Pearson, *Nichols Chronicle*, 84.

61. Missouri River Navigation Association, "What the Association Has Accomplished," 3, 4.

62. Missouri River Navigation Association, "The Missouri River Navigation Association, Organized at Kansas City, Missouri, October 19–20, 1925 (Kansas City: Missouri River Navigation Association, 1925), 3, 4.

63. Ibid., 5; *Kansas City Star*, 4 December 1925; *Kansas City Times*, 14 January 1926; Arthur J. Weaver to Major C. C. Gee, 26 January 1926, Arthur J. Weaver Papers, Falls City, Nebraska; *Kansas City Star*(?), "Upper River Boosters to Press Fight in Congress," 30 April 1926.

64. Missouri River Navigation Association, "The Missouri River Navigation Association," 5.

65. *Kansas City Star*, 22 January 1926.

66. *Sioux City Journal*, "River Meetings at Sioux City and Yankton: Governor Gunderson, J. C. Nichols and A. J. Weaver Among Speakers at Meetings in Upper Missouri River Cities," 28(?) February 1926.

67. *Kansas City Star*(?), 30 April 1926; *Kansas City Times*, 14 January 1926.

68. *Sioux City Journal*, "Dr. Roost Explains Upper Missouri Project," October 1926; *Columbus (NE) Telegram*, "Edgar Howard on the Missouri River," 10 August 1926.

69. *Kansas City Star*, 15 June 1926.

70. Ibid.

71. George R. Call, *Missouri River As I Have Known It*, chap. 5, 5.

72. *ARCE, 1934*, 833.

73. Missouri River Navigation Association, "What the Association Has Accomplished," 6.

74. "President Coolidge Signs the Bill, Nebraska Comment," *Nebraska History Magazine* 8, no. 1 (January–March 1925, printed 15 February 1927): 60, 61.

7. The Dry Years, 1927–1942

1. *Kansas City Times*, 17 March 1927.

2. Ibid., 28 February 1928.

3. Ibid., 7 March 1929.

4. Ibid.; *Kansas City Star*, 16 May 1929.

5. *Kansas City Star*, 6 October 1929.

6. Ibid., 16 May 1929.

7. *Kansas City Journal-Post*, 8 October 1929; *Kansas City Times*, "Our Turn Comes Next, with Ohio River Job Done, the Missouri River Needs a 9-Foot Channel," 26 October 1929.

8. *Kansas City Times*, "High Points in the President's Waterways Address," 24 October 1929.

9. *Kansas City Journal-Post*, 8 October 1929; *Kansas City Times*, "River Days Back, Hoover Visions Great Era," 24 October 1929.

10. *Kansas City Times*, "River Days Back."

11. *Kansas City Star*, "Sees Great River Hope, J. C. Nichols Enthusiastic over Hoover's Speech," 24 October 1929.

12. *Kansas City Journal-Post*, 11 October 1929; *Kansas City Times*, "9-Foot Plea Today, Major Young Will Hear Case for the War Department, to Meet at C. of C.," October 1929; *Kansas City Star*, "A Long River Link," 10 October 1929; and "Oil in River Plea," 15 October 1929; *Kansas City Times*, "Channel Plea Is In," 16 October 1929.

13. *Kansas City Star*, "A Long River Link"; *Kansas City Times*, "Channel Plea Is In."

14. *Kansas City Star*, "For Big Barges," 19 January 1929.

15. Ibid., "A 9-Foot Channel Delay, Lower Missouri Project May Be Held Over," 23 January 1929.

16. Ibid., "Speed in River Hearing, Engineers' Board to Hurry Channel Report to Congress," 23 February 1930.

17. Ibid., "Delay Deep River, the Army Engineers Announce They Will Not Recommend 9-Foot Channel This Year," 13 March 1930.

18. Ibid., "River Development Makes Great Strides, Congress Gives More to Missouri than to Any Other Inland Project," December 1930.

19. Ibid., "Concern on Rivers Bill," 20 March 1930 and "A Threat To River Work, Failure of Congress to Grant Funds May Cause a Halt," 22 March 1930.

20. Ibid., "A Great Water-Highway," 16 September 1930.

21. Ibid., "1000 River Jobs, Appropriation Saturday Means More Work in the Kansas City District This Winter," 22 December 1930.

22. *Kansas City Times*, "$25,000,000 Will Be Spent Immediately," 17 November 1930.

23. *Sioux City Journal*, "Midwest Asks River Project Aid, Campbell," 26 November 1930.

24. Ibid., "To Fight for River Money," 3 December 1930.

25. *Sioux City Tribune*, "Men Named to River Meeting," 3 December 1930; and *Sioux City Journal*, "To Fight for River Money"; *Omaha World Herald*, "Hoover Pledges Support to Work on Upper River, Calls Improvement an Aid to Farmers," 9 December 1930.

26. *ARCE, 1934*, 838.

27. *Kansas City Times*, "For Upper River Haste," 9 December 1931.

28. *ARCE, 1934*, 838.

29. Ibid., 831.

30. *Kansas City Star*, 6 October 1929.

31. Ibid., "Upper River Plea Is In," 13 May 1930.

32. Ibid., "1000 River Jobs, Appropriation Saturday Means More Work in the Kansas City District This Winter."

33. Ibid., 3 March 1931.

34. *ARCE, 1934*, 831; *Kansas City Star*, 6 October 1929, and "Upper River Plea Is In."

35. Ferrell, *Soundings*, 59; *Kansas City Star*, "Great Days on Missouri River in Life of 'Steamboat Bill,'" 12 February 1950, "A Threat to River Work," 22 March 1930, and "Hopeful of River Bill," 21 May 1930; *Kansas City Times*, "Government Action to Assist Jobless," 17 November 1930.

36. *Kansas City Star*, 3 March 1931.

37. Ibid., 6 October 1929.

38. Ibid., 16 May 1930.

39. Ferrell, *Soundings*, 61.

40. *Kansas City Star*, 16 May 1930.

41. Ibid., 1931, untitled article.

42. Ibid., 16 May 1930.

43. *Sioux City Journal*, "Harnessed: Revetment Job Near Salix Illustrates How Uncle Sam Is Preparing Missouri River for Opening of Navigation," 3 March 1940.

44. *Kansas City Star*, 9 August 1929, 6 October 1929, "Setback to River, Failure of June Rise Is a Blow to Missouri Navigation Plans, Hope for a Fall Flood," 10 July 1930, and 3 March 1931; *Kansas City Journal-Post*, "Hurley's Party Glad to Battle Strong Current," 22 June 1932.

45. *Kansas City Times*, "Tie at St. Charles," 22 June 1932.

46. Ibid.

47. *Kansas City Journal-Post*, "Hurley's Party Glad to Battle Strong Current," and *Kansas City Times*, "Revive the River," 23 June 1932.

48. *Kansas City Star*, "Recalls a Hoover Vision," 25 June 1932.

49. *Kansas City Times*, "Tie At St. Charles"; *Kansas City Star*, 24 June 1932; *Kansas City Times*, "Revive the River."

50. *Kansas City Times*, "Eyes Up the River Now," 28 June 1932; *Kansas City Journal-Post*, "Important Dates in Missouri River History," 26 June 1932; *Kansas City Star*, 24 June 1932.

51. *Kansas City Times*, "Eyes Up the River Now."

52. John M. Blum, ed., *The National Experience*, Part 2, *A History of the United States Since 1865*, 8th ed. (Fort Worth, TX: Harcourt Brace Jovanovich, 1993), 688.

53. Ibid., 692.

54. *Kansas City Star*, "Gigantic Job Plan, President-Elect Roosevelt Has Scheme Designed to Solve Unemployment," 2 February 1933.

55. Ibid.

56. *ARCE, 1934*, 827, 831.

57. U.S. Army Corps of Engineers, *Missouri River*, H. Doc. 238, 194, 195, 518.

58. Ibid., 194–200.

59. Ibid., 527.

60. Ibid., 199, 518, 519, 526, 527, 852, 855, 857; *ARCE, 1934*, 842.

61. *Kansas City Star*, "A Halt on River Work," 28 March 1933 and "No Open River Policy," 29 March 1933.

62. *Kansas City Star*, "Plan to Harness River," 30 March 1933.

63. Ibid.

64. *Kansas City Times*, "The Missouri Left Out," 2 May 1933.

65. Ibid.

66. William E. Leuchtenburg, *Franklin D. Roosevelt and the New Deal* (New York: Harper and Row, 1963), 70.

67. *Kansas City Star,* "River Advocates Plead for Work as Valley's Need," 19 June 1933.

68. Ferrell, *Soundings,* 75; Arthur J. Weaver to J. C. Nichols, 8 June 1933, Weaver Papers.

69. *Kansas City Star,* "River Advocates Plead for Work as Valley's Need."

70. Ibid.

71. Ibid., "Asks River Funds," 29 June 1933.

72. Ibid., "Pledge to River," 8 August 1933.

73. *Kansas City Times,* "8000 River Jobs, Work Early Next Month," 25 August 1933.

74. Ibid.; Mayor Hayes to President Roosevelt, 25 January 1935, Proposal by the Municipal Government, Sioux City, Ia., to National Emergency Council, February 1935(?), and Telegram to President Franklin Roosevelt from W. D. Hayes, 5 May 1933, Weaver Papers.

75. *Kansas City Times,* "The Missouri Left Out."

76. Ibid., "Woodring a River Ally," 31 August 1933.

77. Ibid., "8000 River Jobs."

78. Ibid.

79. Ibid., "U.S. Out to 'Finish Job,' Allotment Indicates an Eventual 9-Foot Channel, Miller Says," 25 August 1933.

80. Ibid., "Woodring a River Ally."

81. *Kansas City Star,* "For a Nine-Foot Channel," 6 October 1933, and "Ask Speed on Dam," 30 September 1933.

82. *Kansas City Times,* "Ickes May Oppose River," 4 October 1933.

83. Ibid.

84. *Kansas City Star,* "For a Nine-Foot Channel"; *Kansas City Times,* "Ask Speed on Dam," and "Ready for a River Plea."

85. Ibid.

86. *Kansas City Star,* "River Men Alert, Immediate Action on 104½ Million Allotment for Missouri and Ft. Peck Planned, the President an Aid, Kiro Dam Has Hit A Snag," 8 October 1933, and "A River and Jobs, Fort Peck Dam Also Up," 10 October 1933.

87. Ibid.

88. *Kansas City Star,* "A River and Jobs."

89. *Kansas City Times,* "Push Fort Peck Fight," 12 October 1933; *Kansas City Star,* "A Ft. Peck Fund, Public Works Administration Allots 15½ Million for First Year's Work on Project," 14 October 1933, and "River to Its Own, Fort Peck Allotment Means the Missouri Will Be a Vital Waterways Factor, Roosevelt Is a Big Aid," 15 October 1933; Arthur J. Weaver to Rufus E. Lee, 13 October 1933, Weaver Papers.

90. Ferrell, *Soundings,* 76, 77, and *Big Dam Era,* 5, 7, 8; *Kansas City Times,* "A Vast Fort Peck Plan," 17 October 1933; *Kansas City Star,* "Job Hunters to Fort Peck," 29 October 1933; *Kansas City Times,* "Where 287 Miles of Power Line Will Be Built as Part of the Ft. Peck Dam Project," 16 April 1934, and "To Speed River Work," 9 June 1934.

91. *Kansas City Star,* "River to Its Own," 15 October 1933; George Call to Arthur J. Weaver, 14 October 1933, Weaver Papers.

92. *Kansas City Times,* "A Year's Work On Peck Dam," 19 October 1934; *ARCE, 1934,* 842.

93. *Kansas City Star,* "Job Hunters To Fort Peck."

94. *ARCE, 1934,* 842; *Kansas City Star,* "Work Begins On a 72-Million-Dollar Flood Control Project for the Missouri Valley," 27 February 1934, and "Work Goes Ahead on the Huge Missouri River Project at Fort Peck, Montana," 4 March 1934; *Kansas City Times,* "Where 287 Miles of Power Line Will Be Built as Part of the Ft. Peck Dam Project."

95. *Kansas City Times,* "25 Millions to Ft. Peck, Work on Dam Thus Is Financed for Second Year," 13 July 1934.

96. *Kansas City Star,* "On to the Fort Peck Dam, Inspection Tour Takes Roosevelt to Glasgow, Montana," 6 August 1934.

97. *Kansas City Times,* "Gay Start to Tame River," 13 October 1933.

98. *Kansas City Star,* "400 Men and the River," 21 December 1933.

99. Ibid., "An Upper River Plea In," 2 February 1935, and "To Roosevelt on River," 2 February 1935; Proposal by the Municipal Government, Sioux City, Ia., to National Emergency Council, February 1935(?), Weaver Papers.

100. *Kansas City Star,* "Ask Early River Money," 6 May 1935.

101. *Kansas City Times,* "New River Work Boost," 14 September 1935.

102. *Kansas City Star,* "End of River Job," 10 October 1936.

103. *Kansas City Times,* "Upper River Work Soon," 11 May 1931.

104. Hallberg, Harbaugh, and Witinok, *Changes in the Channel Area of the Missouri River,* 7.

105. Lindner, "Channel Improvement and Stabilization Measures," 8:25, 26; Branyan, *Taming the Mighty Missouri,* 22; *Sioux City Journal,* "They're Fixing the Missouri," 22 July 1938, and "Army Engineers Harnessing Missouri River Here to Confine Channel," 27 March 1940.

106. *Sioux City Journal,* "Harnessed: Revetment Job Near Salix Illustrates How Uncle Sam Is Preparing Missouri River for Opening of Navigation," 3 March 1940, and "Army Engineers Harnessing Missouri River Here to Confine Channel."

107. Branyan, *Taming the Mighty Missouri,* 24.

108. U.S. Army Corps of Engineers, *Federal Engineer,* 49; Lindner, "Channel Improvement and Stabilization Measures," 8:10.

109. *ARCE, 1939,* 1300.

110. Ferrell, *Soundings,* 85, 87.

111. U.S. Army Corps of Engineers, *Federal Engineer,* 47.

112. *ARCE, 1935,* 1002; *ARCE, 1936,* 998; *ARCE, 1937,* 1006.

113. *ARCE, 1940,* 1312.

114. *Sioux City Journal,* "Two Boosters for Missouri River Transportation," 27 June 1940.

115. Ibid., "KSCJ Announcer Paints Picture of Possibilities of River Navigation," 27 June 1940.

116. *ARCE, 1940,* 1312; *Sioux City Journal,* "Big Crowd Cheers Tow-Barge Arrival at Sioux City Port," 27 June 1940.

117. U.S. House, *Missouri River Channel Stabilization and Navigation Project, Hearings Before the Subcommittee of the Committee on Appropriations, 30 June 1952* (Washington, DC: GPO, 1952), 18; *Sioux City Journal,* "KSCJ Announcer Paints Picture of Possibilities in River Navigation," "Sioux City Owned Barge on Maiden Voyage," 3 August 1940, and "Sioux City Towboat on Way Home," 20 August 1940.

118. *ARCE, 1937,* 994.

119. *New York Times,* 14 April 1935.

8. South Dakota Attempts to Develop the River

1. Louis N. Hafermehl, "To Make the Desert Bloom: The Politics and Promotion of Early Irrigation Schemes in North Dakota," *North Dakota History, Journal of the Northern Plains* 59, no. 3 (summer 1992): 13–27.

2. Missouri River Improvement Association, Proceedings, iii; Missouri River Improvement Convention, Official Report, 3; Missouri River Navigation Congress, Proceedings, 93.

3. Charles E. DeLand, Chairman of the Publicity Committee of the Pierre Waterways Convention to Kansas City District Engineer Edward H. Shulz, 17 March 1910, *Correspondence of the Kansas City District, U.S. Army Corps of Engineers, 1907–1930,* RG 77, National Archives, Kansas City, Missouri; William G. Robinson, "The Development of the Missouri Valley," *South Dakota Historical Collections* 22 (1946): 452.

4. Donald L. Miller, "The History of the Movement for Hydro-Electric Development on the Missouri River in South Dakota" (Master's thesis, University of South Dakota, 1930), 11, 11a.

5. Ibid., 15. The cost-to-benefit ratio refers to the cost of the project in comparison to its long-term financial benefits.

6. Major General M. Taylor to Executive Secretary, Federal Power Commission, 15 March 1926, *Correspondence,* RG 77, NA, Kansas City.

7. *Sioux City Journal,* "Engineer Says Missouri Big Bend Is Best Power Site," 16 June 1916 or 1917; Miller, "Hydro-Electric Development," 17.

8. Miller, "Hydro-Electric Development," 19.

9. Ibid., 23.

10. Doane Robinson, *Dam Sites on the Missouri River in South Dakota* (Pierre: South Dakota Department of Immigration, 1918), 3.

11. Ibid., 19.

12. Ibid., 23.

13. Ibid.

14. Daniel W. Mead and Charles V. Seastone, *Report on the Feasibility of the Development of Hydro Electric Power from the Missouri River in the State of South Dakota* (1920; reprint, Pierre: Lawrence K. Fox, 1929), 21.

15. Ibid., 23–25.

16. Ibid., 56.

17. *Mobridge Tribune,* "Cheap Electric Power for Home, Farm, and Factory," 1922; Miller, "Hydro-Electric Development," 62.

18. *Sioux Falls Argus Leader,* 11 November 1957.

19. Miller, "Hydro-Electric Development," 71a.

20. Ibid., 71.

21. *Sioux Falls Argus Leader,* 23 May 1954.

22. Robinson, "Development of Missouri Valley," 455.

23. Pierre Commercial Club, "Navigation of the Missouri River Through the Dakotas" (Pierre: Hipple, 1931), 1.

24. Ibid., 2.

25. Ibid., 1–3.

26. Robinson, "Development of the Missouri Valley," 456, 458.

27. Ibid., 460, 461.

28. Mrs. Sam Weller, interview by author, phone conversation, Mitchell, South Dakota, 12 June 1993.

29. Robinson, "Development of the Missouri Valley," 463.

30. Ibid., 464.

31. Ibid., 463.

32. Chamberlain Commercial Club, "Big Bend Hydro-Electric Project" (Chamberlain, SD: Register, 1935[?]).

33. Reuben Estes to Francis Case, 16 May 1937, File Folder 157, Special Collections, Dakota Wesleyan College, Mitchell, South Dakota.

34. Estes to Case, 16 May 1937, Case Papers; Mrs. Sam Weller, interview.

35. Case to Arnold Sukrow, 2 July 1937, Case Papers.

36. Ibid., Case to Estes, 1 June 1937.

37. Ibid.

38. Ibid., Case to John Herrick, 12 July 1940.

39. Ibid., Frederick L. Kirgis to Secretary of the Interior Harold Ickes, 10 July 1940.

40. Ibid., J. W. Jackson to Case, 17 January 1940.

41. Ibid., Case to John Herrick, 12 July 1940.

42. Ibid., Case to J. W. Jackson, 11 October 1940.

43. Call, *Missouri River As I Have Known It,* chap. 8:3, 4, 5; letter from Cong. Vincent F. Harrington to George R. Call, 29 January 1937 in idem; program for the Upper Missouri Valley Association meeting in the Elks Hall, Huron, South Dakota, 8 February 1937 in idem.

44. Ferrell, *Big Dam Era,* 4.

45. Merrill Q. Sharpe, "History of the Missouri River States Committee," *South Dakota Historical Collections* 22 (1946): 400.

46. Merrill Q. Sharpe, "Missouri River States Committee: Its Origin and Work," in *The Future Development of the Missouri River Valley, A Report on the Program and Activities of the Missouri River States Committee* (Chicago: Council of State Governments, 1944), 8.

47. Sharpe, "History of the Missouri River States Committee," 404.

9. *The Wet Years, 1943–1951*

1. *Sioux City Journal,* "Serious Overflows at Yankton, Stevens Seen," 5 April 1943.

2. Ibid., "Dike Breaks, Large Area Inundated," 11 April 1943.

3. Ibid., "Sea of Water Extends from South Sioux City to Jackson," 10 April 1943.

4. Ibid., "Nearby Lakes 'Lost' in General Flood Airview," 10 April 1943.

5. Ibid., "Find the Victory Garden," 11 April 1943.

6. Ibid., "Hospitalized After Futile Fight to Save His Farm," 11 April 1943.

7. Ibid., "Act to Thwart Flood Disease: Health Authorities Take Steps to Avoid Outbreaks," 11 April 1943.

8. Ibid., "Flood Waters Creep Higher Near Onawa," 8 April 1943.

9. Ibid., "Not Venice; It's Blencoe, Ia.," 13 April 1943.

10. Ibid., "Flood Waters Recede at Omaha Airport," 16 April 1943.

11. Lewis A. Pick, "A Valley-Wide Program of Development," in *Future Development of the Missouri River Valley*, 12.

12. U.S. Army Corps of Engineers, *Federal Engineer*, 75.

13. Pick, "Valley-Wide Program," 12.

14. Paul L. Harley, "The Gestation Period of the Pick-Sloan Missouri Basin Plan," in Pick-Sloan Missouri Basin Plan, proceedings of conference held in Des Moines, Iowa, 10–11 August 1983, by the Missouri Basin States Association, 7; Branyan, *Taming the Mighty Missouri*, 45.

15. *ARCE, 1944*, 1022.

16. Pick, "Valley-Wide Program," 13.

17. *ARCE, 1944*, 944, 1022.

18. Sharpe, "History of the Missouri River States Committee," 405.

19. Marian E. Ridgeway, *The Missouri Basin's Pick-Sloan Plan: A Case Study in Congressional Policy Determination* (Urbana: University of Illinois Press, 1955), 173.

20. Ibid., 212, 213.

21. Charles B. Hoeven, "What Congressmen Say," in *Future Development of the Missouri River Valley*, 29; Bennett C. Clark, "What Congressmen Say," in *Future Development of the Missouri River Valley*, 33, 34.

22. Hart, *Dark Missouri*, 120.

23. Pick-Sloan Missouri Basin Plan, Proceedings, x; U.S. Congress, House, *Statement of M. Q. Sharpe, Governor of South Dakota: Hearing Before the Committee on Flood Control*, 78th Cong., 2d sess., 16–17 February 1944, 3.

24. Sharpe, "History of the Missouri River States Committee," 405.

25. Robert Hipple, interview by author, tape recording, Pierre, South Dakota, 20 May 1992.

26. *Sioux City Journal*, "Flood Control More Than a Dream," 24 August 1943.

27. Ibid.

28. Hipple interview.

29. Max Schwabe, "What Congressmen Say," in *Future Development of the Missouri River Valley*, 35, 36.

30. Sharpe, "History of the Missouri River States Committee," 407; Schwabe, "What Congressmen Say," 35.

31. Gerald P. Nye, "What Congressmen Say," in *Future Development of the Missouri River Valley*, 38.

32. Arthur Svendby, "The Opinions of Organizations in the Valley," in *Future Development of the Missouri River Valley*, 60.

33. U.S. Congress, House, *Statement of M. Q. Sharpe*, 16–17 February 1944, 9; Ridgeway, *Missouri Basin's Pick-Sloan Plan*, 212, 213.

34. U.S. Army Corps of Engineers, *Federal Engineer*, 75.

35. Ibid., 76.

36. Hipple interview; Hart, *Dark Missouri,* 121–25.

37. Department of the Army, U.S. Army Corps of Engineers, Omaha District, *Comprehensive Report, Appendix 8, Plan of Improvement,* 4.

38. Ibid., 20.

39. Hipple interview; Congress, House, *Statement of M. Q. Sharpe,* 3.

40. Hipple interview.

41. Congress, House, *Statement of M. Q. Sharpe,* 9.

42. Ibid., 11.

43. Ibid.

44. Hart, *Dark Missouri,* 127.

45. Ibid., 125.

46. Pick-Sloan Missouri Basin Plan, Proceedings, 12.

47. Ibid., 13.

48. Congress, House, *Statement of M. Q. Sharpe,* 11.

49. Ridgeway, *Missouri Basin's Pick-Sloan Plan,* 173.

50. Corps of Engineers, *Plan of Improvement,* 16.

51. Department of the Army, U.S. Army Corps of Engineers, U.S. Army Engineer District, Omaha, *Missouri River, Big Bend Reservoir, South Dakota, Design Memorandum Number MB-1, Site Selection* (Omaha: U.S. Army Corps of Engineers, 1957), 4–7.

52. Corps of Engineers, *Plan of Improvement,* 15.

53. Corps of Engineers, *Design Memorandum Number MB-1,* 4–8.

54. Ibid., 4–5.

55. Corps of Engineers, *Plan of Improvement,* 17.

56. Ibid., 17.

57. Ibid.

58. Hipple interview.

59. Ferrell, *Soundings,* 97.

60. *Sioux City Journal,* 1 August 1946.

61. *Des Moines Register,* "160-Ft. Fort Randall Dam to Control Flood Waters," 14 September 1947; U.S. Army Corps of Engineers, Missouri River Division, *Missouri River Master Water Control Manual, Review and Update Study, Draft Environmental Impact Statement, Description of Existing Environment, 3.0* (Omaha: U.S. Army Corps of Engineers, Missouri River Division, 1994), 3–5.

62. *Omaha World Herald,* "Fort Randall Dam Is Ready to Guard River," 26 October 1952.

63. U.S. Army Corps of Engineers, Missouri River Division, "Current and Alternative Water Control Plans," in *Draft Environmental Impact Statement,* 2–4.

64. *Des Moines Register,* "160-Ft. Fort Randall Dam to Control Flood Waters."

65. *Sioux City Journal,* "Journal Photographer Helps Fort Randall Celebrate," 1 August 1946.

66. U.S. Army Corps of Engineers, *Federal Engineer,* 107.

67. *Des Moines Register,* "6,000 to Live Here While Dam Is Built," 14 September 1947.

68. U.S. Army Corps of Engineers, *Federal Engineer,* 108.

69. *Des Moines Register,* "Fort Randall Dam Sets Off Dakota Boom," 18 July 1948.

70. *Sioux City Journal-Tribune,* "'Muddy Mo' Meets Master As Dredge Outsilts Silt," 21 July 1952; *Des Moines Register,* "Mighty Missouri Rolls Quietly Under Shackles," 8 August 1952.

71. *Des Moines Register,* "Missouri River Dam Is Growing," 18 July 1948.

72. U.S. Army Corps of Engineers, *Federal Engineer,* 108.

73. *Des Moines Register,* "Missouri River Moves in Tunnels as Spillway Work Goes On," 3 August 1952.

74. U.S. Army Corps of Engineers, *Federal Engineer,* 108; *Des Moines Register,* "Missouri River Dam Is Growing," and "Missouri River Moves in Tunnels as Spillway Work Goes On."

75. *Sioux City Journal,* "Man-Made Walls Curb Wild River," 23 November 1952; Martha Sutherland Coon, *Oahe Dam: Master of the Missouri* (New York: Harvey House, 1969), 35.

76. *Des Moines Register,* "Missouri River Dam Is Growing," and "Mighty Missouri Rolls Quietly Under Shackles."

77. U.S. Army Corps of Engineers, *Federal Engineer,* 110.

78. Ibid., 109.

10. *The Mighty Missouri and the Final Quest for Control*

1. *Des Moines Register,* 14 December 1951.

2. Ibid., 21 December 1951.

3. *Sioux City Journal,* 13 February 1952.

4. Ibid., 5 March 1952.

5. Ibid., 6 March 1952.

6. Ibid., 24 March 1952.

7. Ibid., 28 March 1952.

8. *Omaha World Herald,* 6 April 1952; *Des Moines Register,* 8 April 1952.

9. Ibid., 2 April and 8 April 1952.

10. Ibid., 9 April 1952.

11. Ibid., 10 April 1952.

12. Ibid., "River Volume Here 15 Times as Great as Its Normal Flow," 14 April 1952.

13. Ibid., 8 April 1952.

14. Ibid., 9 April 1952.

15. Ibid., "Peak Is Even Higher Than Was Feared," 14 April 1952.

16. Ibid., "Man 69, Rescued After 5 Days in South Sioux Attic," 16 April 1952.

17. Ibid., 15 April 1952.

18. Ibid.

19. Ibid., 17 April 1952.

20. Ibid., "Peak Is Even Higher Than Was Feared," 13 July 1952.

21. Ibid., "Hectic Flowers Island Survives Another Crisis," 13 July 1952; *Omaha World Herald,* "Record Flood Damage Listed," 13 July 1952.

22. *Sioux City Journal,* 13 July 1952.

23. Ibid., "2 Cities Watch River Tensely, Fear Disaster," 18 April 1952, and "Omaha Waging Winning Fight Against Flood," 18 April 1952.

24. Ibid., "Estimate Cost of April Flood at 179 Million," 14 September 1952, and "Pick Sees Fight Just Beginning," 21 April 1952.

25. *ARCE, 1952,* 1244.

26. *ARCE, 1944,* 994, 995, 1021, 1022; *ARCE, 1952,* 1244, 1245, 1304; House, *Missouri River Channel Stabilization and Navigation Project, Hearing,* Corps of Engineers maps, *Missouri River, Kansas City to Mouth,* and *Missouri River, Kansas City to Sioux City,* with indications of river miles.

27. Ibid.

28. U.S. Army Corps of Engineers, *Federal Engineer,* 228.

29. *ARCE, 1953,* 1150; *Sioux City Journal,* 31 December 1952, and 21 February 1954.

30. *Omaha World Herald,* "2 River Jobs on at Yankton," 11 May 1952; *Sioux City Journal,* "House Trims River Funds 200 Million," 28 March 1952.

31. *Sioux City Journal,* "Pick Sees Fight Just Beginning."

32. Ibid., "10,000 Attend Historic Opening Work On Gavin's Dam," 19 May 1952, and "Pick Sees Fight Just Beginning."

33. Ibid., "Says Reservoir Could Have Stopped Big Flood," 25 June 1952.

34. Ibid., "Truman Urges United Battle to Aid Valley," 17 April 1952.

35. Ibid., "Work on Huge Dams Assured," 16 July 1952.

36. *Omaha World Herald,* "Dredge Helps Move River," 27 July 1952; U.S. Army Corps of Engineers, *Federal Engineer,* 109.

37. *Sioux City Journal,* "'Muddy Mo' Meets Master as Dredge Outsilts Silt," 21 July 1952.

38. Ibid.; U.S. Army Corps of Engineers, *Federal Engineer,* 110.

39. *Sioux City Journal,* "Fort Randall Dam Closure Near Climax," 17 July 1952.

40. *Omaha World Herald,* "Fort Randall Dam Is Ready to Guard River," 26 October 1952, and "Boat Dozer Helps Keep Out Trash from Ft. Randall Dam," 30 August 1953.

41. Ibid., "Randall Lake Grows Fast," 17 October 1954.

42. *ARCE, 1944,* 1024; *ARCE, 1951,* 1363; *ARCE, 1955,* 775; *ARCE, 1956,* 931.

43. *Sioux City Journal-Tribune,* "'Muddy' No Longer Fits the Missouri," 17 April 1959; W. W. Sayre and J. F. Kennedy, "Degradation and Aggradation of the Missouri River," Proceedings of a workshop held in Omaha, Nebraska, 23–25 January 1978, Iowa Institute of Hydraulic Research Report no. 215 (Iowa City: University of Iowa, 1978), 8; *Omaha World Herald,* "'Wild' River Funds Urged," 16 February 1954; *Sioux City Journal-Tribune,* "River Erosion Danger Imminent in This Area, Senator Case Declares," 20 March 1954; *Omaha World Herald,* "Farmer Loses Again to Wandering Missouri," 11 April 1954; *Des Moines Register,* "Missouri Speed-up Is Needed," 30 March 1956; *Sioux City Journal,* "Sioux City Man Argues Against Slashing of River Work Funds," 29 March 1956, and "Waltonians Boost for River Projects," 8 April 1957; *Sioux City Journal-Tribune,* "Congress Urged to Okay Missouri Channel Funds," 15 May 1957.

44. *Sioux City Journal-Tribune,* "Engineers See Dam Progress," 9 July 1952, and "Nice Trip Anyway, Say Discouraged South Sioux Men," 21 July 1953; *Sioux City*

Journal, "Sioux City Man Argues Against Slashing of River Work Funds," 29 March 1956; D. C. Bondurant, "Channel Stabilization on the Missouri River," in *Technical Report no. 1,* Vol. 1, *Symposium on Channel Stabilization Problems,* Committee on Channel Stabilization, Corps of Engineers (Vicksburg, MS: U.S. Army Corps of Engineers 1963), 48, 50, 51; Lindner, "Channel Improvement and Stabilization Measures," 8:9, 14, and 29.

45. Photo of work at Decatur Bend, Monona County, Iowa, provided by Tom Bruegger to author; *Omaha World Herald,* "Missouri River Will Be Led, Rather Than Pushed, Under Dry-Land Bridge," 1 May 1955; John Manning, "River Control Structures," in *Technical Report no. 1,* Vol. 2, *Symposium on Channel Stabilization Problems* (1964), 2:2.

46. U.S. Army Corps of Engineers, *Federal Engineer,* 232; *Sioux City Journal,* "Missouri Channel Entering Decisive Phase," 20 August 1961.

47. Photos of work at channelization structures, Monona County, Iowa, circa 1955–1965, provided by Tom Bruegger to author; *Sioux City Journal,* "Harnessing the Missouri," 16 June 1957, and "Missouri Channel Entering Decisive Phase."

48. *Omaha World Herald,* "Blast Sends Missouri River into New Channel at St. Joseph," 5 October 1952, and "New Bend in the River: Here's How Water Will Flow Under Decatur Bridge," 24 July 1955; *Sioux City Journal,* "Missouri Diversion Creating Two Lakes Near Sioux City," 16 October 1960, "Plug Pulled; Missouri River Near Decatur Flows Straight," 30 July 1961, and "Missouri Channel Entering Decisive Phase."

49. *Sioux City Journal,* "Missouri Bridge at Decatur, Neb., to Have Impact," 5 January 1947; *Des Moines Register,* "War May Change Plans to Move River Bridge," February 1951; *Sioux City Journal-Tribune,* "Hope Nature Will Aid Bridge Without River at Decatur," 2 February 1952; *Sioux City Journal,* "This Is a Fine Bridge, But—It's Bone Dry," summer 1954; *Des Moines Register,* "Seek to Move River to Flow Under Bridge," 2 February 1952; *Sioux City Journal,* "Agree on Funds for Dry Bridge," 22 June 1954, and "Dry Bridge Work Slated," 2 July 1954.

50. *Omaha World Herald,* "Moving River Major Effort," 4 July 1954, and "Missouri River Will Be Led, Rather Than Pushed, Under Dry-Land Bridge."

51. Ibid., "New Bend in the River: Here's How Water Will Flow Under Decatur Bridge."

52. *Sioux City Journal,* "Missouri's Flow Cut for Closure," 30 July 1955.

53. Ibid., "Missouri River Choked to Trickle by Upstream Dams," 7 August 1955.

54. *Des Moines Register,* "Blast Sends Water Under 'Dry' Bridge," 2 August 1955.

55. *ARCE, 1976,* 20.17, 21.15; *ARCE, 1970,* 656.

56. Department of the Army, U.S. Army Corps of Engineers, Office of the District Engineer, Omaha District, *Missouri River, Oahe Reservoir, South Dakota, Design Memorandum no. MO-27, Preliminary Study, Big Bend Dam and Reservoir* (Omaha: U.S. Army Corps of Engineers, 1954), 1–1, 1–4; Robert Hipple, interview.

57. Corps of Engineers, *Missouri River, Oahe Reservoir, MO-27,* 2–1.

58. U.S. Congress, Senate, *Missouri River Basin,* 78th Cong., 2d sess., 1944, S. Doc. 247, 6.

59. Corps of Engineers, *Missouri River, Oahe Reservoir, MO-27,* 2–1; Senate, *Missouri River Basin,* 6.

60. *Sioux Falls Argus Leader,* 13 October 1955; letter from Philip Byrnes to Karl E. Mundt, 16 December 1955, RG 13, Box 1453, File Folder 2, 1958–1959, Karl E. Mundt Papers, Dakota State College, Madison, South Dakota.

61. Lower Brule Resolution, 4 January 1956, Mundt Papers.

62. Mundt to William M. Potts, 16 August 1955, and Chamberlain Commercial Club to Mundt, 31 January 1956, Mundt Papers; Hipple, interview; *Sioux Falls Argus Leader,* 22 June 1956.

63. Corps of Engineers, *Missouri River, Oahe Reservoir, MO-27,* 2–1, 2–2, 4–2; Mundt to William M. Potts, 16 August 1955, and Mundt to John F. Lindley, 30 June 1956, Mundt Papers.

64. U.S. Army Corps of Engineers, U.S. Army Engineer District, Omaha, *Missouri River, Big Bend Reservoir, South Dakota, Design Memorandum No. MB-1, Site Selection,* 4–1, 4–3, 4–4, 4–5, 4–7, 4–9.

65. *Huron Daily Plainsman,* clipping, 1955, "Case Says Let's Demand Power for South Dakota"; letter of 23 July 1955, Case Papers; *Huron Daily Plainsman,* "South Dakota REA Attacks Case and State Reclamation Association on Power Stand; Says REA Endangered," 1955(?).

66. Case to Jarvis Davenport, 19 August 1957, copy of Case's original proposal for Senate bill 2822, 20 August 1957, General E. C. Itschner to Case, 11 September 1957, and Case to Jarvis Davenport, 19 August 1957, all in Case Papers.

67. Letter, 19 August 1958, Mundt Papers.

68. General E. C. Itschner to Mundt, 9 September 1958, and 14 October 1958, Mundt Papers; Newsletter, 9 March 1959, Case Papers.

69. Congress, Senate, Subcommittee of the Committee on Public Works, *Plans for Big Bend Dam, South Dakota: Hearing before the Subcommittee of the Committee on Public Works,* 86th Cong., 1st sess., 16 February 1959, 18.

70. Ibid., 93.

71. *Sioux Falls Argus Leader,* "Big Bend Closure Marks New Era," 21 July 1963; *Huron Daily Plainsman,* "Rusk's Speech Given Bipartisan Praise," 16 September 1966.

72. U.S. Army Corps of Engineers, Missouri River Division, *Missouri River Master Water Control Manual, . . . Description of Existing Environment,* 3–1, 3–3, 3–5.

11. The Untamable Missouri

1. *ARCE, 1944,* 1021; *ARCE, 1952,* 1304.

2. Sayre and Kennedy, "Degradation and Aggradation," 5.

3. Hallberg, Harbaugh, and Witinok, *Changes in the Channel Area of the Missouri River,* 6, 7; U.S. Army Corps of Engineers, Missouri River Division, *Missouri River Bank Stabilization and Navigation Project Final Feasibility Report and Final EIS for the Fish and Wildlife Mitigation Plan* (Omaha: U.S. Army Corps of Engineers, Missouri River Division, 1981), 3, 4.

4. Hallberg, Harbaugh, and Witinok, *Changes in the Channel Area of the Missouri River,* 16.

5. Ibid., 15, 16.

6. U.S. Army Corps of Engineers, Missouri River Division, *Missouri River Bank Stabilization and Navigation Project Final Feasibility Report and Final EIS for the Fish and Wildlife Mitigation Plan*, 3.

7. Number of acres and square miles calculated by taking the 364,000 acres and dividing by total river miles between Sioux City and mouth (762.5 in 1952), which equals 447.37 acres per mile; then multiply 447.37 by the number of river miles in western Iowa before the navigation projects in 1923 (200.8) and divide by two for the half in Nebraska and the half in Iowa.

8. The figure of 186.4 square miles was derived by adding the 66.6 square miles of channel area, the 70.1 square miles of the active erosion zone, and the 49.7 square miles of the meander belt.

9. John L. Funk and John W. Robinson, "Changes in the Channel of the Lower Missouri River and Effects on Fish and Wildlife," in *Aquatic Series no. 11* (Jefferson City: Missouri Department of Conservation, 1974), 15.

10. *Sioux City Journal*, "Missouri Yields a 93-Pound 'Cat,'" 23 June 1959.

11. U.S. Fish and Wildlife Service, Field Office, Division of Ecological Services, *Missouri River Stabilization and Navigation Project, Sioux City, Iowa to Mouth, Detailed Fish and Wildlife Coordination Act Report* (North Kansas City: Kansas City Area Office, U.S. Fish and Wildlife Service, 1980), 42; Jack Merwin, "Research Gives Paddlefish a Chance," *South Dakota Conservation Digest* (January 1974[?]): 12; Donald Friberg, "Living Relics: Because of Little Natural Reproduction, Paddlefish May Be on the Decline in South Dakota," *South Dakota Conservation Digest* (n.d.): 28(?).

12. U.S. Fish and Wildlife Service, Field Office, Division of Ecological Services, *Detailed Fish and Wildlife Coordination Act Report*, 42, 43; U.S. Fish and Wildlife Service, Missouri River Basin Studies, *Distribution and Status of the Important Fish and Wildlife, Missouri River Basin, 1952* (Billings, MT: U.S. Fish and Wildlife Service, 1953), 25, 26, 52, 53, 56, 57, 67, 68.

13. U.S. Fish and Wildlife Service, Missouri River Basin Studies, *Distribution and Status of Waterfowl in the Missouri River Basin* (Billings, MT: U.S. Fish and Wildlife Service, 1957), 50, 51, 54, 55, 56, 57, 60, 61, 100, 101, 114, 115.

14. U.S. Fish and Wildlife Service, *Distribution and Status of the Important Fish and Wildlife*, 152, 155, 162, 166, 173, 176, 179, 182, 188, 197, 200, 204; Donald Frank Johnson, "Plant Succession on the Missouri River Floodplain Near Vermillion, South Dakota" (Master's thesis, University of South Dakota, 1950), 22–25.

15. U.S. Geological Survey, *Monona County, Iowa, 1:100,000-scale Topographic Map* (Denver: U.S. Geological Survey, 1987).

16. *Sioux City Journal Tribune*, "'Muddy' No Longer Fits the Missouri," 17 April 1959.

17. Sayre and Kennedy, "Degradation and Aggradation," 8.

18. *Des Moines Register*, "Newest Iowa Playground: The Missouri, Tamed River Offers Boating, Fishing," 26 August 1956.

19. *Sioux City Journal*, "Missouri River No Longer 'Big Muddy,'" 18 April 1959.

20. U.S. Fish and Wildlife Service, Field Office, Division of Ecological Services, *Detailed Fish and Wildlife Coordination Act Report*, 9.

21. These bends included Omadi, Snyder, Winnebago, Blackbird, Tieville, Decatur, Louisville, and DeSoto.

22. U.S. Army Corps of Engineers, Omaha District, *Investigation of Channel Degradation, 1985 Update, Missouri River, Gavin's Point Dam to Platte River Confluence* (Omaha: U.S. Army Corps of Engineers, 1985), 2:5.

23. *Sioux City Journal,* "ICC Staff Told, 'Time Is Running Out for River,'" 20 October 1980.

24. Hallberg, Harbaugh, and Witinok, *Changes in the Channel Area of the Missouri River,* 16.

25. Ibid., 16; *Kansas City Times,* "Agency Decries Missouri River, U.S. Urged to Alter Policy to Aid Fish, Wildlife," 18 June 1980.

26. *Omaha World Herald,* "R.F.D.: River Work Opens New Frontier," 7 February 1954.

27. U.S. Fish and Wildlife Service, Field Office, Division of Ecological Services, *Detailed Fish and Wildlife Coordination Act Report,* 22.

28. *Omaha World Herald,* "R.F.D.: River Work Opens New Frontier," and "Land Cleared in Flood Plain, New Machinery Speeds Reclamation Job," 7 February 1954; *Sioux City Journal,* "Clearing Accretion Land of Missouri Is Hardy Winter Job," 24 January 1954, and "Land Clearing—1955 Style," 24 January 1955; *Des Moines Register,* "They've Harnessed the Missouri, but It's Still a Problem River," 10 June 1956; *Sioux City Journal,* "Irrigating from Missouri River," 2 July 1956, "Decisions Crucial in Fate of Missouri," 29 December 1980, and "River Research Reveals Habitat Losses," 28 January 1980; *Des Moines Register,* "Promises Drown in Muddy Mo," from series, "The Once Mighty Missouri," 1 October 1989, "The Mo Gnaws Deeper into its Bed," from same series, and "Dry Lakes, Less Wildlife—but a More Navigable River," same series.

29. Thomas B. Bragg and Annehara K. Tatschi, "Changes in Flood-Plain Vegetation and Land Use Along the Missouri River from 1826–1972," *Environmental Management* 1, no. 4 (1977): 346.

30. *Sioux City Journal,* "River Research Reveals Habitat Losses."

31. *Omaha World Herald*(?), "'River Vital to Industry,' Potter Gives Views to Foundation," 28 January 1955.

32. Ibid., "River Project Must Be Used," 17 November 1955.

33. *Sioux City Journal,* "River Site Fill Slated," 17 June 1958, and "Annexation Area," 2 November 1959; *Sioux City Journal-Tribune,* "I.P.S. to Build 25-Million-Dollar Plant on Missouri West of Salix," 10 December 1959; *Rapid City Journal,* "Municipal, Utility Projects Tap River," in series, "Missouri River Row," 18 September 1991.

34. *Omaha World Herald,* "Industry Site Needn't Spoil Good River View," 30 January 1955, and "Tamed River Booms Industry Chance," 15 January 1956.

35. Ibid., "Highway on River Bottom, Bluffs to Mondamin, Plan," 8 February 1956; *Sioux City Journal,* "Supporters of Proposed Interstate Riverfront Highway Outline Benefits," 22 September 1956, "Here's Plan for New Cloverleaf Interchange at Gordon Drive," 21 October 1956, and "Interstate Progresses," 19 April 1959.

36. Ibid., "Once Bitten, Always Interested," 6 October 1957.

37. U.S. Army Corps of Engineers, Missouri River Division, *Missouri River Bank Stabilization and Navigation Project Final Feasibility Report and Final EIS for the Fish and Wildlife Mitigation Plan,* 7.

38. Ibid., 7.

39. Data for calculation: Water area in 1980 estimated at 7,637 acres. Iowa Geological Survey estimated 35,000 acres of the channel area accreted to Iowa side of Missouri River through channelization; this 35,000 is divided by the 33 percent of the land area the Corps estimated remained undeveloped in the former channel area of the entire Missouri south of Sioux City. Thus, 11,550 acres remained undeveloped in the land accreted on the Iowa side. Take 11,550 acres plus the 4,491 acres undeveloped in the active erosion zone (44,915 × 10—Corps estimated that 10 percent of erosion zone was undeveloped), and total acreage undeveloped, including navigation channel water area, equals 23,678 acres or 37 square miles.

40. U.S. Fish and Wildlife Service, Field Office, Division of Ecological Services, *Detailed Fish and Wildlife Coordination Act Report*, 18.

41. Funk and Robinson, "Changes in the Channel of the Lower Missouri," 15, 27.

42. *Sioux Falls Argus Leader*, "Paddlefish Must Depend on Man for Survival," 11 July 1976; Larry W. Kallemeyn, "Paddlefish: Maybe a Future After All," *South Dakota Conservation Digest* (March/April 1975): 12–15.

43. Funk and Robinson, "Changes in the Channel of the Lower Missouri," 27.

44. *Omaha World Herald*, "Missouri River's Duck, Goose Sport on Skids, Up to Hunters to Organize, Help Avert Repeat of Sour Sport in '55," 27 November 1955; U.S. Fish and Wildlife Service, Field Office, Division of Ecological Services, *Detailed Fish and Wildlife Coordination Act Report*, 27.

45. *Sioux Falls Argus Leader*, "For the Birds, Efforts to Save Species Set Policies," in series, "Down by the River: Life Along the Missouri," 25 July 1991; U.S. Fish and Wildlife Service, Region 6, *Draft Biological Opinion on the Preferred Alternative for the Draft Environmental Impact Statement on the Missouri River Master Water Control Manual Review and Study and Operations of the Missouri River Main Stem System* (Denver: U.S. Fish and Wildlife Service, 1994), 40–45.

46. U.S. Army Corps of Engineers, Missouri River Division, *Missouri River Bank Stabilization and Navigation Project Final Feasibility Report and Final EIS for the Fish and Wildlife Mitigation Plan*, 10, 11; U.S. Fish and Wildlife Service, Field Office, Division of Ecological Services, *Detailed Fish and Wildlife Coordination Act Report*, 28.

47. Johnson, "Plant Succession on the Missouri River Floodplain Near Vermillion, South Dakota," 22–25.

48. Funk and Robinson, "Changes in the Channel of the Lower Missouri," 26.

49. Ibid., 21.

50. *Sioux City Journal*, "Sioux City Rediscovers Its Riverfront," 19 September 1991.

51. *Omaha World Herald*, "Missouri River's Duck, Goose Sport on Skids."

52. U.S. Fish and Wildlife Service, Field Office, Division of Ecological Services, *Detailed Fish and Wildlife Coordination Act Report*, 27.

53. Hallberg, Harbaugh, and Witinok, *Changes in the Channel Area of the Missouri River*, 10.

54. *Sioux City Journal*, "South Dakotans Seek Action to Restore McCook Lake Level," 25 April 1955, "McCook Lake Restoration Plea Taken to Congress," 20 May 1955, and "Public Meeting Called to Discuss Improvement of Western Iowa Lakes," 19 September 1955; *Des Moines Register*, "Future Is Dim for Missouri River Lakes," 2 October 1955, and "Oxbow Lakes No Longer Thrive," 2 October 1955; *Sioux City Journal*, "Hope to Save Crystal Lake, Ikes Ask Bids for Second Pump to

Retain Water," 2 June 1955, and "Crystal Lake—Battle of Man Against Nature," 11 August 1957.

55. *Sioux City Journal,* "South Dakotans Seek Action to Restore McCook Lake Level," and "McCook Lake Restoration Plea Taken to Congress."

56. Ibid., "Agree to Raise Level of Lake," 23 March 1954, "Hope to Save Crystal Lake, Ikes Ask Bids for Second Pump to Retain Water," and "Crystal Lake—Battle of Man Against Nature."

57. Ibid., "Area Lakes' Restoration Urged at Meet," 23 September 1955.

58. *Des Moines Register,* "Future Is Dim for Missouri River Lakes."

59. *Sioux City Journal,* "McCook Lake Restoration Plea Taken to Congress."

60. Ibid., "Bill Introduced for Improvements at McCook Lake," 29 May 1955, "State Project at McCook Lake Begins in Fall," 18 August 1955, and "McCook Lake Getting New $300,000 Look," 10 June 1956.

61. Ibid., "Agree to Raise Level of Lake."

62. Ibid., "Crystal Lake—Battle of Man Against Nature," "Back Crystal Lake Project," 13 November 1958, "Army Engineers Oppose Crystal Lake Dredging," 12 April 1961.

63. *Des Moines Register,* "Future Is Dim for Missouri River Lakes."

64. *Sioux City Journal,* "Area Lakes' Restoration Urged at Meet."

65. *Des Moines Register,* "Missouri River Oxbow Lakes," 8 January 1961; *Sioux City Journal,* "River Channel Work Making 'Fun Spots,'" 4 July 1961, "Ding's Idea for a Park On Missouri," 6 August 1961, "Engineers Plan New Lake Near Decatur," 28 July 1961, "New Siouxland Recreational Area—Snyder Bend Lake," 29 May 1961, and "View Missouri Recreation Needs," 20 June 1960; *Omaha World Herald,* "Iowan Will Seek Cash for Refuge on Missouri, DeSoto Bend Help Urged, Appropriations Bill Aid Sought by Jensen," 3 January 1957, "Engineers Poised to Make DeSoto Recreational Outlets Come to Life," 1 March 1959, and "Geese, Ducks, Not Workers, Fly South for Winter; Construction at DeSoto Bend Continues," 9 December 1959; Gerald Jauron, interview by author, tape recording, Earling, Iowa, November 1992; *Des Moines Register,* "They've Harnessed the Missouri, But It's Still a Problem River," 10 June 1956; *Sioux City Journal,* "Hoeven Sees River's Recreation Potential," 12 August 1960.

66. *Omaha World Herald,* "Iowa Recreation Project Will Benefit Nebraskans," 2 April 1961, and "Refuge Chain on Missouri Boon to Fowl, Hunters," 5 April 1961; *Sioux City Journal,* "New Siouxland Recreational Area—Snyder Bend Lake"; *Des Moines Register,* "View River's Play Areas," 17 June 1960. "Decatur Bend O.K. Indicated," 9 November 1967, "Decatur Bend Lake Approved," 18 November 1961, "DeSoto Bend Silt Work Set," 6 April 1961; *Sioux City Journal,* "Missouri Diversion Creating Two Lakes Near Sioux City," 16 October 1960; Jauron, interview.

67. Jauron, interview.

68. Sayre and Kennedy, "Degradation and Aggradation," 54.

69. *Des Moines Register,* "West Iowa Waterways Get Revenge. They Cut Deep, Wide Paths in the Erodible Soil that Are 'Not Bottomless, but You Can Get a Heck of a Canyon.'" 22 August 1993.

70. U.S. Army Corps of Engineers, Omaha District, *Investigation of Channel Degradation, 1991 Update, Missouri River, Gavin's Point Dam to Platte River Confluence*

(Omaha: U.S. Army Corps of Engineers, 1991), 6, 10; *Des Moines Register,* "West Iowa Waterways Get Revenge."

71. *Des Moines Register,* "Dry Lakes, Less Wildlife—but a More Navigable River," in series, "The Once Mighty Missouri," 1 October 1989.

72. Ibid., "S.D. Town Sags When Dams Dry Up Its Sand," 8 October 1956.

73. House, *Missouri River Channel Stabilization and Navigation Project,* 44.

74. *Kansas City Star,* "Dams and Levees Built to Resist River," 19 August 1980.

75. Ibid.; Young, "That Dammed Missouri River," 406; *Des Moines Register,* "Floods Knock Out Water in More Towns Minnesota to Missouri, Midwest River Rising," 26 July 1993; U.S. Army Corps of Engineers, North Central Division, *The Great Flood of 1993, Post-Flood Report, Upper Mississippi River and Lower Missouri River Basins* (St. Paul, MN: U.S. Army Corps of Engineers, 1994), 22.

76. House, *Missouri River Channel Stabilization and Navigation Project,* 22, 25.

77. *Kansas City Star,* "Missouri River's Impact Lags," 22 February 1977; U.S. Fish and Wildlife Service, Field Office, Division of Ecological Services, *Detailed Fish and Wildlife Coordination Act Report, Appendix, Economics,* 2.

78. *Kansas City Star,* "Some River Barge Firms Scraping Bottom," 27 October 1985.

79. *Sioux City Journal,* "River Repair Plans Move Ahead," 13 September 1991.

80. Ibid., 8 December 1981, and "Corps Warns More Water Coming Our Way," 29 April 1995.

81. *Kansas City Star,* "Saving Missouri Barge Traffic a Vital Issue, Danforth Says," 22 March 1992, "Taming the Meandering Missouri," 18 October 1993, and "GAO to Review River Study," 8 February 1992; *Sioux City Journal,* "Daschle Suggests Change in Missouri River Management," 10 June 1990, "Change in River Level Unlikely," 20 July 1987, "River Plans Threaten Ponderosa," 2 August 1995, and "Wildlife Will Benefit from Western Iowa Plantings," 12 June 1972.

Bibliography

Manuscript Collections

Benecke, Louis. Family Papers. Western Historical Manuscript Collection, Columbia, Missouri.
Case, Francis. Papers. Special Collections, Dakota Wesleyan College, Mitchell, South Dakota.
Mundt, Karl E. Papers. Karl E. Mundt Archives, Dakota State College, Madison, South Dakota.
Trail, E. B. Scrapbooks. Western Historical Manuscript Collection, Columbia, Missouri.
Weaver, Arthur J. Papers. Falls City, Nebraska.

Interviews

Chicoine, Blair. Interview by author. Sioux City, Iowa, 14 June 1996.
Estes, Joyce. Interview by author. Tape recording. Lower Brule, South Dakota, 12 March 1992.
Hipple, Robert. Interview by author. Tape recording. Pierre, South Dakota, 20 May 1992.
Jauron, Gerald. Interview by author. Tape recording. Earling, Iowa, 21 November 1992.
Weller, Sam, Mrs. Interview by author. Phone conversation. Mitchell, South Dakota, 12 June 1993.

Government Documents

Department of the Army, U.S. Army Corps of Engineers. *Annual Report of the Chief of Engineers*. Washington, DC: GPO, 1876–1979.
———. Committee on Channel Stabilization. C. P. Lindner, "Channel Improvement and Stabilization Measures," in *State of Knowledge of Channel Stabilization in Major Alluvial Rivers, Technical Report no. 7*. Vicksburg, MS: U.S. Army Corps of Engineers, 1969.
———. Committee on Channel Stabilization. D. C. Bondurant, "Channel Stabilization on the Missouri River," in *Symposium on Channel Stabilization Problems, Technical Report no. 1, vol. 1*. Vicksburg, MS: U.S. Army Corps of Engineers, 1963.
———. Committee on Channel Stabilization. John Manning, "River Control Structures," in *Symposium on Channel Stabilization Problems, Technical Report no. 1, vol. 2*. Vicksburg, MS: U.S. Army Corps of Engineers, 1964.

———. *The Federal Engineer, Damsites to Missile Sites: A History of the Omaha District, U.S. Army Corps of Engineers.* Omaha: U.S. Army Corps of Engineers, Omaha District Office, 1984.

———. *Missouri River.* 73d Cong., 2d sess., H. Doc. 238. Washington, DC: GPO, 1935.

———. Missouri River Division. *Controlling the Missouri.* Omaha: U.S. Army Corps of Engineers, Missouri River Division, 1951.

———. Missouri River Division. *Missouri River Master Water Control Manual, Review and Update Study, Draft Environmental Impact Statement.* Omaha: U.S. Army Corps of Engineers, Missouri River Division, 1994.

———. Missouri River Division. *Missouri River Master Water Control Manual, Review and Update Study, Environmental Studies, Reservoir Fisheries, Main Report, Appendix A—Description of Resource, Appendix B—Reservoir Fish Reproduction Impact Methodology.* Omaha: U.S. Army Corps of Engineers, Missouri River Division, 1994.

———. Missouri River Division. *Water Resources Development in South Dakota.* Omaha: U.S. Army Corps of Engineers, 1955.

———. Missouri River Division. *1991–1992 Missouri River Main Stem Reservoirs Annual Operating Plan and Summary of Actual 1990–1991 Operations.* Omaha: U.S. Army Corps of Engineers, 1991.

———. North Central Division. *The Great Flood of 1993, Post-Flood Report, Upper Mississippi River and Lower Missouri River Basins, Main Report.* Chicago: U.S. Army Corps of Engineers, North Central Division, 1994.

———. Office of the District Engineer, Omaha. *Missouri River, Oahe Reservoir, South Dakota, Design Memorandum no. MO-27, Preliminary Study, Big Bend Dam and Reservoir.* Omaha: U.S. Army Corps of Engineers, 1954.

———. Omaha District. *Comprehensive Report on Missouri River Development, Appendix 8, Plan of Improvement.* Omaha: U.S. Army Corps of Engineers, 1944(?).

———. Omaha District. *Investigation of Channel Degradation, 1985 Update, Missouri River, Gavin's Point Dam to Platte River Confluence.* Omaha: U.S. Army Corps of Engineers, 1985.

———. U.S. Army Engineer District, Omaha. *Missouri River, Big Bend Reservoir, South Dakota, Design Memorandum no. MB-1, Site Selection.* Omaha: U.S. Army Corps of Engineers, 1957.

———. U.S. Army Engineer Division, Missouri River. *Water Resources Development in South Dakota.* Omaha: U.S. Army Corps of Engineers, 1957.

———. U.S. Army Office of the District Engineer, Omaha. *Missouri River, Big Bend Reservoir, South Dakota, Transcript of Dictaphone Recording taken at [the] Meeting of the Board of Consultants Held at Pierre, South Dakota, 21 and 22 October 1958.* Omaha: U.S. Army Corps of Engineers, 1958.

———. U.S. Army Office of the District Engineer, Omaha. Real Estate Division. *Real Estate Memorandum, Big Bend Project, Buffalo, Hughes, Hyde, Lyman, and Stanley Counties, South Dakota, MB-21.* Omaha: U.S. Army Corps of Engineers, 1960.

Department of the Interior, Fish and Wildlife Service. Field Office, Division of Ecological Services. *Missouri River Stabilization and Navigation Project, Sioux City, Iowa to Mouth, Detailed Fish and Wildlife Coordination Act Report.* North Kansas City, MO: Kansas City Area Office, Division of Ecological Services, 1980.

————. *Fish and Wildlife Technical Report 8, Limnological and Fishery Studies on Lake Sharp, a Main-stem Missouri River Reservoir, 1964–1975.* Washington DC: GPO, 1987.

————. Missouri River Basin Studies. *Distribution and Status of the Important Fish and Wildlife, Missouri River Basin, 1952.* Billings, MT: Fish and Wildlife Service, 1953.

————. Missouri River Basin Studies. *Distribution and Status of Waterfowl in the Missouri River Basin.* Billings, MT: Fish and Wildlife Service, 1957.

————. Region 6. *Draft Biological Opinion on the Preferred Alternative for the Draft Environmental Impact Statement on the Missouri River Master Water Control Manual Review and Study and Operations of the Missouri River Main Stem System.* Denver: U.S. Fish and Wildlife Service, 1994.

Missouri Basin Inter-Agency Committee. *The Missouri: A Great River Basin of the United States, Its Resources and How We Are Using Them.* Washington DC: GPO, 1954(?).

Missouri Basin Inter-Agency Committee and the Missouri River States Committee. *The Missouri River Basin Development Program.* Washington, DC: GPO, 1952.

Missouri River State Committee. *The Future Development of the Missouri River: A Report on the Program and Activities of the Missouri River States Committee.* Chicago: Council of State Governments, 1944.

Robinson, Doane. *Dam Sites on the Missouri River in South Dakota.* Pierre: South Dakota Department of Immigration, 1918.

U.S. Congress. House. Committee on Flood Control. *Statement of M. Q. Sharpe, Governor of South Dakota: Hearing Before the Committee on Flood Control.* 78th Cong., 2d sess., 16–17 February 1944.

————. Committee on Rivers and Harbors. *Missouri River.* 60th Cong., 2d sess., 1908. H. Doc. 1120.

————. *Missouri River Channel Stabilization and Navigation Project: Hearing Before the Subcommittee of the Committee on Appropriations.* 82d Cong., 2d sess., 30 June 1952. Washington, DC: GPO, 1952.

U.S. Congress, Senate. *Missouri River Basin.* 78th Cong., 2d sess., 1944. S. Doc. 247.

————. Subcommittee of the Committee on Public Works. *Plans for Big Bend Dam, South Dakota: Hearing Before the Subcommittee of the Committee on Public Works.* 86th Cong., 1st sess., 16 February 1959.

Proceedings

Aitken, Walter W. "Probable Effect of Reservoir Construction on Flora and Fauna of the Missouri River Region. Paper presented at South Dakota Ornithologists Union. Sioux Falls, South Dakota, 15 January 1949. Photocopy.

Case, Francis. "Review Report on the Missouri River in North Dakota, South Dakota and Nebraska." Supplement 5, vol. 3. Transcript of Proceedings, Public Hearing. Pierre, South Dakota, 15 March 1940.

Pick-Sloan Missouri Basin Plan. Proceedings of conference held in Des Moines, Iowa, 10–11 August 1983. Missouri Basin States Association, 1983.

Sayre, W. W., and J. F. Kennedy. "Degradation and Aggradation of the Missouri River." Proceedings of a workshop held in Omaha, Nebraska, 23–25 January 1978, Iowa Institute of Hydraulic Research Report no. 215. Iowa City: University of Iowa, 1978.

Newspapers

Chamberlain (SD) Register. 1956–1958
Des Moines (IA) Register, 1955–1995
Huron (SD) Daily Plainsman, 1950–1970
Kansas City (MO) Star, 1900–1975
Kansas City (MO) Times, 1900–1980
Mobridge (SD) Tribune, 1922
Omaha (NE) World Herald, 1955–1980
Pierre (SD) Capital Journal, 1950–1965
Sioux City (IA) Journal, 1930–1995
Sioux Falls (SD) Argus Leader, 1950–1995

Journals

Abel, Annie Heloise, ed. *Tabeau's Narrative of Loisel's Expedition to the Upper Missouri.* Norman: University of Oklahoma Press, 1939.
Account of a Steamboat Voyage on the Missouri River, St. Louis to Fort Benton, May–August, 1859, by Elias J. Marsh, M.D. South Dakota Historical Review 1, no. 2 (1936): 79–127.
Audubon, Maria R. *The Missouri River Journals, 1843.* In *Audubon and His Journals.* Edited by Elliot Coues. Vol. 1. 1897. Reprint, New York: Dover Publications, 1960.
Bell, Gordon H. *Down the Big Muddy.* Sioux Falls, SD: Published by author, 1958.
Brackenridge, Henry Marie. *Views of Louisiana; Together with a Journal of a Voyage Up the Missouri River, in 1811.* 1814. Reprint, Ann Arbor, MI: University Microfilms, 1966.
Bradbury, John. *Travels in the Interior of America, in the Years 1809, 1810, and 1811; Including a Description of Upper Louisiana, Together with the States of Ohio, Kentucky, Indiana, and Tennessee, with the Illinois and Western Territories, and Containing Remarks and Observations Useful to Persons Emigrating to Those Countries.* 1817. Reprint, Ann Arbor, MI: University Microfilms, 1966.
Bray, Edmund C., and Martha Coleman Bray, eds. and trans. *Joseph N. Nicollet on the Plains and Prairies: The Expeditions of 1838–39, with Journals, Letters, and Notes on the Dakota Indians.* St. Paul: Minnesota Historical Society, 1976.
Coues, Elliot, ed. *The History of the Lewis and Clark Expedition by Meriwether Lewis and William Clark.* 3 vols. 1893, Reprint. New York: Dover Publications, n.d.
Culbertson, Thaddeus A. *Journal of an Expedition to the Mauvaises Terres and the Upper Missouri in 1850: by Thaddeus A. Culbertson.* In Smithsonian Institution, *Fifth Annual Report, 1850.* Edited by John Francis McDermott. 1952. Reprint, Lincoln: J and L Print Company, Reprints in Anthropology, 1981.

Gass, Patrick. *A Journal of the Voyages and Travels of a Corps of Discovery, Under the Command of Capt. Lewis and Capt. Clarke of the Army of the United States, from the Mouth of the River Missouri through the Interior Parts of North America to the Pacific Ocean, During the Years, 1804, 1805, and 1806*. Minneapolis: Ross and Haines, 1958.

James, Edwin, ed. *Account of an Expedition from Pittsburgh to the Rocky Mountains, Performed in the Years 1819 and '20, by Order of the Hon. J. C. Calhoun, Sec'y of War: Under the Command of Major Stephen H. Long, from the Notes of Major Long, Mr. T. Say, and Other Gentlemen of the Exploring Party*. 1823. Reprint, Ann Arbor: University Microfilms, March of America Facsimile Series, no. 65, 1966.

Larpenteur, Charles. *Forty Years a Fur Trader on the Upper Missouri: The Personal Narrative of Charles Larpenteur, 1833–1872*. 1933. Reprint, Minneapolis: Ross and Haines, 1962.

Moulton, Gary E., ed. *The Journals of the Lewis and Clark Expedition*. 6 vols. to date. Lincoln: University of Nebraska Press, 1983–.

Nichols, Roger L., ed. *The Missouri Expedition, 1818–1820: The Journal of Surgeon John Gale with Related Documents*. Norman: University of Oklahoma Press, 1969.

Oehler, Gottlieb F., and David Z. Smith. *Description of a Journey and Visit to the Pawnee Indians who live on the Platte River, a tributary to the Missouri, 70 miles from its mouth by Brn. Gottlieb F. Oehler and David Z. Smith, April 22–May 18, 1851, to which is added A Description of the Manners and Customs of the Pawnee Indians by Dr. D. Z. Smith*. 1851–1852. Reprint, New York: N.P., 1914.

Reid, Russell, and Clell G. Gannon, eds. *Journal of the Atkinson-O'Fallon Expedition*. North Dakota Historical Quarterly 4 (October 1929): 5–56.

Riggs, Stephen Return. *Journal of a Tour from Lac-qui-Parle to the Missouri River*. South Dakota Historical Collections 13 (1926): 330–44.

Robbins, Willard. Recollections of Monona County Pioneers. Published by author, n.d.

Trudeau, Jean Baptiste. *Trudeau's Description of the Upper Missouri*. Mississippi Valley Historical Review 8 (1921): 149–79.

Warren, G[ouverneur]. K[emble]. *Explorer on the Northern Plains: Lieutenant Gouverneur K. Warren's Preliminary Report of Explorations in Nebraska and Dakota, in the Years 1855–56–57*. Introduction by Frank N. Schubert. Washington, DC: Office of the Chief of Engineers, 1981.

Books

Ambrose, Stephen. *Undaunted Courage: Meriwether Lewis, Thomas Jefferson, and the Opening of the American West*. New York: Simon and Schuster, 1996.

Ashton, Diane E., and Eileen M. Dowd. *Fragile Legacy: Endangered, Threatened and Rare Animals of South Dakota*. Pierre, SD: Department of Game, Fish and Parks, 1991.

Athearn, Robert G. *Forts of the Upper Missouri*. Lincoln: University of Nebraska Press, 1967.

Baumhoff, Richard G. *The Dammed Missouri Valley, One Sixth of Our Nation*. New York: Alfred Knopf, 1951.

Blum, John M., ed. *The National Experience*. Part 2, *A History of the United States Since 1865*. 8th ed. Forth Worth, TX: Harcourt Brace Jovanovich, 1993.

Branyan, Robert L. *Taming the Mighty Missouri: A History of the Kansas City District, Corps of Engineers, 1907–1971*. Kansas City, MO: U.S. Army Corps of Engineers, 1974.

Chittenden, Hiram. *History of Early Steamboat Navigation on the Missouri River*. 2 vols. New York: F. P. Harper, 1903.

Coon, Martha Sutherland. *Oahe Dam: Master of the Missouri*. New York: Harvey House, 1969.

Cronon, William. *Nature's Metropolis: Chicago and the Great West*. New York: W. W. Norton, 1991.

Cutright, Paul Russell. *Lewis and Clark: Pioneering Naturalists*. Lincoln: University of Nebraska Press, 1969.

Dietrich, William. *Northwest Passage: The Great Columbia River*. New York: Simon and Schuster, 1995.

Dinsmore, James J. *A Country So Full of Game: The Story of Wildlife in Iowa*. Iowa City: University of Iowa Press, 1994.

Ewers, John C. *Indian Life on the Upper Missouri*. Norman: University of Oklahoma Press, 1968.

Ewers, John C., Marsha V. Gallagher, David C. Hunt, and Joseph C. Porter. *Views of a Vanishing Frontier*. Omaha: Center for Western Studies, Joslyn Art Museum, 1984.

Ferrell, John R. *Big Dam Era: A Legislative and Institutional History of the Pick-Sloan Missouri Basin Program*. Omaha: Missouri River Division, U.S. Army Corps of Engineers, 1993.

———. *Heartland Engineers: A History of the Kansas City District, U.S. Army Corps of Engineers*. Washington, DC: GPO, 1992.

———. *Soundings: One Hundred Years of the Navigation Project*. Washington, DC: GPO, 1996.

Gilmore, Melvin Randolph. *Uses of Plants by the Indians of the Missouri River Region*. Foreword by Hugh Cutler. Lincoln: University of Nebraska Press, 1977, 1991.

Hallberg, George R., Jayne M. Harbaugh, and Patricia M. Witinok. *Changes in the Channel Area of the Missouri River in Iowa, 1879–1976*. Iowa City: Iowa Geological Survey, 1979.

Hanson, Joseph M. *The Conquest of the Missouri: Being the Story of the Life and Exploits of Captain Grant Marsh*. 1909, 1937. Reprint, New York: Murray Hills Books, 1946.

Hart, Henry C. *The Dark Missouri*. Madison: University of Wisconsin Press, 1957.

Heckman, William, L. *Heckman's Hand Book of Information About the Missouri River*. Hermann, MO: published by author, 1933.

Holder, Preston. *The Hoe and the Horse on the Plains: A Study of Cultural Development Among North American Indians*. Lincoln: University of Nebraska Press, 1970.

Hoover, Herbert T. "The Missouri River." In *Rolling Rivers: An Encyclopedia of America's Rivers*. Edited by Richard A. Bartlett, 211–16. New York: McGraw-Hill, 1984.

Hoover, Herbert T., Karen P. Zimmerman, and Christopher J. Hoover. *South Dakota History: An Annotated Bibliography*. Westport, CT: Greenwood Press, 1993.

Hundley, Norris Jr. *The Great Thirst: Californians and Water, 1770s–1990s*. Berkeley: University of California Press, 1992.

Iverson, Peter, ed. *The Plains Indians of the Twentieth Century*. Norman: University of Oklahoma Press, 1985.

Jackson, Donald. *Voyages of the Steamboat Yellow Stone*. New York: Ticknor and Fields, 1985.

Joslyn Art Museum and the University of Nebraska Press. *Karl Bodmer's America*. Omaha: Joslyn Art Museum, 1984.

Ladner, Mildred D. *William de la Montagne Cary: Artist on the Missouri River*. Norman: University of Oklahoma Press, 1984.

Lass, William E. *A History of Steamboating on the Upper Missouri River*. Lincoln: University of Nebraska Press, 1962.

Lathrop, A. H. *Life in Vermillion Before the 1881 Flood and Shortly After*. Vermillion, SD: Clay County Historical Society, 1970.

Lawson, Michael L. *Dammed Indians: The Pick-Sloan Plan and the Missouri River Sioux, 1944–1980*. Norman: University of Oklahoma Press, 1982.

Lehmer, Donald J. *Introduction to Middle Missouri Archeology*. In Anthropological Papers no. 1, National Park Service, U.S. Department of the Interior. Washington, DC: GPO, 1971.

Leuchtenburg, William E. *Franklin D. Roosevelt and the New Deal*. New York: Harper and Row, 1963.

Lowitt, Richard. *The New Deal and the West*. Norman: University of Oklahoma Press, 1984.

Malone, Michael P., and Richard W. Etulain. *The American West: A Twentieth Century History*. Lincoln: University of Nebraska Press, 1989.

Marcus, Alan I., and Howard P. Segal. *Technology in America: A Brief History*. New York: Harcourt Brace Jovanovich, 1989.

Mead, Daniel Webster, and Charles V. Seastone. *Report on the Feasibility of the Development of Hydro Electric Power from the Missouri River in the State of South Dakota*. 1920. Reprint, Pierre, SD: Lawrence K. Fox, 1929.

Mutel, Cornelia F. *Fragile Giants: A Natural History of the Loess Hills*. Iowa City: University of Iowa Press, 1989.

Nash, Roderick. *Wilderness and the American Mind*. 3d ed. New Haven: Yale University Press, 1982.

———, ed. *American Environmentalism: Readings in Conservation History*. 3d ed. New York: McGraw-Hill, 1990.

Neihardt, John G. *The River and I*. 1910. Reprint, Lincoln: University of Nebraska Press, 1938, 1968.

Nelson, Bruce. *Land of the Dacotahs*. Minneapolis: University of Minnesota Press, 1946.

Opie, John. *Ogallala: Water for a Dry Land*. Lincoln: University of Nebraska Press, 1993.

Pearson, Robert, and Brad Pearson. *The J. C. Nichols Chronicle*. Lawrence: University Press of Kansas for Robert Pearson and Brad Pearson, 1994.

Perlin, John. *A Forest Journey: The Role of Wood in the Development of Civilization*. Cambridge: Harvard University Press, 1991.

Pitzer, Paul C. *Grand Coulee: Harnessing a Dream.* Pullman: Washington State University Press, 1994.

Prior, Jean C. *Landforms of Iowa.* Iowa City: University of Iowa Press, 1991.

Reiger, John F. *American Sportsmen and the Origins of Conservation.* Norman: University of Oklahoma Press, 1986.

Ridgeway, Marian E. *The Missouri Basin's Pick-Sloan Plan: A Case Study in Congressional Policy Determination.* Urbana: University of Illinois Press, 1955.

Schell, Herbert S. *History of South Dakota.* Lincoln: University of Nebraska Press, 1961.

Sherow, James. *Watering the Valley: Development Along the High Plains Arkansas River, 1870–1950.* Lawrence: University Press of Kansas, 1991.

Stewart, Rick, Joseph D. Ketner II, and Angela L. Miller. *Carl Wimar: Chronicler of the Missouri River Frontier.* Fort Worth, TX: Amon Carter Museum, 1991.

Stine, Jeffrey K. *Mixing the Waters: Environment, Politics, and the Building of the Tennessee-Tombigbee Waterway.* Akron, OH: University of Akron Press, 1993.

Terral, Rufus. *The Missouri Valley: Land of Drouth, Flood, and Promise.* New Haven: Yale University Press, 1947.

Thorson, John E. *River of Promise, River of Peril: The Politics of Managing the Missouri River.* Lawrence: University Press of Kansas, 1994.

Todd, John. *Early Settlement and Growth of Western Iowa, or Reminiscences.* Des Moines: Historical Department of Iowa, 1906.

Vestal, Stanley. *The Missouri.* 1945. Reprint, Lincoln: University of Nebraska Press, 1964.

Webb, Walter Prescott. *The Great Plains.* 1931. Reprint, Lincoln: University of Nebraska Press, 1981.

White, Richard. *The Organic Machine: The Remaking of the Columbia River.* New York: Hill and Wang, 1995.

Will, George F., and George E. Hyde. *Corn Among the Indians of the Upper Missouri.* St. Louis: William Harvey Miner, 1917.

WNAX Radio, Yankton, SD. *Disaster 1952.* Sioux City, IA: Record Printing Company, 1952.

Works Progress Administration, Federal Writer's Project. *Sodbusters: Tales of Southeastern South Dakota.* Alexandria, SD: South Dakota Writer's League, 1938.

Worster, Donald. *Rivers of Empire: Water, Aridity, and the Growth of the American West.* 1985. Reprint, New York: Oxford University Press, 1992.

Yankton (SD) Herald. The Great Flood. Yankton, SD: Herald Press, 1881.

Articles

Anderson, Hattie M. "The Evolution of a Frontier Society in Missouri, 1815–1828, Part 1." *Missouri Historical Review* 32 (April 1938): 298–326.

———. "Missouri, 1804–1828: Peopling a Frontier State." *Missouri Historical Review* 31 (January 1937): 150–80.

Armstrong, Moses Kimball. "History and Resources of Dakota, Montana and Idaho." *South Dakota Historical Collections* 14 (1928): 9–70.

Bannon, John Francis, S. J. "Lewis and Clark Came Late." *South Dakota History* 4, no. 2 (1974): 222–37.

Best, Louis B., Kenneth L. Varland, and Robert B. Dahlgren. "Effects of Stream Channelization on Land-Use Practices in Iowa." *Iowa State Journal of Research* 52, no. 4 (May 1978): 411–23.

Bradley, L. E. "Government Ice Harbors on the Upper Missouri." *North Dakota History* 60, no. 3 (1993): 28–37.

Bragg, Thomas B., and Annehara K. Tatschi. "Changes in Flood-Plain Vegetation and Land Use Along the Missouri River from 1826 to 1972." *Environmental Management* 1, no. 4 (1977): 343–48.

Bratton, Sam T. "Inefficiency of Water Transportation in Missouri—A Geographical Factor in the Development of Railroads." *Missouri Historical Review* 14 (October 1919): 82–88.

Briggs, Harold E. "The Settlement and Economic Development of the Territory of Dakota." *South Dakota Historical Review* 2, no. 2 (1937): 151–66.

Brown, Richard Maxwell. "The Enduring Frontier: The Impact of Weather on South Dakota History and Literature." *South Dakota History* 15, nos. 1 and 2 (1985): 27–65.

Campbell, David C. "The Pick-Sloan Program: A Case of Bureaucratic Economic Power." *Journal of Economic Issues* 18, no. 2 (June 1984): 449–56.

Cass, Edward C. "Flood Control and the Corps of Engineers in the Missouri Valley, 1902–1973." *Nebraska History* 63, no. 1 (spring 1982): 108–21.

Chamberlain Commercial Club. "Big Bend Hydro-Electric Project." Chamberlain, SD: Register Printing Company, 1935(?).

Chittenden, Hiram M. "Report on Steamboat Wrecks on Missouri River." *Nebraska History Magazine* 8, no. 1 (January–March 1925): 21–22.

Clow, Richmond L. "Tribal Populations in Transition: Sioux Reservations and Federal Policy, 1934–1965." *South Dakota History* 19, no. 3 (fall 1989): 362–91.

Corbin, Annalies. "Shifting Sand and Muddy Water: Cartography and River Migration as Factors in Locating Steamboat Wrecks on the Far Upper Missouri River." *Historical Archaeology* 32, no. 4, in press.

Corbin, Annalies, and Kenneth W. Karsmizki. "Steamboats in Montana: Wrecks of the Far Upper Missouri–Yellowstone River Drainage Area, Phase 1—The Search for Historical Evidence." *Underwater Archaeology* (1997): 64.

DeLand, Charles E. "Papers and Communications upon Internal Waterways and Navigation, Comprising a Portion of Part III of the Author's Book Entitled 'Thoughts Afield.'" Pierre, SD: Charles E. DeLand, 1911.

Ferrell, John. "Developing the Missouri: South Dakota and the Pick-Sloan Plan." *South Dakota History* 19, no. 3 (fall 1989): 306–41.

Fite, Gilbert C. "Agricultural Pioneering in Dakota: A Case Study." *Great Plains Quarterly* 1, no. 3 (1981): 169–80.

Freedom, Gary S. "Moving Men and Supplies: Military Transportation on the Northern Great Plains, 1866–1891." *South Dakota History* 14, no. 2 (1984): 114–33.

Freeman, Lewis R. "Trailing History down the Big Muddy." *National Geographic* 54, no. 1 (July 1928): 73–120.

Friberg, Donald. "Living Relics: Because of Little Natural Reproduction, Paddlefish May Be on the Decline in South Dakota." *South Dakota Conservation Digest* (n.d.): 28(?).

Funk, John L., and John W. Robinson. "Changes in the Channel of the Lower Missouri River and Effects on Fish and Wildlife." *Missouri Department of Conservation, Aquatic Series, No. 11* (November 1974).

Gerber, Max E. "The Steamboat and the Indians of the Upper Missouri." *South Dakota History* 4, no. 2 (1974): 139–60.

Hafermehl, Louis N. "To Make the Desert Bloom: The Politics and Promotion of Early Irrigation Schemes in North Dakota." *North Dakota History, Journal of the Northern Plains* 59, no. 3 (summer 1992): 13–27.

Hamburg, James F. "Railroads and the Settlement of South Dakota During the Great Dakota Boom, 1878–1887." *South Dakota History* 5, no. 2 (spring 1975): 165–78.

Harvey, Mark W. T. "North Dakota, the Northern Plains, and the Missouri Valley Authority." *North Dakota History, Journal of the Northern Plains* 59, no. 3 (summer 1992): 28–39.

————. "North Dakota's Water History: An Introduction." *North Dakota History, Journal of the Northern Plains* 59, no. 3 (summer 1992): 2–4.

Hoover, Herbert. "The Need of Inland Waterways for Agriculture and Industry." Address, Missouri River Navigation Conference, Kansas City, MO, 19 October 1925. In *Inland Waterways and Missouri River Navigation.* Kansas City, MO: Missouri River Navigation Association, 1925.

Hoover, Herbert T., John Rau, and Leonard Bruguier. "Gorging Ice and Flooding Rivers: Springtime Devastation in South Dakota." *South Dakota History* 17, nos. 3 and 4 (1987): 181–201.

Hunt, William J. "Fort Floyd: An Enigmatic Nineteenth-Century Trading Post." *North Dakota History, Journal of the Northern Plains* 61, no. 3 (summer 1994): 7–20.

The Journal of Charles LeRaye. South Dakota Historical Collections 4 (1908): 149–80.

Kallemeyn, Larry W. "Paddlefish: Maybe a Future After All." *South Dakota Conservation Digest* (March/April 1975): 12–15.

"Land of the Big Muddy." *Time,* 1 September 1952, 36, 45.

Langevin, Thomas H. "Development of Multiple-Purpose Water Planning by the Federal Government in the Missouri Basin." *Nebraska History* 34, no. 1 (1953): 1–19.

Lasch, Robert. "Harnessing the Missouri." *Reporter,* 29 August 1950, 32–34.

Lass, William E. "The History and Significance of the Northwest Fur Company, 1865–1869." *North Dakota History, Journal of the Northern Plains* 61, no. 3 (summer 1994): 21–40.

————. "Missouri River Steamboating." *North Dakota History, Journal of the Northern Plains* 56, no. 3 (summer 1989): 3–16.

Lawson, Michael L. "Federal Water Projects and Indian Lands: The Pick-Sloan Plan, a Case Study." *American Indian Culture and Research Journal* 7, no. 1 (1983): 23–40.

Lehmer, Donald J. "Climate and Culture History in the Middle Missouri Valley." In *Pleistocene and Recent Environments of the Central Great Plains.* Edited by Wakefield Dort and J. Knox Jones, 117–30. Lawrence: University Press of Kansas, 1970.

Mattison, Ray H. "The Indian Frontier on the Upper Missouri to 1865." *Nebraska History* 39, no. 3 (1958): 241–66.

Merwin, Jack. "Research Gives Paddlefish a Chance." *South Dakota Conservation Digest* (January 1974[?]): 12.

Miller, George J. "Making the Missouri River Navigable: How It Is Accomplished and What the Engineers Say." Kansas City, MO: Missouri River Navigation Association, November 1928.

Missouri River Improvement Association. Proceedings of the Missouri River Improvement Convention, Held at Kansas City, Missouri, December 15 and 16, 1891. Kansas City, MO: Missouri River Improvement Association.

Missouri River Improvement Convention. Official Report of the Proceedings of the Missouri River Convention, Held in Kansas City, Missouri, December 29 and 30, 1885. Kansas City, MO: Lawton and Havens, 1885.

Missouri River Navigation Association. "The Missouri River Navigation Association, Organized at Kansas City, Missouri, October 19–20, 1925." Kansas City, MO: Missouri River Navigation Association, 1925.

———. "Railways and Waterways." Kansas City, MO: Missouri River Navigation Association, 1931.

———. "What the Missouri River Navigation Association Has Accomplished." Kansas City, MO: Missouri River Navigation Association, 1927.

Missouri River Navigation Congress. Proceedings of the First Annual Convention of the Missouri River Navigation Congress at Sioux City, Iowa, Wednesday and Thursday, January 22–23, 1908. Sioux City(?): Missouri River Navigation Congress, 1908.

Missouri Valley River Improvement Association. "The Way to Navigate Is to Navigate: The Deep Water Project for the Missouri River, a 12-Foot Channel Would Save Its Cost Every Year." Report of the Missouri Valley River Improvement Association. Kansas City, MO: Missouri Valley River Improvement Association, 1908.

———. "The Way to Navigate Is to Navigate: The Missouri, a Deep Waterway, a 12-Foot Channel Would Save Its Cost Every Year." Work of Missouri Valley River Improvement Association for the Development of River Navigation. Kansas City, MO: Missouri Valley River Improvement Association, 1907.

Nebraska History Magazine. "The Missouri River: Its Discovery, Its Region and Resources, Its Navigation, Its Future." Lincoln: Nebraska State Historical Society, 1927.

Nichols, J. C. "The Missouri River, the Mississippi Waterways, and Their Relation to Agriculture and Industry." Address, Mississippi Valley Association, 10th Annual Convention, St. Louis, Missouri, 27 November 1928. In *The Missouri River, the Mississippi Waterways, and Their Relation to Agriculture and Industry.* Kansas City, MO: Missouri River Navigation Association, 1928.

Nichols, Roger L. "Martin Cantonment and American Expansion in the Missouri Valley." *Missouri Historical Review* 64 (October 1969): 1–17.

Parker, Donald D. "Expeditions up the Missouri, 1818–1825." *South Dakota Historical Collections* 33 (1966): 458–87.

Pierre Commercial Club. "Navigation of the Missouri River Through the Dakotas." Pierre: Hipple, 1931.

Robinson, William G. "Big Bend of the Missouri." Photocopy. Pierre: South Dakota State Historical Society, 1963.

———. "The Development of the Missouri Valley." *South Dakota Historical Collections* 22 (1946): 445–544.

Roy, Sydney J. "The Value of Missouri River Navigation to the Consumers and Producers of the Missouri River Valley." Address, "Farmers Week" Conference, Jessie Hall, University of Missouri, Columbia, 21 January 1926. In *Navigation and Agriculture*. Kansas City, MO: Missouri River Navigation Association, 1925.

Ruhe, R. V., T. E. Fenton, and L. L. Ledesma. "Missouri River History, Floodplain Construction, and Soil Formation in Southwestern Iowa." *Iowa Agriculture and Home Economics Experiment Station, Research Bulletin 580* (September 1975): 738–91.

Schell, Herbert S. "The Dakota Southern: A Frontier Railway Venture of Dakota Territory." *South Dakota Historical Review* 2, no. 3 (1937): 99–125.

———. "Early Manufacturing Activities in South Dakota, 1857–1875." *South Dakota Historical Review* 2, no. 2 (1937): 73–95.

Sharpe, M. Q. "History of the Missouri River States Committee." *South Dakota Historical Collections* 22 (1946): 400–409.

Shimek, B. "Geology of Harrison and Monona Counties." Iowa Geological Survey Annual Report, 20. Des Moines: Emory H. English, 1910.

Shortridge, James R. "The Expansion of the Settlement Frontier in Missouri." *Missouri Historical Review* 75 (October 1980): 64–90.

Simpich, Frederick. "Taming the Outlaw Missouri." *National Geographic*, November 1945, 569–98.

Thomas, Raymond D. "Missouri Valley Settlement—St. Louis to Independence." *Missouri Historical Review* 21 (October 1926): 24–40.

Viles, Jonas. "Old Franklin: A Frontier Town of the Twenties." *Mississippi Valley Historical Review* 9, no. 4 (March 1923): 269–82.

Voss, Stuart F. "Town Growth in Central Missouri, Part 1." *Missouri Historical Review* 64 (October 1969): 64–80.

———. "Town Growth in Central Missouri, Part 2." *Missouri Historical Review* 64 (January 1970): 197–217.

———. "Town Growth in Central Missouri, Part 3." *Missouri Historical Review* 64 (April 1970): 322–50.

Welsh, Michael. "Western Historians, the U.S. Army Corps of Engineers, and the Rivers of Empire." *North Dakota History, Journal of the Northern Great Plains* 59, no. 3 (summer 1992): 5–12.

White, Edward J. "A Century of Transportation in Missouri." *Missouri Historical Review* 15 (October 1920): 126–62.

Wilson, Frederick T. "Old Fort Pierre and Its Neighbors." *South Dakota Historical Collections* 1 (1902): 257–379.

Windell, Marie George, ed. "The Road West in 1818: The Diary of Henry Vest Bingham, Part 2." *Missouri Historical Review* 40 (January 1946): 174–204.

Wood, Raymond W. "An Introduction to the History of the Fur Trade on the Northern Plains." *North Dakota History, Journal of the Northern Plains* 61, no. 3 (summer 1994): 2–6.

Young, Gordon. "That Dammed Missouri River." *National Geographic,* September 1971, 374–412.

Theses and Dissertations

Call, George R. *The Missouri River Improvement Program As I Have Known It.* Manuscript, Sioux City (IA) Public Library, 1967.

Collins, Edward. "A History of Union County, South Dakota, to 1880." Master's thesis, University of South Dakota, 1937.

Goetz, Anna M. "The History of Yankton County to 1886." Master's thesis, University of South Dakota, 1927.

Johnson, Donald Frank. "Plant Succession on the Missouri River Floodplain Near Vermillion, South Dakota." Master's thesis, University of South Dakota, 1950.

Koerselman, Jon D. "The Origins of Sioux City, Iowa, 1850–1870." Master's thesis, University of South Dakota, 1975.

Miller, Donald L. "The History of the Movement for Hydro-Electric Development on the Missouri River in South Dakota." Master's thesis, University of South Dakota, 1930.

Nichol, Ralph E. "Steamboat Navigation on the Missouri River with Special Reference to Yankton and Vicinity." Master's thesis, University of South Dakota, 1936.

Pope, James Sterling. "A History of Steamboating on the Lower Missouri: 1838–1849, Saint Louis to Council Bluffs, Iowa Territory." Ph.D. diss., St. Louis University, 1984.

Rees, Ida Mae. "Sioux City as a Steamboat Port, 1856–1873." Master's thesis, University of South Dakota, 1967.

Rogge, Charles H. "Early History of Sully County." Master's thesis, University of South Dakota, 1936.

Schneiders, Robert K. "To Dam the Missouri River: Big Bend Dam and the Lakota Indians." Master's thesis, Iowa State University, 1993.

Wyman, Walker Demarquis. "The Missouri River Towns in the Westward Movement." Ph.D. diss., University of Iowa, 1935.

Index